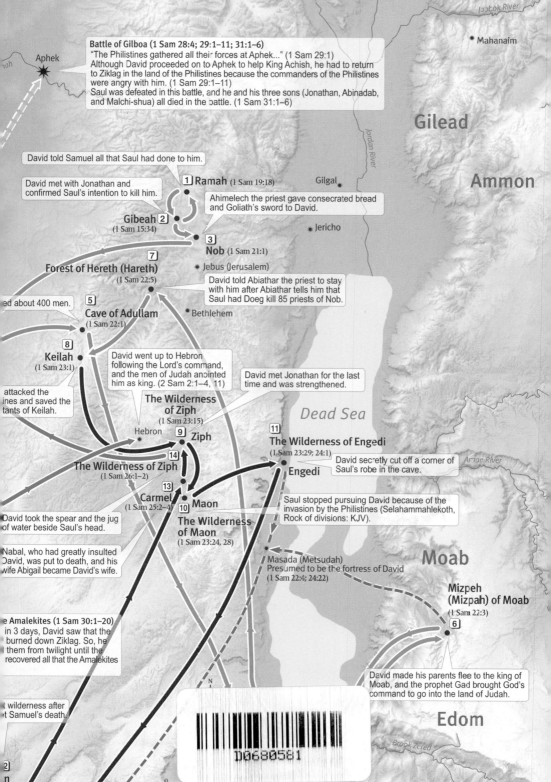

The Unquenchable Lamp of the Covenant

"Remember the days of old,
Consider the years of all generations.
Ask your father, and he will inform you,
Your elders, and they will tell you."

—Deuteronomy 32:7

The Unquenchable Lamp of the Covenant

The First Fourteen Generations in the Genealogy of Jesus Christ

Rev. Abraham Park D.Min., D.D.

PERIPLUS EDITIONS
Singapore • Hong Kong • Indonesia

Published by Periplus Editions (HK) Ltd.

www.periplus.com

Copyright © 2010 Periplus Editions (HK) Ltd.
First Korean edition published by Huisun in 2007. www.pyungkang.com

Photographs © 2010 Hanan Isachar /www.isachar-photography.com

Scripture quotations taken from the New American Standard Bible®, Copyright © 1960, 1962, 1963, 1968, 1971, 1972, 1973, 1975, 1977, 1995 by The Lockman Foundation.

Library of Congress Cataloging-in-Publication Data

Park, Abraham.
The unquenchable lamp of the Covenant : the first fourteen generations in the genealogy of Jesus Christ / Abraham Park. -- 1st ed.
    p. cm.
Includes bibliographical references (p.   ) and index.
ISBN 978-0-7946-0670-1 (hardcover)
1. Jesus Christ--Genealogy. 2. Economy of God. 3. Covenants--Biblical teaching. I. Title.
BT314.P37 2011
231.7'6--dc22
                              2010021941

ISBN 978-0-7946-0670-1

Distributed by:

North America, Latin America & Europe
Tuttle Publishing
364 Innovation Drive,
North Clarendon,
VT 05759-9436 U.S.A.
Tel: 1 (802) 773-8930; Fax: 1 (802) 773-6993
info@tuttlepublishing.com
www.tuttlepublishing.com

Asia Pacific
Berkeley Books Pte. Ltd.
61 Tai Seng Avenue #02-12
Singapore 534167
Tel: (65) 6280-1330; Fax: (65) 6280-6290
inquiries@periplus.com.sg
www.periplus.com

Japan
Tuttle Publishing
Yaekari Building, 3rd Floor,
5-4-12 Osaki, Shinagawa-ku,
Tokyo 141-0032
Tel: (81) 3 5437 0171; Fax: (81) 3 5437 0755
sales@tuttle.co.jp
www.tuttle.co.jp

Indonesia
PT Java Books Indonesia
Jl. Rawa Gelam IV No. 9
Kawasan Industri Pulogadung
Jakarta 13930
Tel: (62) 21 4682-1088; Fax: (62) 21 461-0206
cs@javabooks.co.id

Printed in Singapore

14 13 12 11   10 9 8 7 6 5 4 3 2 1

Contents

PART FIVE

From Saul to David • 207

List of Abbreviations

Bible Versions

ASV	American Standard Version
KJV	King James Version
MT	Masoretic Text
NASB	New American Standard Bible*
NET	New English Translation
NIV	New International Version
NJB	The New Jerusalem Bible
NKJV	New King James Version
NLT	New Living Translation
NRSV	New Revised Standard Version (1989)
RSV	Revised Standard Version (1952)

Reference Works

BDAG Bauer, Walter. *A Greek-English Lexicon of the New Testament and Other Early Chrisitan Literature*. Revised and augmented by F. Wilbur Gingrich and Frederick W. Danker. Chicago, 1979

BDB Brown, F., S. R. Driver, and C. A. Briggs. *A Hebrew and English Lexicon of the Old Testament: With an Appendix Containing the Biblical Aramaic*. Oxford, 1952

HALOT Koehler, L., W. Baumgartner, and J. J. Stamm. *The Hebrew and Aramaic Lexicon of the Old Testament*. Translated and edited under the supervision of M. E. J. Richardson. 4 vols. Leiden: 1994–1999

ISBE *International Standard Bible Encyclopedia*. Edited by G. W. Bromiley. 4 vols. Grand Rapids, 1979–1988

TDOT *Theological Dictionary of the Old Testament*. Edited by G. Johannes Botterweck, Helmer Ringgren, and Heinz-Josef Fabry. Translated by Douglas W. Stott. 15 vols. Grand Rapids, 1999

TWOT *Theological Wordbook of the Old Testament*. Edited by R. L. Harris and G. L. Archer. 2 vols. Chicago, 1980

---

* Bible verses quoted in this book are from the New American Standard Bible unless indicated otherwise.

Foreword

As the third book in a planned series of twelve, *The Unquenchable Lamp of the Covenant* is a bright testimony to the marvelous gospel of Jesus Christ. Indeed, it is a bold witness to Jesus himself, the King of Kings and the Lord of lords, the One promised and long awaited in the history of redemption. This latest work from Rev. Park is a careful reading of the Gospel genealogies of Jesus that demonstrates the tremendous significance of the genealogies in revealing the providence of God in accomplishing the redemption of God's people through the Lord Jesus.

The Unquenchable Lamp is a refreshing exposition for its assumption of the unity of scripture, the unity of history of redemption, in its big-picture approach that pays serious attention to the details. Also refreshing is the author's obvious love of revelation and the Lord of revelation. Just as one theologian wrote, "the theologian who does not love God is in grave danger," it can be asserted that the author of the *The Unquenchable Lamp* is a theologian who deeply loves God and his Word.

The Unquenchable Lamp is a beautiful and passionate exposition of the *sovereignty* of God as it unfolds the revelation of redemption in scripture. In this sense, the author persuasively shows this sovereignty in God's works of redemption in a way that abstractly theologizing cannot convey. This is seen in the evidences of God's sovereign choice of men and women who were 'practically imperfect' in every way, Jews and Gentiles alike as both vehicles and partakers of the gospel of the promises. That is, the gospel of redemption has since Eden been going to all the peoples on earth, without discrimination, as God's mercy extends to the *unworthy*.

Most importantly, *The Unquenchable Lamp* testifies to Jesus Christ; it proclaims that Christ is utmost, pre-eminent in the history of creation and redemption. Rev. Park's passion is to preach Christ and not himself (2 Cor 4:5). *The Unquenchable Lamp* lifts up Christ as the only One *who can* raise up men and women from the pits of pride and despair, from the curse of death and destruction. To that end, honesty pervades this work, yet not in an overly self-focused style so popular today, since all admissions of human frailty and failings are given only to magnify the Lord Jesus and to praise him and his glorious grace.

The Unquenchable Lamp is a superb example of Biblical Theology (in both senses of the word); it is theologically sound and it also seeks to trace out this story of redemption-history as scripture itself outlines and presents it. This is done through exposition of the often ignored genealogies of scripture, indicating a desire to take all of scripture as the Word of God. This is not to say that there will be no discussion or debate about some of the author's exegesis or interpretations (especially when based on word studies), but that he has provided excellent material to stimulate much fruitful study of the Word. Even my limited knowledge of Rev. Park and his work assures me that he would never want his readers stopping with *his* word, but rather that his diligent research and writings would challenge us to study *God's* Word more faithfully ourselves. This is the fruit of faithfully adhering to such an ideal in his lifetime of ministry.

The author writes with a pastor's heart and an evangelist's zeal, since he has long labored in love, prayer, and preaching for the church of the Lord Jesus. Yet even more than this, his writings extol the *zeal of God* for his divine purposes and his covenanted people. We become enthralled with God in this presentation in no small part because we are shown the power and love of God in fulfilling his ancient covenant promises to make a people for himself and to restore his creation through the Messiah. This God-centered approach is a much needed antidote to the *selfism* of our times, the me-centered nature of so much teaching and thinking. Rev. Park is to be commended for pointing us first and foremost to "the One who is, the One who was, and the One who is coming" (Rev 1:8).

I would be remiss not to mention the very fine maps, charts, and diagrams that compliment this work. These vital components, and the entire project, are consistently informed by the fruit of much archaeological, geographical, linguistic, and historical study.

In conclusion, in stark contrast to the widespread deleterious presuppositions of Historical Criticism, the verse that characterizes the edifying tone and assumptions of *The Unquenchable Lamp* is that "All Scripture is inspired by God and profitable for teaching, for reproof, for correction, for training in righteousness; so that the man of God may be adequate, equipped for every good work" (2 Tim 3:16–17).

Stephen T. Hague
Academic Dean, Faith Theological Seminary

Introduction

Moses proclaimed to the Israelites just before the entry into the land of Canaan, "Remember the days of old, consider the years of all generations. Ask your father, and he will inform you, your elders, and they will tell you" (Deut 32:7; cf. Job 8:8; 15:18; Deut 4:32). "The days of old," which is the divine history of salvation, and the "years of generations," which include God's administration of redemption that appears in that history, are all recorded in the Bible. Thus, the prophets of old carefully studied the Scriptures to understand God's work of salvation and discern God's administration suitable to the fullness of the times (Eph 1:9–10; 1 Pet 1:10–11).

The Bible, from Genesis to Revelation, is the Word of the living God, which reveals His total sovereignty and enfolds the great history of redemption in which He saves fallen mankind. The links between generation to generation in this history of redemption are the covenants that God made with His people, and these covenants became the lamp, shining upon each era (2 Chr 21:7; Ps 119:105).

Having begun with the promise of the "woman's seed (or offspring)" in Genesis 3:15, the lamp of God's covenant to save fallen mankind continued to burn and shine through each time period, being renewed through each generation. Finally when the fullness of the time came, Jesus Christ came to this world as the fulfillment of the covenant (Gal 4:4). Jesus Christ, the mystery of God hidden from the past ages and generations, has now been revealed to His saints (Col 1:26–27; 2:2).

The genealogy of Jesus Christ is a synopsis of the divine history of redemption and God's work through the covenant. The New Testament begins with the introduction, "The book of the genealogy of Jesus Christ, the son of David, the son of Abraham" (Matt 1:1). This is a great proclamation that Jesus Christ is the completion and fulfillment of the Old Testament history and the beginning of the New Testament history (John 1:17). Thus, the genealogy of Jesus Christ is the epitome of the history of redemption, which crosses the boundaries of the Old and New Testaments and opens up a new path to interpreting the entire Bible from the redemptive perspective.

Since 1968, I organized what God's grace has helped me realize through the genealogy of Jesus Christ and proclaimed it from the pulpit through many worship services. I later revised and supplemented my sermons and preached it numerous times. Each time I preached, many believers who were blessed by the sermons encouraged me to publish the material in a book, but I refused. I thought it would be unthinkable to write a book regarding the genealogy of Jesus Christ which can be called the apex of the Old and New Testaments. However, I did not want any of the grace that I had received to be lost just as our Lord said, "Gather up the leftover fragments that nothing may be lost" (John 6:12). Furthermore, in earnest hope that my writing would be of some help to my fellow pastors and laborers, I now carefully lay out this book entitled *The Unquenchable Lamp of the Covenant*.

In my mission to understand God's plan for salvation as revealed in Matthew 1, I carefully searched from cover to cover all the writings and research on the genealogies written by my predecessors of faith. Moreover, I continually researched and studied in order to gain insight about the times in which the people in the genealogies had lived and learn the significant meanings hidden in the original languages of the Bible. However, researching the genealogy of Jesus Christ is an enormous task that covers the entire Old Testament. Thus, I apologize that I was unable to clarify and deliver all the precious treasures hidden in the messages regarding the genealogy. This book is not a perfect piece of work, so I welcome and greatly appreciate any constructive criticism aimed at improving this book.

The God whom we serve and believe in is greater than all (John 10:29) and this great God sent His only begotten son, Jesus Christ. He sent Jesus Christ, who was in the bosom of the Father, to save each one of us who is no greater than a speck of dust (John 1:18). Jesus bore all our sins and subjected Himself to indescribable shame and curses unbearable even for sinful creatures and was nailed on the cross. On the cross, His flesh was torn and subject to torment as He shed His precious blood and died to complete the great work of salvation. Without the redemption of Jesus Christ, there is no one who can escape God's wrath or receive salvation from sin.

Indeed, this cross is a testimony of the love of our great God for mankind who was filled with sin and heading toward death (Rom 5:8). It is a brandmark of a love that will not fade for all eternity. Thus, we who have been saved must kneel before the cross of Jesus Christ and confess in tears that we are the foremost of all sinners (1 Tim 1:15). We must remember the cross for all eternity, give thanks for the cross, know only the cross, and boast only of the cross (1 Cor 2:2; Gal 6:14).

The cross is not something we carelessly use to receive salvation and dispose of like a paper cup, thrown out after its usage. Rather, it is the power of God that ceaselessly manifests in those who receive salvation (1 Cor 1:18). The cross is the fountainhead wherein the eternal life that Jesus Christ has promised to us springs forth unceasingly (1 Jn 2:25). During the last supper with His disciples the night before the cross, Jesus took the cup, gave thanks, and gave it to His disciples saying, "This is My blood of the covenant, which is poured out for many for forgiveness of sins" (Matt 26:28; Mark 14:24; Luke 22:20; 1 Cor 11:25; Heb 9:20; 10:29; 12:24; 13:20).

The precious blood on the cross is the blood of the covenant, which gives eternal life. The spirit of the man whose sins have been forgiven through this precious blood is the lamp of God (Prov 20:27). The believers of Jesus Christ must break the power of darkness and become lamps that brighten all the nations; their flames must blaze brightly until the grand fulfillment of redemption.

I poured out my heart and soul into writing this book with Jesus Christ's blood-stained cross on my heart and with prayer that my unworthy writings may testify of Jesus' blood. There would be no greater joy than to see the readers of this humble book become true people of the cross who follow in the steps of Christ (1 Pet 2:21), and become living lamps of God. People of the cross are those who have their names recorded in the book of life. Those who dwell on the earth and whose names are not recorded in the book of life will worship the beast (Rev 13:8) and will be thrown into the lake of fire which burns for all eternity (Rev 20:15). However, those whose names are recorded in the book of life of the Lamb will enter the glorious New Jerusalem (Rev 21:27).

I pray that we may all fight the good fight each day and never lose heart, finish the course and keep our faith until the end (2 Tim 4:7), and overcome this world through faith and become victorious (1 Jn 5:4–5). Then, when the Lord says, "Come, you who are blessed of My Father, inherit the kingdom prepared for you from the foundation of the world" (Matt 25:34), it is my prayer that you are able to boldly answer, "Amen."

As an unworthy sinner, I am not only grateful for the salvation I have received through the precious blood of Jesus Christ, but also for the immense grace of God which has allowed me to work as His steward preaching His Word for over 50 years. Furthermore, my heart is moved with gratitude for the grace that has allowed me to confess my faith and express the essence of my theological beliefs through these books before the sun sets on my life. Though I am planning to write 12 books as part of The History of Redemption series, God must direct my steps in order for me to accomplish this (Pro 16:9), so I entrust all plans and authority into His hands.

It is not by the efforts of this old man alone that these books were published. It was made possible by the wonderful work of God's hands and the help of many people around me that my age-worn manuscripts could be put into book format and testify of God's Word.

I thank my beloved fellow pastors, elders, and all the members of the congregation for their prayers without which I would not have been able to publish my first book, *The Genesis Genealogies*; my second book, *The Covenant of the Torch*; and now, *The Unquenchable Lamp of the Covenant*. Moreover, I earnestly thank President Taek-Joong Kim of Samyoung Printing and his staff and the staff of Huisun Books, giving all the glory to God.

I sincerely hope and pray that all the godly servants of God who read this book and all the churches around the world that have been purchased with the cost of Jesus Christ's blood will come to understand God's redemptive administration through the genealogy of Jesus Christ, share the same inspiration in God's word, and respond to His call with "Amen."

Abraham Park
March 7, 2009
Servant of Jesus Christ on the pilgrim's path to heaven

מדבר צין הוא קדש

מדבר סיני

מדבר פארן

מדבר שור

ארץ פלשתים

ים המלח

עיר כרמל

שבט שמעון

שבט

באר שבע

עמלק

אלכסנדרי

ארץ גשן

פתם

לוח המסעות במדבר
אשר על פי יסעו ועל פי יחנו

א׳ רעמסס	טו׳ רתמה	לט׳ חרהגדגד
ב׳ סכת	טז׳ רמן פרץ	ל׳ ימבתה
ג׳ אתם	יז׳ לבנה	לא׳ עברנה
ד׳ פיהחירת	יח׳ רסה	לב׳ עציןגבר
ה׳ מרה	יט׳ קהלתה	לג׳ מדברצין
ו׳ אילם	כ׳ הרספר	לד׳ ההרהר
ז׳ ים סוף	כא׳ חרדה	לה׳ צלמנה
ח׳ מדברסין	כב׳ מקהלה	לו׳ פונן
ט׳ רפקה	כג׳ תחת	לז׳ אבת
יו׳ אלוש	כד׳ תרח	לח׳ דיבןגר
יא׳ רפידם	כה׳ מתקה	לט׳ עלמן דבלתים
יב׳ מדברסיני	כו׳ חשמנה	מ׳ הרי עברים
יג׳ קברת התאו	כז׳ מסרות	מא׳ ערבת מואב
יד׳ חצרת	כח׳ בני יעקן	

PART ONE

God Who Is Greater Than All

CHAPTER 1

God Who Is Greater than All

We often say that God is great and mighty. The Bible also refers to God as the "great God" or "the LORD who is great" (Ezra 5:8; Neh 4:14; Ps 95:3; Dan 2:45; Titus 2:13).

How great is our God? To the unbelieving Jews, Jesus described God as "My Father, who is...greater than all" (John 10:29).

> **John 10:29** My Father, who has given them to Me, is greater than all; and no one is able to snatch them out of the Father's hand.

The word *all* (πᾶς: *pas*) used in this verse includes the universe and all things in it—both seen and unseen. In other words, it includes all tangible and intangible, material and immaterial things (Neh 9:6; Col 1:16–17; Acts 14:15; 17:24–25; Rev 5:13, 10:6).

God created all things through His mighty Word (Gen 1:7, 15, 24, 30; Ps 33:6–9; Heb 11:3); He created out of nothing (Gen 1:1); He created every creation instantaneously (Gen 1:3, 11–12, 16, 21, 25; 2:7, 19, 22); and He created for six days (Gen 1:3–31). The God who created this immense universe is too great to be compared with anything since nothing is greater than God. He is truly the "great God" (Ps 48:1; 96:4–5; 135:5; 145:3; 147:5). David confessed, "For great is the LORD, and greatly to be praised; He also is to be feared above all gods" (1 Chr 16:25). The Hebrew word for *great* in this verse is גָּדוֹל (*gādôl*), which means "great in magnitude and extent" or "big." In this passage, this word conveys the greatness that cannot be compared with anything or fathomed by the human mind. This God, who is greater than all, is so great that neither the vast land nor the infinite universe can serve as His dwelling place (1 Kgs 8:27).

1. The Most High Ruler, the Maker of All

The great and awesome God that we serve and believe in is our Father who is greater than all (John 10:29). He is the head of all (1 Chr 29:11); the Father of all (Eph 4:6); and the Most High Ruler (Gen 1:1; 14:19, 22; Exod 20:11; 2 Chr 2:12; Neh 9:6; Ps 102:25; 124:8; 134:3; 136:6; 146:6; Matt 11:25; Acts 4:24; 17:24).

The word *all* refers to all things, inclusive of all kinds of phenomena and everything that exists in the entire universe. In a narrower sense, the expression *all things* may refer to all things that are physically visible. However, the word comprehensively embraces everything in heaven and on earth. Thus, the word *all* includes the entire human race and all that exists within God's special grace and mercy (Ps 145:9).

The title *Lord* or *Most High* describes the sovereign ruler who governs and administers through His providence. The title *Ruler of all* reveals the absolute inimitability of God who is the Lord of creation, the sovereign ruler who gives breath and life to all creatures and reigns over all creation (Ps 103:19).

2. The Vast Universe

The universe that the *Most High Ruler* created is wondrous and unfathomable. We cannot help but admire its vastness and boundlessness. Even if we combine the strength of the human eye and the most powerful telescope to look at the farthest outreaches, we will still see only a small part of its vast space. We can get a little glimpse of the wonders of God's greatness and love simply by examining the size of our solar system, though it is only a fraction of the entire universe.

(1) The sizes of the earth, sun, moon, and stars

The earth is the third planet from the sun in our solar system. It is about 6,400 km (3,977 mi) in radius, 40,000 km (24,855 mi) in circumference, 514.5 million km^2 (198 million mi^2) in surface area, 1.0975 trillion km^3 (263 billion mi^3) in volume, and 6.6 sextillion tons (6×10^{24} kg) in mass.

The sun, which appears the largest to the naked eye, is about 700,000 km (435,000 mi) in radius, which is more than 100 times the size and about 330,000 times the mass of the earth. Furthermore, the sun's volume is about 1.3 million times that of the earth. This means that about 1.3 million earth-size planets can fit inside the sun. Most of the earth's energy comes from the sun, whose external temperature is about 6,000°C (11,000°F) and internal temperature is about 15 million°C (27 million°F). Astronomers estimate that this energy is comparable to about 40 million explosions of one-megaton atomic bomb in one second.

The moon, which lights up the night sky, is about one-fourth the size of the earth. It has a radius of 1,738 km (1,080 mi), and is located about 380,000 km (236,121 mi) from the earth. The moon's external temperature rises to an average of 107°C (224.6°F) during the day and falls to a bitter −153°C (−243°F) at night. Because the moon rotates about its axis in about the same amount of time it takes to orbit the earth (synchronous rotation), we only see one side of the moon. To this day, no one, except for those who have explored the moon, has ever seen the far side of the moon.

In the universe, there are countless numbers of stars that are hundreds of times larger than the sun. About 6,000 stars are visible to the naked eye, and about 124 million are visible through the 100-inch telescope at the Mount Wilson Observatory, which was once the largest telescope in the early 1900s. However, there are too many stars that still cannot be observed with our eyes or technology.

The galactic system that can be seen from the earth through the naked eye is known as our galaxy. Our galaxy is made up of about 200 billion stars, including the sun, and it is classified as a barred spiral galaxy. The entire galaxy is roughly 100,000 light years across in diameter and about 50,000 light years thick.

Since it is reported that there are about 100 billion galaxies that are like ours in the universe, there must be at least about 2×10^{22} stars (200 billion stars x 100 billion galaxies). Albert Einstein estimated that the actual size of the universe is probably 10 times the size that we can identify. He also estimated that there are probably about 10^{25} stars in the whole universe, which would take us about 10^{17} (100 quadrillion) years to count if we were to count 20 stars per second. God said to Abraham, "Now look toward the heavens, and count the stars, if you are able to count them" (Gen 15:5), and to Jeremiah, "As the host of heaven cannot be counted" (Jer 33:22). Genesis 1:16 states that God made all the stars, and we cannot help but stand in awe before the immensity of God's creation.

Furthermore, not one of these innumerable stars is like another. Each is different in size, color, and brightness. Only the brightest stars (Class 1) have proper names, while most others are classified with letters of the alphabet. The stars that are not classified with a name or an alphabet are numerically labeled. Still, most stars are not named. However great the number of the stars may be, God leads them forth by number, counts them each one by one, and calls them all by name without missing one of them. Psalm 147:4 states, "He counts the number of the stars; He gives names to all of them."

> **Isaiah 40:26** Lift up your eyes on high and see who has created these stars, the One who leads forth their host by number, He calls them all by name; because of the greatness of His might and the strength of His power not one of them is missing.

These innumerable stars move and follow their courses according to the command of God, their commander who also created each of them like soldiers who follow the order of their commander-in-chief. Therefore, none of the stars moves on their own random courses; they move according to the rules in their designated place and will come to a complete halt when God gives His call.

How large are stars? There are countless number of stars that are hundreds of times bigger than the sun. Red giant stars are about 10 times the size of the sun. Super giant stars are more than 100 times the size of the sun, and the star Antares in Scorpio is about 230 times larger than the sun. There is a star that catches the eye on clear winter evenings—the Betelgeuse in Orion. This star is so large that it is about 950 to 1,000 times greater than the sun in its diameter, 20 times in mass and 512 million times in volume. Truly, the planet earth, on which we live, is like a tiny speck of dust compared to the size of the great universe (Isa 40:15).

(2) The Immeasurable Distance between the Stars

To the naked eye, the stars in our galaxy are all clustered closely together. In actuality, each star is distanced approximately five light years apart. The astronomical unit *light year* is used to measure the distance between the stars because it would be impossible to measure them in meters or kilometers. One light year is the distance that light travels in one year at the approximate speed of 300,000 km/s (186,000 mi/s). Light can travel around the earth 7 times in 1 second. At this speed, light can travel about 9.4608×10^{12} km (5.9 trillion mi) in a single light year. Since the sun is 1.5 billion km from the earth, it would take a plane traveling at about 900 km/h (560 mi/h) 19 years to reach the sun while light would take about 8 minutes. Furthermore, the distance covered by one light year is 65,000 times the distance from the earth to the sun. It is a distance that would take an automobile, traveling at the speed of 100 km/h (62 mi/h), about 10 million years to cover. One light year is like an infinite distance to us for it is too great to conceptualize. Now, it is mind-boggling to think about the vastness of the entire universe given the fact that the average distance between stars in the sky, which seem to be gathered up so close to each other, is about 5 light years.

The closest star to the earth, Alpha Centauri in the Centaurus constellation, is located 4.3 light years away. Sirius, the brightest star in the night sky, is 8.7 light years away, and Polaris, the North Star located very close to the north celestial pole, is 400 light years away from the earth. There are planets around the Scorpius constellation that are about 5,600 light years away from the earth.

The discussion on the vastness of the universe goes further. We can think of it in a scale, beginning with stars. Stars make up a galaxy; galaxies make up a cluster of galaxies; clusters of galaxies make up a supercluster of galaxies; and lastly, superclusters of galaxies make up the structures of the vast universe. The universe is not just a group of galaxies scattered around without any order; its arrangement is that of a net-like structure. The average distance between galaxies is approximately two million light years. Just imagine how vast the universe is! Thus, the "expanse" that God created on the second day (Gen 1:6–8) is infinitely vast and surpasses the limits of human understanding. Compared to this vast universe, a human being is a mere drop in the ocean.

When we cannot even fully understand this earth in which we live, how can we, as Job confessed, comprehend the infinite power and greatness of our God, who created the universe and governs all things in it? Henceforth, it is merely impossible for man to fathom all the works of God (Job 9:8–10; 11:7–9; 37:23; Eccl 3:11).

Job 5:9 Who does great and unsearchable things, wonders without number.

We cannot help but grieve deeply at the ignorance of mankind and praise the infinite wisdom of our God every time we look upon the sky and consider the greatness of His creation. God once scolded Job, "Who is this that darkens counsel by words without knowledge?" (Job 38:2). Job 26:14 also states, "Behold, these are the fringes of His ways; and how faint a word we hear of Him! But his mighty thunder, who can understand?"

Mankind is so lowly that we cannot handle a faint word we hear of God even with all the knowledge of the world. What would happen then, if they hear a voice like great thunder? The psalmist exclaimed, "O LORD, how many are Your works! In wisdom You have made them all; the earth is full of Your possessions" (Ps 104:24).

The work of God cannot be understood by the shallow wisdom of man, and it is naturally impossible for man to judge His works (Eccl 8:17; 1 Cor 1:21). All we can do is give thanks and praise God for His providence that rules over the vast universe and keeps it in order day by day (Ps 136).

3. God Who Upholds All

(1) God who governs the galaxy

Man on the earth is traveling through the universe along with the earth at a great speed of the earth's rotation of about 0.46 km/s (0.29 mi/s, twice the speed of a passenger airplane), plus the speed of its revolution around the sun at about 30 km/s (18.6 mi/s, 3 times the speed of the fastest missile), plus the speed of the movement of our solar system around the galaxy at about 220 km/s (136.7 mi/s).

It is also known that the rotation of our galaxy around its center takes approximately 200 million years (1 cosmic year). The central hub of our rotating galaxy is an enormous black hole, an area of space with a gravitational field so intense that interstellar matters collapse together and are endlessly condensed. The black hole in our galaxy is approximately four million times larger than the sun and rotates at a speed close to the speed of light, causing space to rotate with it.

All of these phenomena are examples of how God "upholds all things by the Word of His power and preserves His creation" (Heb 1:3). "Preserving" is God's continuing work of maintaining all that He has created. Hence, the word *uphold* (φέρω, *phero*) signifies the management of God's creation in its preserved condition. If God takes away the Word of His power, the order of the entire universe will be destroyed in a moment (2 Pet 3:10). From this we can witness the mercy and compassion of God, who is good to all. Isaac Newton described the force that pulls masses together as "universal gravitation." The law of universal gravitation shows the power of God's Word that upholds all bodies of the universe precisely in their orbits.

(2) The grand symphony of the stars in the universe

The report on the Cassini-Huygens Mission put out by the National Aer-
onautics and Space Administration (NASA) reveals the existence of sound
waves collected from the planet Saturn and its vicinity. Sound waves are
produced when an object rotates at a fast rate. Unimaginably deafening
sounds must resound between the infinite number of stars that rotate
and move about at the tip of God's fingers. The sound, however, is not a
thundering noise but a harmonious song in God's ears (Job 38:7). Thus,
the universe is a symphony of billions of sounds and instruments of the
Great Sovereign.

Because man can only hear sounds within a limited range, we cannot
hear the great symphony of the universe now. However, we will be able
to praise the Lord accompanied by this cosmic symphony in the heavenly
world (Rev 4:10–11; 5:11–14; 14:3).

The psalmist describes this symphony of the universe in Psalm 19:2,
"Day to day pours forth speech, and night to night reveals knowledge."
The verb *pours forth* in this verse is נָבַע (*nāba'*) in Hebrew and it means
"to pour," "to gush forth," "to spring up," or "to bubble up." This signifies
that all things in the heavens and on earth will praise God's providence of
creation during the day and will continue to pour forth His glory from
day to day. Thus, in awe we must praise God that the divine order of the
universe remains even when a day passes and another day comes. This
divine order is according to the arrangement that God established during
the creation (Gen 1:14) and according to the promise of preservation that
God made with Noah and his family (Gen 8:20–22; 9:11). This is what
God called "My covenant for the day and My covenant for the night"
through Jeremiah (Jer 33:20).

(3) The perfect order and harmony of the universe

The entire universe is not in chaos, but is a world of complete order and
perfect harmony under one God. This is so because the vast universe was
created on the basis of perfect and precise design, and all things were arranged accurately in their own place according to the divine administration of God's providence for salvation (Ps 103:19; Prov 3:19; Jer 10:12).

It can be said that such orderly movement and beautiful harmony is
a testimony to God's greatness, faithfulness, and goodness for the salvation of fallen mankind. The alternation of night and day, the change of
seasons, and the wondrous changes in the world of creation are proof

that God's mercy for the salvation of this world continues (Gen 8:22; Deut 4:19; Ps 136:5, 9).

In Psalm 19:1, the psalmist confessed, "The heavens are telling of the glory of God; and their expanse is declaring the work of His hands," and praise for the works of God's hands has been sung without ceasing ever since the time of creation. God's divinity is undeniably revealed as long as we are willing to witness it by opening our eyes and our ears to God's providence of creation found in the "day" that consists of night and day (Rom 1:20).

4. The Agape Love of the God of All

God, who is greater than all, gave His love to save us. His love is immeasurable for it is infinite. The greatness of God reflected through the enormous universe is not irrelevant to us. It is deeply linked to our life—the very platform where the history of salvation for mankind is taking place. Beholding the heavenly bodies in the night sky is sufficient in itself to cause amazement and astonishment. However, what is even more unbelievably inspirational is having God, who created the great universe and keeps all movements and activities in order, give special attention to mankind—we who are as insignificant as dust—by bestowing the grace of salvation upon us. The psalmist declares that He is the God "who is enthroned on high, who humbles Himself" (Ps 113:5–6). David, when he saw the providence of redemption hidden in the heavens, the moon and the stars that God ordained, also exclaimed, "What is man, that You take thought of him…" (Ps 8:4). Truly, the works that the Lord carries out to save one soul are so great and His thoughts are so deep (Ps 92:5) that even the boundlessly vast universe cannot be compared to one soul, which is more precious than the heavens and the earth (Matt 16:26; Luke 9:25).

The Bible verse that sums up this essence of salvation is John 3:16.

> **John 3:16** For God so loved the world, that He gave His only begotten Son, that whoever believes in Him should not perish, but have eternal life.

This is truly the quintessence of the gospel and the way of salvation and eternal life. This is the great Bible passage that contains God's sovereign administration and providence of redemption to save each one of us who deserved to fall into the brimstone of hell.

(1) "God"

The word for *God* in this verse refers to God the Father. The Greek word for God is θεός (*theos*), equivalent to אֱלֹהִים (*'ĕlōhim*) in the Old Testament. He is the God of Trinity. There are three persons in the Trinity: Father, Son, and the Holy Spirit (Matt 28:18–20; 2 Cor 13:14[1]). Also, God is the one and only God (John 5:44; 1 Cor 8:4, 6; 1 Tim 2:5; Jas 2:19), and He is the Almighty, who surpasses time and space (Eph 4:6). He is the God who not only created all things (Acts 17:24; Heb 3:4), but also maintains and governs them.

(2) "so loved"

In Greek, *so loved* is οὕτως γὰρ ἠγάπησεν (*houtōs gar ēgapesen*), a powerful declaration that begins this verse. The motivating power for redeeming sinners is God's love and the degree of that love is expressed as "so loved."

Οὕτως (*houtōs*: "so") signifies "thus," "as follows," and "so."[2] The word *so* or *so much* emphasizes the degree of sincerity in one's act of giving his heart and efforts.

Also, ἠγάπησεν (*ēgapēsen*) is a verb form of ἀγάπη (*agapē*), which signifies the immense love given to sinful mankind. This is the love that surpasses all limits and conditions. It is the love everlasting, sacrificial, unfailing, loathing of sin, and unconditionally given by God (1 Jn 4:10, 19).[3]

The great love of God, who had predestined the salvation of fallen mankind from before creation and fulfilled His love by giving His life on the cross, continues today as the motivating power that brings world history into existence. It is also the strong driving force that leads us to salvation.

(3) "the world"

The Greek word for *world* is κόσμος (*kosmos*). This word is used 185 times in the New Testament: the Apostle John used it 78 times in the Gospel of John and 24 times in his epistles. The word *kosmos* means "universe," which includes all sinners.

First, *kosmos* is the universe. It is a synonym of "heaven and earth" in the Old Testament (Acts 17:24).

Second, *kosmos* is the dwelling place of mankind—the territory of their habitation, which is the earth (John 21:25; 1 Tim 6:7).

Third, *kosmos* refers to the human race, which is the "world" in John 3:16. It signifies all mankind, the people who live in bondage of sin, including us (John 1:10; 3:17; 4:42; 2 Cor 5:19). John 1:29 mentions "the Lamb of God who takes away the sin of the world." The "sin of the world" in this verse refers to "sins of the people of the world." John 3:17 also says, "For God did not send the Son into the world to judge the world, but that the world should be saved through Him." The "world" in this verse also refers to people in this world. In other words, only by believing in Jesus can the people of this world be saved (Acts 4:12).

Even great and powerful nations on this earth are like "a drop from a bucket" and "a speck of dust on the scales"; even islands that seem immovable are only like "fine dust" to God (Isa 40:15). All the nations put together are like nothing before God (Isa 40:17). Therefore, the fact that God who is greater than all, the creator of the universe has come just to find me, who is unworthy as a speck of dust, is the mystery of salvation and the love that cannot be measured.

(4) "gave"

The verb *gave* is ἔδωκεν (*edōken*) in Greek, an aorist tense in the indicative mood of δίδωμι (*didōmi*), which means to "give or bestow." The aorist tense, in the indicative mood, refers to a completed event. Essentially, this word explains that our God of love and mercy has already given us His only begotten Son Jesus Christ as the greatest gift. The gift that God gives to mankind is a free gift apart from any human work, merit, or effort.

Our salvation is not a result of man's righteous works, but a gift freely given by the grace of God (Rom 5:15; Eph 2:8–9). The greatest gift of all is our Lord Jesus Christ.

(5) "only begotten Son"

Generally, an *only begotten son* means "a son without a brother or sister." However, saying that Jesus Christ is God's "only begotten Son" signifies that Jesus Christ is the one and only Son of God (John 1:14, 18; 3:16, 18; 1 Jn 4:9). This expression conveys the love of Jesus Christ, who existed in the form of God and had equality with God but came down in the incarnate form as God's only begotten Son in order to save sinners (John 10:30; Phil 2:6). Thus, John 1:18 states, "…the only begotten of God, who is in the bosom of the Father, He has explained Him."

When Abraham gave his only son Isaac, God said, "For now I know that you fear God, since you have not withheld your son, your only son, from Me," and God acknowledged Abraham's faith (Gen 22:12). Likewise, sending the only begotten Son whom He loved so much to this world and letting him die so wretchedly on the cross is a demonstration of His love toward us (1 Jn 4:9; Rom 5:8).

(6) "whoever believes in Him"

The word *believe* is πιστεύω (*pisteuo*), the verb form of πίστις (*pistis*), which means "faith." Faith is the means of salvation. To have faith is to believe in God, and to believe in God is to receive Him. John 1:12 states, "But as many as received Him, to them He gave the right to become children of God, even to those who believe in His name." The word *receive* in this verse does not mean to receive as to welcome a customer or visitor at a reception counter, but to accept the only begotten Son Jesus Christ perpetually and continue to serve Him as the Savior of life. It is by God's perfect grace and gift that we can believe in Jesus as our personal Lord of salvation (Eph 2:8).

The Greek word for *whoever* is πᾶς (*pās*), meaning "all or every." This is to say that all, including Jews and Gentiles, rich and poor, men and women, and old and young, can receive salvation from sin and death.

(7) "should not perish, but have eternal life"

Granting eternal life is the sole reason of His love. It is the liberation from sin that we find in Jesus Christ and the promise of eternal life through Him (Rom 8:1; 1 Jn 2:25). This is the ultimate purpose of Jesus' coming onto this earth (Heb 9:28; 1 Jn 3:5). Having "eternal life" is not simply having a life that lasts forever. Eternal life begins by starting a new relationship with God (John 17:3; Rom 5:21) and then receiving new life (John 5:24). Furthermore, it is entering into an eternal fellowship with God in the kingdom of heaven through resurrection and transfiguration at the end of the world and being liberated from death (John 6:40; 1 Cor 15:51–52; 1 Thes 4:16–17). This is the promise of a blessed life that entails eternal continuation and heavenly quality of life.

Therefore, Jesus Christ is the greatest gospel and the good news of great joy (Luke 2:10). He is the only mediator for sinners (1 Tim 2:5; Gal 3:19–20; Heb 8:6; 9:15) and the grace upon grace that is desperately needed by all sinners (John 1:16). Thus, anyone who does not believe in Jesus Christ, the only begotten Son and Lord of salvation, will perish. To perish is to be cast away from God and receive the punishment of hell. Hell is the place where fire burns endlessly, the smoke of torment goes up forever, and even worms do not die (Mark 9:43, 48; Rev 14:11).

According to a recent discovery, there are shrimp, clams, bacteria, and other living things found in scalding-hot water at a temperature of about 407°C (764.6°F) in the ocean bed near a volcanic crater. Imagining how it would be for these creatures to live in this high-temperature environment helps one picture those in hell suffering in burning fire without being able to die. However, those who believe in Jesus will not perish, but will receive eternal life and enjoy everlasting blessings in the kingdom of heaven.

It is a great honor just to have God, who is greater than all, come down to our lowly and obscure human history and become the Immanuel for us. Moreover, He who is without sin humbled Himself as a worm and allowed His holy body to be torn on the cross, and every drop of His blood poured out for us (Rom 8:3; 2 Cor 5:21; Heb 4:15; 7:26; 9:14; 1 Pet 2:22–24; 1 Jn 3:5; Ps 22:6). By the blood He shed on the cross, we are forgiven of our sins and are redeemed (Matt 20:28; Eph 1:7; 1 Pet 1:18–19). Jesus Christ, who died on the cross and rose again the third day, still intercedes for us on the right hand of God's throne so that we can overcome sin and receive final salvation (Rom 1:4; 1 Cor 15:3–4). Can we ever sufficiently express His great love with our limited words?

We have received the greatest treasure called "eternal life," which cannot be compared in value to any worldly treasure (Ps 49:7–8; Matt 13:44–46; John 10:28; 17:2; 1 Jn 2:25; 5:11). This eternal life is Jesus Christ Himself (1 Jn 5:20). Thus, the fact that God, who is greater than all, came down to save people, who are sinners as lowly as worms, is truly a great gospel. He gave all of this as a free gift. This is something we cannot repay even with all of our lives; we are indebted to this gospel and His love (Rom 1:14). Debt inevitably entails the responsibility to repay. Though He gave to us freely, it is our duty as mature children of God to reciprocate His love as much as possible.

The only appropriate way for us to respond to this debt is to share this gospel (Matt 28:18–20). This is also the Great Commission that the Lord gave to us (Mark 16:15; Titus 1:3). The first proclamation of Jesus Christ and John the Baptist was "Repent, for the kingdom of heaven is at hand" (Matt 3:1–3; 4:17; Mark 1:14–15). The Apostle Paul confessed that he was called as an apostle for the gospel (Rom 1:1) and that he had nothing to boast of in preaching the gospel, for woe to him if he does not preach the gospel (1 Cor 9:16). Likewise, it is our task to live the rest of our lives with the resolution that we will die daily like the Apostle Paul (1 Cor 15:31), testify to this gospel (Acts 20:24; Rom 1:14–15; 2 Tim 4:1–2), and be faithful until our very last breath (Rev 2:10).

CHAPTER 2

The History of
Redemption and the Covenant

The Bible testifies of the greatness of God's absolute sovereignty for He is greater than all, and of His work of saving mankind through the redemptive work of our Lord Jesus Christ. Covenants are the links and the means of fulfilling this work in actual history. The Bible is a record of the redemptive history that is connected by covenants; therefore, it can be called a covenantal book that promises salvation. God took Israel out of Egypt, "from the midst of the iron furnace," to make them His people and become their God under the covenant (Deut 4:20; 1 Kgs 8:51; Jer 11:4).

A covenant is a promise that God made especially with mankind because of His love for them (Lev 26:9). Accordingly, mankind can become united with God and have a personal relationship with God through His covenant. The key point and purpose of the covenant that God established with mankind is for Him to make them His own people. Mankind can become His people through the covenant just as God declares in Jeremiah 31:33 and Ezekiel 36:28, "I will be their God, and they shall be My people" (Gen 17:7; Exod 6:7; 19:5–6; Lev 26:11–12; Deut 29:13; 2 Kgs 11:17; 2 Chr 23:16; Ezek 37:27; 2 Cor 6:16).

The word *covenant* is defined as "an agreement or promise usually under seal between two or more parties especially for the performance of some action." A covenant is usually ratified when it is beneficial to both parties. However, God's covenant is a pronouncement of God's unilateral grace. This promise of God is unchangeable (Heb 6:17) and faithful (Rom 3:3; 1 Cor 1:9; 10:13; 2 Cor 1:18; 1 Thes 5:24; 2 Thes 3:3; 2 Tim 2:13; Titus 1:9; 3:8; Heb 11:11; 1 Pet 4:19; 1 Jn 1:9). When His people keep the covenant, God will surely fulfill that covenant and respond with lovingkindness and truth (Ps 103:17–18).

> **Psalm 25:10** All the paths of the LORD are lovingkindness and truth to those who keep His covenant and His testimonies.

What are the most distinctive features in the covenant that God made with mankind?

First, it is unilateral and sovereign.

Fallen mankind absolutely does not qualify to have a covenantal relationship with God (Ps 14:3; Jer 17:9; Rom 3:10). Nevertheless, God who is greater than all came and unilaterally established the covenant to achieve the great administration, that is salvation for His elect. Through God's unconditional grace, this covenant was given to Adam when Adam was in a state of total depravity because of his fall. This is the reason that the Bible describes as "covenant" that which God "commanded" (Josh 7:11), "confirm[ed]" (Lev 26:9; Deut 5:2), and "gave" (Acts 7:8). Since God's covenant is sovereignly administered, it is an eternally unchangeable and utterly unbreakable promise.

Second, it is eternal.

It is stated in Deuteronomy 7:9 that God "keeps His covenant...to a thousandth generation" (see also 1 Chr 16:15). The psalmist in Psalm 105:8 also confesses, "He has remembered His covenant forever, the word which He commanded to a thousand generations." The expression *thousand generations* mentioned in these verses is not a literal number of generations, but a symbol of "eternity." Thus, it conveys the perpetuity of God's covenant. The covenant that God made with Abraham not only continued in the covenants of Moses and David, but also in many more covenants in the following generations. Hence, the efficacy of God's covenant ceaselessly continues throughout all generations. Even human covenants cannot be nullified nor can conditions be added after they have been established (Gal 3:15). God's covenant is definitely firmer than man's covenants, and it is eternally binding. God did not forsake His people even when they broke the covenant, and He protected them because it was His covenant (Jer 29:10).

Moreover, God renewed His covenant in every generation. These covenants are not mutually exclusive. They are all founded upon and linked to the covenants that were already established. Thus, there is continuity and unity in all the covenants of God.[4] He had to renew and reestablish His covenant in every era in order to reaffirm and bring to light His redemptive will to save His chosen people. Also, it was to seal the relationship firmly between God and His people.

Hence, the fact that God made a covenant with mankind shows God's unchanging grace and infinite love. Because of this covenant, we can look forward to the hope of heaven that will ultimately lead us to salvation. Our hope does not falter, for God's covenant is steadfast and it is not shaken by any challenge. Even the turning of the ages and the flow of time cannot challenge the perpetuity of the covenant, and the faithfulness of the covenant is never nullified or withdrawn under any circumstance (Deut 4:31; Gal 3:17).

Let us now consider the covenants of God found in the Bible. In the Garden of Eden, God told Adam, "but from the tree of the knowledge of good and evil you shall not eat, for in the day that you eat from it you shall surely die" (Gen 2:17). According to this promise, Adam's life and death depended on his act (or work) of obedience. Thus, this promise is called the "covenant of works." Since the covenant of works is the covenant that God made with the first man Adam who represents all mankind, it is known as the "federal headship."[5]

However, Eve listened to the serpent and ate the fruit from the tree of the knowledge of good and evil. Adam also ate the fruit that she gave him. As a result, they both fell (Gen 3:1–6). Because of their disobedience, Adam and Eve could not keep their places. Consequently, death came upon all mankind through the sin of one man, Adam, "for as in Adam all die" (1 Cor 15:22).

God made a covenant for the redemption of mankind since the fall of Adam. This covenant began with the promise of the woman's seed (Gen 3:15) and continued until the time of Noah (Gen 6:18; 9:8–17). It was valid in the time of Abraham (Gen 15; 17) and also in the times of the successive patriarchs (Gen 26:2–5; 28:10–22). The covenant became more concrete through the exodus generation and its succeeding generation in the wilderness (Exod 19:5; 24:1–7; Deut 29; 30). Then it continued into the time of David (2 Sam 7:12–16) and finally was completed through Jesus Christ (Matt 26:26–28; Mark 14:22–25; Luke 22:19–20; 1 Cor 11:23–25; Heb 7:22; 8:13).

1. The First Revelation of the Covenant (Proto-gospel)

To Adam and Eve who had fallen, God promised the seed of the woman. Although this promise is not a formal covenant, it is the first revelation of God's covenant for it clearly expresses God's intention of saving mankind from their sins. In this promise God vowed, "…I will put enmity between you and the woman, and between your seed and her seed; he shall bruise you on the head, and you shall bruise him on the heel" (Gen 3:15). Because this is the first promise in the Bible that reveals God's will for Jesus Christ to destroy the powers of Satan and save us from sin and death (i.e., Satan's powers), it is called the *proto-gospel*.

The seed of the woman promised in this covenant refers to the Messiah who is to come and save fallen mankind. The head is the most important member of the body. The promise that he will "bruise…the head" signifies a complete defeat without any possibility of restoration. It prophesies that Jesus Christ, the woman's offspring, will defeat Satan and his forces to triumph completely (1 Cor 15:22, 25–26; Rev 20:9–10).

God confirmed this covenant with Adam and Eve by making garments of skin and clothing them Himself (Gen 3:21). The garments of skin obtained through the sacrifice of an animal that died in place of the man, who actually deserved death, foreshadow the atoning work of Jesus Christ on the cross; they were an assurance of the promise of the woman's seed (John 1:29; 1 Cor 5:7). All of God's covenants in the Bible are established on this foundation of His administration for redemption—that He will save mankind through the Messiah, the seed of the woman.

2. The Noahic Covenant (Covenant of the Bow)

After commanding Noah to build an ark, God said that He would establish a covenant with him (Gen 6:14). This is the first occurrence of the word "covenant" in the Bible.

> **Genesis 6:18** But I will establish My covenant with you; and you shall enter the ark—you and your sons and your wife, and your sons' wives with you.

God established the covenant with Noah to secure the path through which the seed of the woman could come, even in the midst of the judgment of the world. When the flood covered the world, "all flesh that moved on the earth perished, birds and cattle and beasts and every swarming thing that swarms upon the earth, and all mankind…all in whose nostrils was the breath of the spirit of life, died" (Gen 7:21–22). In the midst of this destruction, "only Noah was left, together with those that were with him in the ark" (Gen 7:23). After the flood, God established a covenant with Noah through a bow (rainbow). He put a bow in a cloud and made it a sign that He would not judge mankind again by a flood, but would preserve them until the completion of the history of redemption (Gen 9:8–17).

The covenant that God made before the flood was given to just one person—Noah (Gen 6:18). However, the covenant of the bow established after the flood was a universal covenant given to Noah, his sons, and "all flesh" that were with Noah (Gen 9:10–12, 15–17). Therefore, the universe and all things in it will be restored on the day when the salvation of mankind is complete (Acts 3:21; Rom 8:18–23).

3. The Abrahamic Covenant

First, God chose Abraham through His sovereign grace to effectuate His promise with Adam. Then, God established a covenant with Abraham with a plan to bless all nations and people of the world through him. In light of this, the Abrahamic covenant can be considered the blueprint of God's plan of salvation, which would be carried out in history. Hence, the Abrahamic covenant is the basic model and structure of all covenants.

God established covenants with Abraham seven times:[6]

(1) God called Abraham and made the first promise in Genesis 12:1–3.
(2) God made the first promise of the land of Canaan in Genesis 12:7.
(3) God made another promise of the land of Canaan and about Abraham's descendants in Genesis 13:15–18.
(4) God reaffirmed His promise of the descendants and the land of Canaan through the covenant of the torch in Genesis 15:12–21.
(5) God established the "covenant of circumcision" in Genesis 17:9–14.
(6) God promised the birth of Isaac once again in Genesis 18:10.
(7) After Abraham had offered up Isaac, God made the final confirmation of all the covenants He had made previously.

The covenants that God made with Abraham were repeatedly confirmed with Isaac (Gen 26:3, 24), and Jacob (Gen 28:13–15; 35:12). Also, the covenants not only applied to Abraham's descendants, but also applied universally to all nations (Ps 105:8–11; Gal 3:7–9, 29).

4. The Sinaitic Covenant

God established the Sinaitic covenant with the Israelites as He gave the Ten Commandments when they had been camping in the Wilderness of Sinai for about 11 months. The Ten Commandments are the core and essence of the entire Law. They are not merely a set of commandments, but God's covenant (Exod 19:5; 24:7). In other words, the Ten Commandments are more than just commandments or law (Exod 24:12)—they are God's covenant of salvation which include His promises. Therefore, the ark that contained the Ten Commandments was called the "Ark of the Covenant" (Deut 31:26; 1 Sam 4:5; Heb 9:4; Rev 11:19), or the "Ark of God" (1 Sam 3:3), and the book where the commandments were recorded was called the "Book of the Covenant" (Exod 24:7; 2 Kgs 23:21; 2 Chr 34:30).

In the Sinaitic covenant, Moses read the book of the covenant in the hearing of the people of Israel (Exod 20:22–23:33) and they responded, "All that the LORD has spoken we will do, and we will be obedient!" (Exod 24:7). This covenant was a promise that God would be their protector as long as they remained under God's rule and sincerely served Him. After the covenant was established, Moses took the blood and sprinkled it on the people, and said, "Behold the blood of the covenant, which the LORD has made with you in accordance with all these words" (Exod 24:8).

The Sinaitic covenant that was given to the first generation of the Israelites in the early stage of the wilderness journey was reestablished on the first day of the eleventh month in the fortieth year since the Exodus. This covenant is called the "covenant of the Plains of Moab," distinct from the Sinaitic covenant (Deut 29:1–29).

However, the people of Israel completely forgot about those covenants after Joshua, who was Moses' successor, and all of the people from that generation were gathered to their fathers (Judg 2:6–10). They forsook God, committing abominable sins in the sight of the Lord. As a result of not keeping the Sinaitic covenant, they were punished through other nations (Ps 78:10–11, 37). Nevertheless, God, who is faithful to the covenant, restrained His anger many times and did not forsake His people (Ps 78:38). Rather, He guided and held onto them until the end, and He eventually established the Davidic covenant (Ps 78:70–72).

5. The Davidic Covenant

God established this covenant with King David after the Israelites' entry into Canaan, the period of the judges, and the reign of King Saul (2 Sam 7:12–16; 1 Chr 17:10–14). When David expressed the desire to build the temple of God and prayed, God gave this covenant through the prophet Nathan as an answer to that prayer (2 Sam 7:3–4).

The central message of the Davidic covenant is that the temple of God will be built by a descendant of David and that God will establish the throne of His kingdom forever (2 Sam 7:12–13). This was a promise about David's son Solomon; moreover, it was about the Messiah, the King of all kings, who would come through the royal line of David and establish the eternal kingdom of God. There are a couple of special characteristics in the covenant that God made with David.

First, it is a covenant made with an oath. An *oath* is generally understood as "a formal promise to achieve a goal or purpose." Also translated as "swear" or "adjure," the Hebrew word שָׁבַע (*shāba'*) shares the same consonant root as שֶׁבַע (*sheba'*), which means "seven." Thus, *swearing* or *making an oath* implies repeating the promise seven times. As a result, a promise with an oath (swear) is certain to be kept by both parties. Psalm 89:3–4 states, "I have made a covenant with My chosen; I have sworn to David My servant...." God continues to use this word to make oaths and swear to David: "Once I have sworn by My holiness..." (Ps 89:35) and "...which You swore to David in Your faithfulness" (Ps 89:49).

An oath is a pledge which is much stronger than a promise. If men have to keep their oaths, how much more certain and steadfast God's decisions must be if He confirms them with an oath (Ps 110:4)! Things decided by imperfect human beings can always change and be amended, but the things decided by the oath of God, who is the perfect sovereign ruler, are perfect and certainly remain immutable.

Second, it is a covenant made through faithfulness.

The word *faithfulness* means "steadfast or true in affection or allegiance." Psalm 89:49 affirms, "...which You swore to David in Your faithfulness."

> **Psalm 132:11** The LORD has sworn to David, a truth from which He will not turn back; "Of the fruit of your body I will set upon your throne."

The word *truth* is אֱמֶת (*'ĕmet*), which is derived from the word אָמַן (*'āman*), meaning "to be faithful" or "to be truthful." God is truthful, and thus it is impossible for God to lie (Heb 6:18). Therefore, the covenant made through God's faithfulness is the promise that will surely be fulfilled. No one can break His covenant (Jer 33:20–21). Isaiah 55:3 refers to the covenant that God established with David as "the faithful mercies shown to David." This is a declaration that the Davidic covenant will certainly be fulfilled, and that no interference—regardless of how strong it may be—can get in the way of its fulfillment.

6. The New Covenant of Jeremiah

This was the covenant that God gave to the prophet Jeremiah in the dismal times before Jerusalem was destroyed in 586 BC (Jer 31:31–34). The giving of a new covenant does not imply that the old covenant was imperfect; rather, it reflects the grace of God, who has compassion upon imperfect mankind and works to grant them perfect salvation. Even though God poured out His grace and renewed the covenant in every generation, the Israelites continued to engage in even greater sins through countless immoral and disobedient acts, eventually facing destruction. The purpose of the new covenant was to keep His people from losing the hope of salvation when taken captive to Babylon (Jer 51:50–53). In this covenant, God expressed His strong will by urging the Israelites to trust firmly in the new covenant and endure the time of the captivity until the end, making it an opportunity to repent, for He would surely save them.

There were two stipulations to this covenant.

First, God would write His law on the hearts of His people.

In Jeremiah 31:33, God declares, "I will put My law within them, and on their heart I will write it." While the old covenant was inscribed on stone tablets, the new covenant is inscribed on tablets of human hearts; thus, we can now become "a letter of Christ" through the gospel (2 Cor 3:1–3). Therefore, His promise that "I will be their God, and they shall be My people," would eventually be fulfilled (Jer 31:33; cf. Exod 6:7; 19:4–6; Ezek 36:25–28).

Second, the least to the greatest would know God.

Jeremiah 31:34 states, "And they shall not teach again, each man his neighbor and each man his brother, saying, 'Know the LORD,' for they shall all know Me, from the least of them to the greatest of them" (cf. Heb 8:8–13). In other words, God will allow people to come to know Him through the work of the Holy Spirit, even without the teaching of men (John 14:26; 15:26; 16:13).

The new covenant that the prophet Jeremiah prophesied was fulfilled at the coming of Jesus Christ, who had the power to fulfill the old covenant (Rom 8:2–4). For that reason, Jesus is described in Hebrews 12:24

as "the mediator of a new covenant" (also Heb 9:15). Jesus also said at the Last Supper, "This cup which is poured out for you is the new covenant in My blood" (Luke 22:20; cf. 1 Cor 11:25).

All of the covenants of the Bible were completed through the new covenant that our Lord Jesus Christ established through His suffering on the cross, which is the only and absolute foundation for the salvation of mankind and the coming of the eternal kingdom of heaven (Matt 26:27–29; Mark 14:24–25; Luke 22:20; Heb 8:10–13; 13:20). Therefore, in Christ all who have become spiritual sons of Abraham are in covenantal relationship with God (Rom 4:11, 16; Gal 3:7–9, 29).

The central theme of all the covenants is that God will take the covenantal people as His own and He will be their God (Gen 17:7; Exod 6:6–7; 19:4–6; Lev 11:45; 26:11–12; Deut 4:20; 29:13; 2 Kgs 11:17; 2 Chr 23:16; 2 Cor 6:16). Therefore, Greeks, Jews, circumcised, uncircumcised, barbarians, Scythians, slaves, and freemen can all receive salvation through faith in Jesus Christ—the mediator of the new covenant (Heb 8:6)—and they can become God's covenantal people (Rom 10:11–13; Col 3:11).

CHAPTER 3

Jesus Christ,
the Fulfiller of the Eternal Covenant

All of the previously discussed covenants are connected to Jesus Christ: every covenant testified about the coming of Jesus Christ and He came according to the promise. The history of redemption is God's work of establishing and fulfilling His covenant. The purpose of God's covenant is to send the Messiah and save mankind. The Bible testifies of the establishment, the succession, and the ultimate fulfillment of the covenant through the coming of Jesus Christ. Thus, we can correctly understand God's administration in the history of redemption when we examine the close relationship between the covenants found in the Bible and Jesus Christ.

When Adam and Eve broke the covenant of works in the beautiful Garden of Eden, an actual place in history, they were expelled (Gen 3:24). All who were born after Adam became children of death and wrath, deserving only to die because of sin (Rom 5:12; Eph 2:3). Founded upon the promise of the "seed of the woman," which God gave to mankind after the fall (Gen 3:15), the various covenants that have since followed have progressively built up toward the coming of Jesus Christ.

1. The Noahic Covenant and Jesus Christ

God established the covenant of the bow with Noah, his descendants, and every living creature. The essence of this covenant is that God would no longer judge the world with water so that the sons of promise would not be cut off (Gen 9:11, 15).

The sign given for this covenant is the bow in the cloud (Gen 9:11–17). While the world was in ruins and despair because of the flood, God gave Noah hope and promise by setting His rainbow in the cloud.

The people during the days of Noah must have trembled in fear of another judgment in the form of a flood every time it rained since the time of the great flood. However, they probably found a sense of security and peace in their hearts when they saw the rainbow. A rainbow stretches across the sky over the land in harmonious order of red, orange, yellow, green, blue, indigo/navy, and violet/purple, and fills us with a deep impression of wonder, joy and peace. This rainbow of eternal hope is Jesus Christ (Col 1:27). Today's Christians should have no fear as well, as long as they have this rainbow of hope. Even when the powers of tribulation encroach upon us, we will find comfort and hope as long as we have the rainbow.

Just as the people in the days of Noah found comfort by beholding the rainbow, and the people during the wilderness journey found life by beholding the bronze serpent, we need to find eternal life by wholeheartedly fixing our eyes upon Jesus Christ (Heb 12:2). The covenant of the bow is our living hope, foreshadowing Jesus Christ, our eternal comforter (2 Cor 1:3–7; 1 Pet 1:3).

2. The Abrahamic Covenant and Jesus Christ

Matthew 1:1 states, "The book of the genealogy of Jesus Christ, the son of David, the son of Abraham." To say that Jesus Christ is the son of Abraham first means that Jesus Christ is the Savior of the Jews who are "sons" of Abraham. However, all who have faith in Christ, regardless of their lineage, whether Jews or Gentiles, are sons of Abraham (Gal 3:7–9, 29). Thus, Jesus is the Savior of all who believe.

God made several covenants with Abraham, wherein only Jesus Christ was promised (Gal 3:16). *First*, God promised Abraham, "And in you all the families of the earth shall be blessed" in Genesis 12:3. The expression *in you* is בְּךָ (*beka*) in Hebrew and does not simply mean that all the families of the earth will be blessed because of the man Abraham, but that all the families of the earth will be blessed through Jesus Christ who will come as a descendant of Abraham.

Second, God promised Abraham in Genesis 15:5, "'Now look toward the heavens, and count the stars, if you are able to count them.' And He said to him, 'So shall your descendants be.'" The Hebrew word for "descendants" (זֶרַע, *zera'*) is in the singular form, initially referring to Isaac, but ultimately to Jesus Christ who was to come in the future (Gal 3:16). Jesus Christ was the true heir of the covenant, who would fulfill the covenant of God given to Abraham (Gen 15:2–4). Therefore, this covenant prophesies that there will be as many saints as there are stars in the heavens who will inherit the kingdom of heaven through Jesus Christ.

Third, God promised Abraham in Genesis 18:18, "…Abraham will surely become a great and mighty nation, and in him all the nations of the earth will be blessed." It means that all the nations of the earth will be blessed through Abraham, but even more so through Jesus Christ who was coming "in him" (בוֹ, *bō*) as his descendant.

Fourth, God promised Abraham in Genesis 22:17–18, "Indeed I will greatly bless you, and I will greatly multiply your seed as the stars of the heavens, and as the sand which is on the seashore; and your seed shall possess the gate of their enemies; and in your seed all the nations of the earth shall be blessed, because you have obeyed My voice."

God promised three things about "your seed" (זֶרַע, *zera*ʿ) in this covenant. In all three of the promises זֶרַע (*zera*ʿ) is used in the singular form, signifying Jesus Christ who is coming. The first promise was "I will greatly multiply your seed as the stars of the heavens, and as the sand which is on the seashore" (Gen 22:17). Again, "your seed" refers to Jesus Christ, who would come as the son of Abraham, and thus a countless number of people would be born again in faith through Him.

The next promise was "your seed shall possess the gate of their enemies" (Gen 22:17). Initially, this means that his seed will possess the enemy's city, but ultimately it is a promise that Jesus Christ will destroy all of Satan's authority and gain victory.

Lastly, God promised, "and in your seed all the nations of the earth shall be blessed" (Gen 22:18). Here again, the expression *in your seed* (בְּזַרְעֲךָ, *bĕzar*ʿ*ākā*) describes Jesus Christ, who will come as the son of Abraham and bring blessings to all the nations of the earth.

3. The Sinaitic Covenant and Jesus Christ

Four hundred and thirty years after the "promises" that God had given to Abraham and his descendants (Gal 3:15, 17), God gave the Ten Commandments and the Law to the Israelites through Moses in the Sinaitic covenant (Exod 20–23). Here, God gave the Law to Moses and Moses recounted to the people all of the Lord's words, and all the people answered that they would do all that God had spoken to them (Exod 24:3, 7). The promise of the coming of Jesus Christ is foreshadowed even in the Sinaitic covenant.

First, the "blood of the covenant" foreshadows that of Jesus Christ's. When the people promised that they would follow the covenant, Moses sacrificed young bulls and sprinkled their blood. In doing so, he confirmed the covenant and declared, "Behold the blood of the covenant which the LORD has made with you in accordance with all these words" (Exod 24:8).

The blood of the covenant that Moses established was a foreshadow of the perfect and eternal blood of the covenant that Jesus Christ would establish on the cross. With the time of the crucifixion drawing near, Jesus said at the Last Supper, "...this is My blood of the covenant, which is poured out for many for forgiveness" (Matt 26:28; Mark 14:24; Luke 22:20; 1 Cor 11:25). The blood of beasts forgave the sins of man only once when it was shed, but the blood of Jesus Christ that was shed on the cross completely removes all sins once for all (Rom 6:10; Heb 7:27; 9:12, 26; 10:2, 10; 1 Pet 3:18).

Second, this "first covenant" foreshadows the "new covenant" through Jesus Christ. The "first covenant" in Hebrews 8:7 is the Sinaitic covenant that God established with the people of Israel through Moses (Heb 8:7; 9:1, 15, 18). Although the people of Israel had vowed to keep this covenant, they could not completely keep it because of the sinfulness and weakness that resulted from the total depravity and fall of mankind. The first covenant caused the people to yearn for the new covenant that would be established through Jesus Christ. Jesus Christ is the mediator of the new covenant (Heb 9:15; 12:24). Therefore, it is not that Christians abide by the covenant with their own strength, but rather through God's power and the work of the Holy Spirit in Jesus Christ (Rom 8:2–4).

4. The Davidic Covenant and Jesus Christ

The New Testament begins with "υἱοῦ Δαυὶδ υἱοῦ Ἀβραάμ (*huiou David huiou Abraam*)" (Matt 1:1). This is a declaration that Jesus Christ is both the son of Abraham and David at the same time. The most important principle in the Davidic covenant is the promise of "a son," the son of David (2 Sam 7:12–14; 1 Chr 22:9–12; Ps 89:28–29). The son that God promised to give David was a "man of rest," and he was to build a house for God, and God would establish the throne of the son's kingdom forever (1 Chr 22:9–10).

This covenant was first fulfilled when David's son Solomon built the Temple of Jerusalem and dedicated it to the Lord. However, the promise that a son would come and establish the throne of the kingdom forever is ultimately the promise of the coming Jesus Christ, who would establish the eternal kingdom of heaven.

The archangel Gabriel said to Mary, "…and the Lord God will give Him the throne of His father David; and He will reign over the house of Jacob forever, and His kingdom will have no end" (Luke 1:32–33). This message is a reassuring testimony that Jesus Christ came as the One to fulfill the Davidic covenant (Ps 2:7, 12; Acts 13:33–34).

5. The New Covenant of Jeremiah and Jesus Christ

God sent the prophet Jeremiah and established a covenant right before Jerusalem perished. The center and the executor of this new covenant was Jesus Christ. Jesus called it "the new covenant in My blood" (Luke 22:20; 1 Cor 11:25) and the author of Hebrews refers to Jesus as "the mediator of a new covenant" (Heb 9:15; 12:24).

How is Jesus described in the new covenant?

First, it foreshadows the changing of the character and hearts of the people through the gospel of Jesus Christ.

> **Jeremiah 31:33** "But this is the covenant which I will make with the house of Israel after those days," declares the LORD, "I will put My law within them, and on their heart I will write it; and I will be their God, and they shall be My people."

The Hebrew word for *within* in this verse is קֶרֶב (*qereb*), meaning "inward part" or "midst." It refers to the inner thought, inward feelings, or character of a man. The Hebrew word for *heart* is לֵב (*lēb*), which means "inner man" or "mind." While the Old Testament law was the covenant that changes the outer aspects of a person, the new covenant is one that changes the character and the inner man of a person (Ps 40:8; Ezek 11:19–20; 2 Cor 3:2–3).

Jesus woke the people to the essence of sin when He spoke about how adultery stems from a person's character and heart. Up until Jesus' teaching, people were condemned only on the basis of their outward behaviors.

He said in Matthew 5:27–28, "You have heard that it was said, 'You shall not commit adultery,' but I say to you, that everyone who looks on a woman to lust for her has committed adultery with her already in his heart."

Until the time of Jesus, the law was not written on the hearts of the people, but the new covenant in Christ is the law that is written upon the heart (Jer 31:33; Heb 8:10). The new law that is written upon the heart is nothing other than the gospel of Jesus Christ.

The word *write* is כָּתַב (*kātab*), meaning "to inscribe." It is ἐπιγράφω (*epigraphō*) in Greek, which also means "to inscribe." The word is used for something that is carved permanently in stone rather than just written down superficially. When the gospel of Jesus Christ is inscribed on our hearts, we can enter into an eternal relationship with God and thus the promise, "I will be their God, and they shall be My people" (Jer 31:33; Heb 8:10), is fulfilled.

When God's law was not inscribed on the Israelites' hearts, they forsook, betrayed, and rebelled against Him. However, when God's law is eternally inscribed on their hearts, they will become faithful people who will never forsake God.

Second, it foreshadows the complete forgiveness that Jesus Christ will give.

> **Jeremiah 31:34** "And they shall not teach again, each man his neighbor and each man his brother, saying, 'Know the LORD,' for they shall all know Me, from the least of them to the greatest of them," declares the LORD, "for I will forgive their iniquity, and their sin I will remember no more."

The word *know* used in this verse is יָדַע (*yāda'*) in Hebrew, signifying a knowledge attained through one's whole personality, not merely through the intellect—knowing fully just as we see "face to face" (1 Cor 13:12).

How is such a phenomenon possible? Jeremiah 31:34 explains that it is possible because God forgives their iniquities and remembers their sins no more. In the Hebrew text of Jeremiah 31:34, there is a subordinating conjunction *for* (כִּי, *kî*), which expresses cause. In other words, people will come to know God personally as a result of His redemptive work (Heb 8:11).

The work of redemption, which grants forgiveness of all sins, is fulfilled through the cross of Jesus Christ (Eph 1:7; Heb 9:12–13, 28). Hence, the cross of Jesus Christ becomes the foundation upon which people can come to know God personally. For this reason, God says that He will establish a covenant with "those who turn from transgression in Jacob" in Isaiah 59:20–21. Those who repent through God's sovereign grace and partake in the redeeming work of the cross of Jesus Christ will receive the new covenant. Isaiah 59:21 presents two kinds of phenomena that result from the new covenant.

> **Isaiah 59:21** "And as for Me, this is My covenant with them," says the LORD: "My Spirit which is upon you, and My words which I have put in your mouth, shall not depart from your mouth, nor from the mouth of your offspring, nor from the mouth of your offspring's offspring," says the LORD, "from now and forever."

According to this verse, God's Spirit and Word will not depart from the mouth of God's people forever once the new covenant is made. The Hebrew word used for *My Spirit* in this verse is רוּחַ (*rûaḥ*), referring to the Holy Spirit (Isa 61:1; 1 Jn 2:27). For *My words*, the Hebrew word דָּבָר (*dābar*) is used, referring to "the Word of God." The Holy Spirit and the Word of God worked together during the time of the early church. When Peter proclaimed the Word, the Holy Spirit came down upon all who were listening to the Word (Acts 10:44). The time of the new covenant has come in Jesus Christ, but the final completion has not yet been achieved. When the new covenant is completely fulfilled through the Second Coming Lord, the Word and the Holy Spirit of God will not depart throughout the generations.

The focus of all the covenants discussed in this chapter is none other than Jesus Christ Himself; Jesus Christ is the final fulfillment and completion of all the covenants in the Bible. Every covenant testified to Jesus Christ progressively through clear revelations in the flow of redemptive history. The genealogy of Jesus Christ is a synopsis of God's redemptive administration by which His covenants have manifested throughout history.

We will be able to understand clearly the essence of the redemptive history in the Bible as we carefully study God's covenant and its fulfillment in the genealogy of Jesus Christ.

עמלק

מדבר צין והוא קדש

ים המלח

עתר

מקדה

עיר כרמל

הצור

שבט

ענב

מדבר סיני

קישברינ

מדבר פארן

מדבר שור

מולדה

אלהלד

שרוחן

באר שבע

שבט שמעון

גת

ביתמרבעות

אשקלון

ארץ פלשתם

ארץ גשן

פתם

שרה

צען

ים אלכסנדרי

לוח המסעות במדבר
אשר על פי ה' יסעו ועל פי ה' יחנו

כט' חרהגדגד	טו' רתמה	א' רעמסס
ל' יטבתה	טז' רמןפרץ	ב' סכת
לא' עברנה	יז' לבנה	ג' אתם
לב' עצינגבר	יח' רסה	ד' פיהחירת
לג' מדברצין	יט' קהלתה	ה' מרה
לד' הרההר	ך' הרספר	ו' אילם
לה' צלמנה	כא' חרדה	ז' ים סוף
לו' פונן	כב' מקהלה	ח' מדברסין
לז' אבת	כג' תחת	ט' דפקה
לח' דיבןגד	כד' תרח	יו' אלוש
לט' עלמןדבלה	כה' מתקה	יא' רפידים
מ' הרי עברים	כו' חשמנה	יב' מדברסיני
מא' מסרות	כז' מסרות	יג' קברתהתאוה
בא' ערבתמואב	כח' בני יעקן	יד' חצרות

PART TWO

God's Administration in the History of Redemption and the Genealogy of Jesus Christ

While Genesis—the first book of the Old Testament—opens with the creation account of the heavens and the earth, Matthew—the first book of the New Testament—opens with the genealogy of Jesus Christ who came to this world to save fallen mankind. The first gateway through which the New Testament introduces the coming of Jesus Christ is the "genealogy."

Generally speaking, a genealogy is a record of a family tree that records physical blood lineage. It is recorded for the purpose of conveying legal rights, verifying the purity of an ethnic heritage, and/or to boast of the achievements of one's ancestors. In order to improve their own genealogies, people have not shied away from "beautifying" them by deleting shameful pasts and highlighting proud achievements. The nation of Korea has about 260 family names and puts great importance on genealogies to the extent that it can almost claim that the concept of genealogy originated from Korea. People used to guard the books of their genealogies with their lives, even if their house was on fire! It was the greatest disgrace to be obliterated from the genealogy of the family. In the case of pairing of marriages, the genealogy of the prospective spouse is scrutinized also.

The genealogies of the Jews have been well preserved even through tumultuous times and many wars (1 Chr 1–9). Land inheritance, birth order, as well as social position and status were all determined according to the genealogies (1 Chr 5:1–3; Num 3:10; 26:55; 33:54).

After returning from the Babylonian exile, those who asserted priestly rights had to prove that they were descendants in the priestly lineage through their genealogy. If their genealogy was uncertain, those people were forbidden from performing priestly duties (Ezra 2:61–63; Neh 7:63–64). Sons of three families among those who returned from the Babylonian exile—the sons of Habaiah, the sons of Hakkoz, and the sons of Barzillai—could not perform priestly duties because they could not prove their genealogical ancestries (Ezra 2:61). There were also sons from three families who were not able to provide evidence that their fathers' households and their descendants were from Israel: the sons of Delaiah, the sons of Tobiah, and the sons of Nekoda—a total of 652 people (Ezra 2:59–60). One had to know his or her genealogy in order to be registered during the New Testament times (Luke 2:1–4). Because the Israelites valued their lineages, they would call a person specifically by mentioning the name of his or her father, grandfather or other direct or collateral relatives (Num 27:1; Josh 17:1; Zeph 1:1; 1 Sam 1:1; 1 Chr 4:37).

A genealogy not only contains the family's roots, but also the history of various events and stories that took place in different times and places. At the same time, it serves as a firm foundation for future generations and the hope for their future. The genealogy is very important because it is the definitive proof that verifies and justifies the identity and social position of an individual.

Therefore, the genealogies in Matthew or Luke initially serve as conclusive evidence of the historicity of the birth of Jesus Christ of Nazareth and the proof of his identity. Jesus was a Jew by birth and an actual person in history, who was known to the people as the son of Mary and Joseph of Bethlehem of Judea (Luke 3:23). In essence, however, he was God the Son, the promised Messiah of the Old Testament, the one who was preordained from eternity according to God's grand plan for the salvation of mankind.

The genealogy of Jesus Christ is the very core of the entire history of redemption. It is a vivid panorama of redemptive history, which awakens us to God's faithfulness in continuing the genealogy and to His zeal in working without resting until the final fulfillment of the covenant.

CHAPTER 4

The Book of the Genealogy of Jesus Christ

Matthew 1:1 The book of the genealogy of Jesus Christ

βίβλος   γενέσεως   Ἰησοῦ   Χριστοῦ
biblos   *geneseōs*   *Iesou*   *Christou*

The phrase, "the book of the genealogy" in Matthew 1:1 is βίβλος γενέσεως (*biblos geneseōs*) in Greek. The word βίβλος (*biblos*) means "book" and γενέσεως (*geneseōs*) is the possessive form of γένεσις (*genesis*), which means "beginning," "origin," "root," or "existence." Therefore, the *book of genealogy* in Matthew 1:1 also means the "book of history" and the "book of the origins." A similar word is used in the first half of Matthew 1:18, "the birth of Jesus Christ took place in this way…." The Greek word for *birth* in this verse is also γένεσις (*genesis*).

In the Old Testament, the word *account* in Genesis 2:4, "the account of the heavens and the earth," and *the book of the generations* in Genesis 5:1, "the book of the generations of Adam," are both translated as βίβλος γενέσεως (*biblos geneseōs*) in the Septuagint just like "the book of the genealogy" in Matthew 1:1. Especially in the case of γένεσις (*genesis*), the same Greek word had already been established as the standard title for the book of Genesis in the Septuagint[7] by the time Matthew's gospel was being recorded. Therefore, using the word γένεσις (*genesis*) to start out the book of Matthew reminds the readers of the beginning of the Old Testament, "Genesis."

In this sense, Jesus Christ's genealogy in Matthew 1 can be viewed as a proclamation of the beginning and the origin of the entire Bible. It parallels the account of the creation of the universe and mankind (Gen 2:4) and the genealogy of the godly patriarchs starting from Adam (Gen 5:1).

In other words, it is the proclamation of the new creation (γένεσις) through Jesus Christ.

The Hebrew word for *genealogy* is תּוֹלְדוֹת (*tôlēdôt*), which is translated as "account" in Genesis 2:4, "generations" in Genesis 5:1, and "records of the generations" in Genesis 6:9; 10:1; 11:10, 27; 25:12, 19; 36:1; and 37:2. All of this confirms that the genealogies in the Bible are not based on myths, symbolisms or parables, but are actual records of events that took place in history.

Accordingly, Matthew 1:1 would read "the *toledoth* of Jesus Christ, son of David, son of Abraham." This signifies that it is the account, history, genealogy and record of Jesus Christ who actually lived in history.

Specifically, the word תּוֹלְדוֹת (*tôlēdôt*) is derived from יָלַד (*yālad*), which means "birth," "offspring," "result," "history of an event or a person." This word means more than "birth" or "offspring," signifying a profound sense of God's administration and providence that is fulfilled throughout the life of the person in reference.

The use of the word βίβλος (*biblos*), which means "book," suggests that the genealogy in Matthew 1 contains enough information to be considered a complete book even though it is only 16 verses long.

Therefore, Matthew 1:1 is not simply a reference to the event of Jesus Christ's birth nor is it merely an introduction to the book of Matthew or the New Testament. Rather, it should be seen as a significant proclamation which reveals the beginning, the origin and the existence of Jesus Christ. At the same time it brings together the entire history of the Old and New Testaments. Further, by recording the genealogy of Jesus Christ, Matthew is declaring that God is in direct control of the entire history of Israel. Moreover, by calling it the "book of the genealogy of Jesus Christ," he has proclaimed that Jesus Christ is the essence of the Old Testament and the basis for the New Testament (John 5:39; Luke 24:27, 44).

Truly, the axis of world history and the centripetal force behind history has been God's sovereign work of redemption through Jesus Christ. Thus, the history of mankind is reflected by the history of salvation as it progressed toward its ultimate purpose—Jesus Christ. Therefore, those who are included in the genealogies are linked to Jesus Christ in God's eyes. It would not be an exaggeration to say that they had been born, had lived, and died for the purpose of fulfilling the divine work of redemption through Jesus Christ.

Two core points in Jesus' genealogy are important for redemptive history: Jesus Christ who came as "the son of David, son of Abraham" and Jesus Christ who came as the seed of the woman.

1. The Son of David, the Son of Abraham

The very opening words of the New Testament are "The book of the genealogy of Jesus Christ, the son of David, the son of Abraham" (Matt 1:1). Why does the New Testament introduce Jesus as the son of Abraham and the son of David?

First, it testifies that Jesus Christ is the Messiah who was promised through Abraham and David. The Jews took more pride in Abraham and David than in any other patriarch because Abraham was regarded as the father of the Jews and David as the king who firmly established the royal lineage.

God had promised that through Abraham's "offspring shall all the nations of the earth be blessed" (Gen 22:18) and through David He promised, "I will raise up your offspring after you, who shall come from your body...I will establish the throne of his kingdom forever" (2 Sam 7:12–13). These are covenants which promise that the Messiah will come as a descendant of Abraham and David.

Therefore, more than anyone else, the Jews eagerly awaited the fulfillment of the promise that the Messiah would come as a descendant of Abraham and David. By opening the genealogy of Jesus Christ with the introduction, "Jesus Christ, the son of David, the son of Abraham," Matthew is emphatically proclaiming that Jesus Christ is the Messiah that was prophesied to Abraham and David.

Second, it testifies of God's faithfulness in fulfilling the covenants. Abraham was born in 2166 BC. The first time that God established a covenant with Abraham was in 2091 BC when he was 75 years old. At that time, God said, "all peoples on earth will be blessed through you" (Gen 12:3 NIV). The phrase, "through you" is בְּךָ (*bēkā*) in Hebrew and means "in you." Therefore, God is saying that all nations will be blessed "in" Abraham through Jesus Christ who will come as Abraham's descendant.

The promise of the Messiah who would come as Abraham's offspring was fulfilled 2,087 years later through Jesus Christ, who was born in 4 BC. By doing this, God proclaimed his faithfulness in fulfilling His covenants.

Furthermore, in 1003 BC, which was after David had finished the seven years and six months of reign in Hebron and started his reign in Jerusalem, God promised in the Davidic Covenant that the Messiah would come as David's descendant. Then, God fulfilled that promise through Jesus Christ about 1,000 years later.

Thus, Matthew's genealogical account explains the Christ-centered administration of redemptive history from the perspective of the establishment and the fulfillment of the covenants with Abraham and David.

2. The Seed of the Woman

After the fall of Adam, the first promise of the coming of the Messiah is the promise of the seed of the woman. Genesis 3:15 says that "he shall bruise the head of the serpent" which actually means that he will completely destroy the serpent's head. Therefore, Genesis 3:15 is the Proto-gospel which promises that Jesus Christ will defeat Satan and be victorious (Rev 12:9).

The genealogy of Matthew 1 does not merely lay out the physical blood lineage or ancestry of Jesus, but shows how the seed of the woman came to this world through the lineage of faith in the history of redemption. To accomplish this end, God had to put on human form and come into this world. It was not done through the union of a man and a woman, but only through the body of a virgin (Isa 7:14; Matt 1:23). Indeed, Jesus was the seed of the woman conceived by the Holy Spirit (Matt 1:18; Luke 1:35).

As the seed of the woman, Jesus essentially does not have a human father. Jesus was conceived through the Holy Spirit, not through sexual relations; He was born of a virgin body. Although He was of the same nature as we are, He was the sinless God-man who became our Savior. All human beings other than Jesus Christ are seeds of men. In other words, they are from and of men (Matt 1:1–17; 1 Cor 11:8). All seeds of men are sinners (Rom 3:10); they have been born into this world through natural reproductive means. However, Jesus is the seed of the woman, conceived by the Holy Spirit and is by no means a seed of man.[8]

Throughout the long history of Israel, God had established covenants in various forms, and He ceaselessly continued the providence for redemption in order to fulfill the covenants. Eventually, Jesus Christ was born through the body of a woman when the fullness of the time came (Gal 4:4).

In reality, Jesus Christ came at the apex of history just as the Bible had promised. Accordingly, He brought the work of Satan to an end by destroying sin and death (Heb 2:14; 1 Jn 3:5; Jude 1:6), thereby redeeming mankind. God saves His people based on the covenants. God has faithfully kept those covenants and has continually advanced His work of salvation without ceasing even until today.

The promises made by an imperfect human being can always be changed or canceled. However, the covenants made by the perfect sovereign God, can never be changed, for God invariably fulfills all that He has promised. Indeed our God is unlike man for He cannot lie (Heb 6:18), nor does He revoke His promises. Moreover, He will certainly fulfill the covenants He has spoken when the time comes (Num 23:19; Deut 8:18). God's covenant is not altered due to human circumstances or to the passage of time, nor is it ever revoked or terminated in mid-course; it will certainly bear fruit (Isa 55:11). Truly, heaven and earth may pass away but not the smallest letter or stroke of God's Word will pass until all is accomplished (Matt 5:18).

Therefore, if we firmly hold on to the authority of the scepter of the Word, then we will be able to overcome any obstacle and find resolution to our problems. Since the One who promised is faithful, we must also be unmoved in the hope of our faith and continue to hold firmly onto the promise of God as we move forward.

CHAPTER 5

The Structure of
Jesus Christ's Genealogy

The genealogy of Jesus Christ is the genealogy of God's covenant and grace. It is the fulfillment of the Triune God's plan and providence, which was established before all ages for the redemption of mankind.

Jesus' genealogy is recorded twice: once in Matthew 1 and again in Luke 3. The genealogy in the Gospel of Matthew continues through David's son Solomon (Matt 1:6) whereas Luke's genealogy continues through Nathan (2 Sam 5:14; 1 Chr 3:5; 14:4), Solomon's full brother (Luke 3:31). Even though the genealogies in Matthew and Luke go through different lines after David, both are true genealogies of Jesus Christ based on historical facts.

Luke, in writing his Gospel, reveals that it was based on "the things that have been accomplished among us" (Luke 1:1), and introduces himself as one who has undertaken to compile a narrative "as those who from the beginning were eyewitnesses and ministers of the word have delivered them to us" (Luke 1:2). As such, not only did Luke write his narrative based on the facts of history, but "having followed all things closely for some time past," he wrote "an orderly account" (καθεξῆς [kathexēs]: "in order"; Luke 1:3). Therefore, we must remember that although the genealogies of Matthew 1 and Luke 3 list two different lineages, they are recorded so as to testify about one man, Jesus Christ.

1. Comparison of the Genealogies in Matthew 1 and Luke 3

The genealogy in the Gospel of Matthew (Matt 1:1–17) is recorded in the prologue of the book. The genealogy in the Gospel of Luke is placed in between two events: the baptism of Jesus Christ (Luke 3:21–22) and the devil's three temptations (Luke 4:1–13). In the Gospel of Luke, the author specifically introduces the genealogy of Jesus Christ with the words,

"Jesus, when He began His ministry, was about thirty years of age" (Luke 3:23). In Greek, the expression "when He began His ministry" is just one word, ἄρχω (archō). It means "to be the first, to be the chief, to rule" (Mark 10:42; Rom 15:12). Thus, the verse can be viewed as a declaration that Jesus Christ's lordship and reign had begun.

The genealogy in the Gospel of Matthew records a total of 41 people from Abraham to Jesus in a linear descending order (going from parent to offspring; Matt 1:1–17), whereas Luke's genealogy records a total of 77 people (including God and Jesus) in a linear ascending order (going from offspring to parent; Luke 3:23–38).

Even though Jesus' genealogy is expressed in terms of three periods each of 14 generations, totaling 42 generations (Matt 1:17), there are actually only 41 persons recorded because David was counted twice (Matt 1:6). The genealogy recorded in Luke is also considered by some to have a total of 78 generations because it includes Ἀδμίν (Admin), who is not mentioned in the genealogy in some translations of the Bible. Ἀδμίν (Admin) is listed in the 4th Revised Edition of the UBS (United Bible Societies) Greek New Testament, but not in the Textus Receptus.[9]

Matthew's genealogy spans 2,000 years, recording the generations beginning with Abraham, whereas Luke's genealogy spans the entire Old Testament period of 4,000 years. The genealogy in the Gospel of Matthew begins with Abraham and ends with Jesus Christ, while the genealogy in the Gospel of Luke starts with Jesus and ends with God Himself. Besides having disparate listing formats, the two genealogies are identical from Abraham to David except for one name (see "Ram" in Matt 1:3; "Arni" in Luke 3:33; ASV, NET, NJB, NLT, NRSV, RSV). However, the names are all different from David to the generation before Jesus' father Joseph. Also, the genealogy in the Gospel of Luke lists a total of 56 generations from Abraham to Jesus, which is significantly more than the number of generations listed in Matthew.

Although these points will be discussed in greater detail later, let us consider a few important points now. The genealogy of Matthew 1 does not record all the generations in continuity; many generations have been omitted. This indicates that the genealogy in Matthew 1 contains a deliberate intention according to God's administration of redemption. Moreover, Matthew's genealogy lists a total of five women—Tamar (Matt 1:3), Rahab (Matt 1:5a), Ruth (Matt 1:5b), Uriah's wife (Matt 1:6), Mary (Matt 1:16); however, the genealogy in the Gospel of Luke mentions no women.

Text	Format	Number of generations	Beginning – End	Unique Features
Matthew 1	Linear descending	41	Abraham – Jesus	Genealogy of Joseph's tribe
Luke 3	Linear ascending	77	Jesus – God	Genealogy of Mary's tribe

The genealogy in the Gospel of Matthew is known to be the genealogy of Joseph's lineage, whereas the genealogy in the Gospel of Luke belongs to the line of Mary, Jesus' mother.[10] The genealogy in the Gospel of Matthew contains 42 generations divided into 3 periods of 14 generations. This structure confirms how God administered in each generation according to the covenants with Abraham and David until the fullness of the time had come when He sent Jesus Christ as the ultimate fulfiller of these covenants (Gal 4:4). Furthermore, the structure of the genealogy in the Gospel of Luke (linear ascending) verifies that Jesus Christ, who came to earth to save sinful mankind (Rom 3:22; Acts 2:21; 10:43; 16:31), is indeed the "Son of God" (Luke 3:22; 4:3, 9; Rom 1:2–4; cf. Luke 1:35; 2:49).

2. Structure of the Genealogy in Matthew 1 (Matt 1:1–17)

Matthew 1:17 "fourteen generations…fourteen…fourteen"

The genealogy of Jesus Christ according to the Gospel of Matthew is introduced in Matthew 1:1, its content is presented in Matthew 1:2–16, and its structure is explained in Matthew 1:17. Thus, Matthew 1:17 is the key to interpreting and understanding the genealogy in Matthew 1.

Matthew 1:17 Therefore all the generations from Abraham to David are fourteen generations; and from David to the deportation to Babylon fourteen generations; and from the deportation to Babylon to the time of Christ fourteen generations.

It was 14 generations from Abraham to David (Matt 1:2–5), 14 from David to the exile to Babylon (Matt 1:6–11), and 14 from the exile to Babylon up to Jesus Christ (Matt 1:12–16).[11] It is clear that Matthew intended to divide the history of Israel into three parts using major historical events as reference points. Furthermore, it is also clear that he used "14 generations" to reveal God's administration in the history of redemption.

There is no need to be overly attached to the meaning of numbers in the Bible. However, it would be a mistake to say that there is no significance to the number "14" here. Obviously, 14 is 7 doubled. In the Bible, the number 7 is the sum of 3 and 4. The number 3 is the heavenly number representing God the Father, God the Son, and God the Holy Spirit; and 4 is the number representing the earth with its 4 cardinal directions of east, west, north and south. Thus, 7 is a symbolic number that signifies fullness, abundance, the entirety, and the time it takes to fulfill a plan.[12] It is a perfect number that lacks nothing; it is a number of completion and wholeness. The Semites[13] gave more weight and significance to 14 than to 7 because 14 is 7 doubled.[14]

The fact that the genealogy in the Gospel of Luke is made up of 77 people also conclusively affirms the perfect integrity of God's administration of redemptive history—that through many generations, God administered His plan without error. Therefore, the genealogy of Jesus Christ, through the use of the numbers "7" and "14," testifies to the complete fulfillment of the plan of salvation through God's Son, Jesus Christ.

Organizing the 42 generations from Abraham to Christ into three periods of 14 generations each conveys a strong message that God's perfect administration was provident in each period. Behind every course of Israel's history, God sovereignly intervened to fulfill His predestined will at the right time (Eph 1:4; 3:11; 2 Tim 1:9).

The genealogy in the Gospel of Matthew is an astonishing proclamation that Jesus Christ came at the preordained time (Hab 2:3; Mark 1:15; Gal 4:2) in accordance with God's plan of redemption. Apostle Paul called this "an administration suitable to the fullness of the times" (Eph 1:10). The word *administration* means "the act of planning, organizing and managing an affair or activity," which would signify God's ruling and managing the entire universe.

We must be able to discover God's perfect and flawless administration of redemption in this genealogy. Moreover, we must receive wisdom to understand that even human history, through which we are living at this moment, is not something that flows in any coincidental or random way. We must understand that history is proceeding toward the second coming of Christ under the administration of the perfect God, the Alpha and Omega of history (1 Tim 2:6; 6:15; Heb 10:37).

3. Structure of the Genealogy in Luke 3 (Luke 3:23–38)

> **Luke 3:23** And when He began His ministry, Jesus Himself was about thirty years of age, being supposedly the son of Joseph, the son of Eli.

> **Luke 3:38** the son of Enosh, the son of Seth, the son of Adam, the son of God.

Unlike the genealogy in the Gospel of Matthew, the genealogy in the Gospel of Luke does not provide any explanation about special dividing points or any explanations about certain people. Rather, the genealogy in the Gospel of Luke simply and systematically lists all 77 people.

In Matthew 1, the genealogy is listed in order from ancestor to descendant, but in Luke 3, the genealogy is listed in reverse order from descendant to ancestor. In the Old Testament, choir members were the only ones whose genealogies were listed in reverse order (1 Chr 6:31–48). This "linear ascending structure" of the genealogy in the Gospel of Luke is its most prominent feature and the key to interpreting the genealogy in the perspective of redemptive history.

When we carefully examine the persons listed in the genealogy of Luke, we can see that these 77 people are listed in 11 groups of 7 people each with important persons serving as dividing points. The people who are listed first in each of the 11 groups (i.e., Jesus, Joseph, Mattathias, Shealtiel, Jesus, Joseph, David, Arni, Terah, Cainan, Jared) generally hold important positions in the history of redemption.

Some assert that the genealogy in the Gospel of Luke was not categorized by birth but by themes. In other words, the genealogy in the Gospel of Luke is not historically (biologically) organized, but is organized according to various theological themes.[15]

Some people also divide up the 77 people listed in the genealogy of Luke's Gospel into groups of four periods: 21 (3x7) generations from the return of the exile to Jesus Christ, then 21 (3x7) generations of the kingdom period, 14 (2x7) generations from David to Abraham, and the final 21 (3x7) generations before Abraham.[16]

(1) The meaning of the 77 names
In the following table, the 77 names that appear in the genealogy of Luke 3 are organized into 11 groups of 7 persons with their names and their meanings listed. Most of the people listed in this genealogy are obscure individuals whose names or achievements cannot be found in the Old Testament.

However, we must remember that in the Bible, all names—without exception—are meaningful. Moreover, the meanings, which these names possess within the administration of redemptive history, are very significant. We can guess the historical identity of a person through the name that appears in the genealogy. Furthermore, because parents bestowed most names in the Bible (Gen 4:1, 25–26; 5:3, 28–29; 16:11, 15; 17:19; 19:37–38; Judg 8:31; 1 Chr 7:23), the names give us insight into the parent's spiritual desires and thankfulness, historical context of the times, and the circumstances surrounding the birth of the child.

When we scrutinize the names and their meanings with the help and inspiration of the Holy Spirit, I am certain that we will receive amazing grace to understand God's administration of redemption as revealed through the genealogies.

4. Chart: The Meanings of the 77 Names

(1) From Jesus to Jannai		
① Jesus / Ἰησοῦς	Luke 3:23	The Lord saves; He who saves His people from their sins (Matt 1:21)
② Joseph / Ἰωσήφ	Luke 3:23	The Lord adds; may the Lord add
③ Eli / Ἡλί	Luke 3:23	Ascent
④ Matthat / Ματθάτ	Luke 3:24	Gift of God
⑤ Levi / Λευί	Luke 3:24	To be joined
⑥ Melchi / Μελχί	Luke 3:24	King
⑦ Jannai / Ἰανναί	Luke 3:24	God is gracious
(2) From Joseph to Maath		
① Joseph / Ἰωσήφ	Luke 3:24	The Lord adds; may the Lord add
② Mattathias / Ματταθίας	Luke 3:25	Gift of God
④ Amos / Ἀμώς	Luke 3:25	Strong
⑤ Nahum / Ναούμ	Luke 3:25	Comfort
⑥ Hesli / Ἐσλί	Luke 3:25	God at my side
⑦ Naggai / Ναγγαί	Luke 3:25	Brilliancy
⑧ Maath / Μάαθ	Luke 3:26	Small, wiping away, breaking

(3) From Mattathias to Zerubbabel

① Mattathias / Ματταθίας	Luke 3:26	Gift of God
② Semein / Σεμεείν	Luke 3:26	The Lord is fame; the Lord hears me
③ Josech / Ἰωσηχ Joseph / Ἰωσήφ	Luke 3:26	He hears
④ Joda / Ἰωδά	Luke 3:26	Praise of the Lord (same as Judah)
⑤ Joanan / Ἰωάννα	Luke 3:27	The Lord has been gracious
⑥ Rhesa / Ῥησά	Luke 3:27	Affection
⑦ Zerubbabel / Ζοροβαβέλ	Luke 3:27	Descended (seed) of Babylon

(4) From Shealtiel to Er

① Shealtiel / Σαλαθιήλ	Luke 3:27	Asked of God
② Neri / Νηρί	Luke 3:27	The Lord is my light (lamp)
③ Melchi / Μελχί	Luke 3:28	King
④ Addi / Ἀδδί	Luke 3:28	Ornament
⑤ Cosam / Κωσάμ	Luke 3:28	Diviner
⑥ Elmadam or Elmodam (KJV) / Ἐλμωδάμ	Luke 3:28	Measure
⑦ Er / Ἤρ	Luke 3:28	Watchful; awake; stir up

(5) From Joshua to Judah

① Joshua / Ἰησοῦς	Luke 3:29	The Lord saves; the Lord is salvation
② Eliezer / Ἐλιέζερ	Luke 3:29	My God is helper; God of help
③ Jorim / Ἰωρείμ	Luke 3:29	The Lord is exalted
④ Matthat / Ματθάτ	Luke 3:29	Gift of God
⑤ Levi / Λευί	Luke 3:29	To be joined
⑥ Simeon / Συμεών	Luke 3:30	Harkening; hearing
⑦ Judah / Ἰούδας	Luke 3:30	Praise; let Him be praised

(6) From Joseph to Nathan

① Joseph / Ἰωσήφ	Luke 3:30	The Lord adds; may the Lord add
② Jonam / Ἰωνάν	Luke 3:30	The Lord is gracious; grace of God
③ Eliakim / Ἐλιακείμ	Luke 3:30	God raises up
④ Melea / Μελεᾶς	Luke 3:31	Fullness; abundance
⑤ Menna / Μεννά	Luke 3:31	Great pain
⑥ Mattatha / Ματταθά	Luke 3:31	Gift; gift of the Lord
⑦ Nathan / Ναθάν	Luke 3:31	Gift; giver

(7) From David to Amminadab

① David / Δαβίδ	Luke 3:31; 1 Chr 2:15; Ruth 4:22	Beloved; friend
② Jesse / Ἰεσσαί	Luke 3:32; 1 Chr 2:12–13; Ruth 4:22	The Lord exists; extant
③ Obed / Ὠβήδ	Luke 3:32; 1 Chr 2:12; Ruth 4:21–22	Worshipper; servant
④ Boaz / Βοόζ	Luke 3:32; 1 Chr 2:11–12; Ruth 4:21	Mental keenness; in him is strength
⑤ Salmon / Σαλμών	Luke 3:32; 1 Chr 2:11; Ruth 4:20–21	Mantel; clothing; garment
⑥ Nahshon / Ναασσών	Luke 3:32; 1 Chr 2:10–11; Ruth 4:20	Enchanter; oracle; one that foretells
⑦ Amminadab / Ἀμιναδάβ	Luke 3:33; 1 Chr 2:10; Ruth 4:19–20	My kinsman is noble; my people are generous

(8) From Arni to Abraham

① Arni (ASV)/ Ἀράμ	Luke 3:33; 1 Chr 2:9–150; Ruth 4:19	Exalted; high
② Hezron / Ἐσρώμ	Luke 3:33; 1 Chr 2:9–10; Ruth 4:18–19	Surrounded by a wall; enclosure
③ Perez / Φάρες	Luke 3:33; 1 Chr 2:4; Ruth 4:18	A bursting forth; breach
④ Judah / Ἰούδας	Luke 3:33; 1 Chr 2:1	Praise; let Him be praised
⑤ Jacob / Ἰακώβ	Luke 3:34; 1 Chr 1:34; 2:1	Heel grabber; supplanter
⑥ Isaac / Ἰσαάκ	Luke 3:34; 1 Chr 1:28, 34	Laughter
⑦ Abraham / Ἀβραάμ	Luke 3:34; 1 Chr 1:27, 34	Father of a multitude; Father of many nations

* For the next 20 generations from Abraham to Adam, please refer to Part 4 in *The Genesis Genealogies: God's Administration in the History of Redemption* by Abraham Park.

(9) From Terah to Shelah

① Terah / Θάρα	Luke 3:34; 1 Chr 1:26	To delay; to station
② Nahor / Ναχώρ	Luke 3:34; 1 Chr 1:26	To snort
③ Serug / Σαρούχ	Luke 3:35; 1 Chr 1:26	Tendril; strength; firmness
④ Reu / Ῥαγαύ	Luke 3:35; 1 Chr 1:25	Friend; neighbor
⑤ Peleg / Φάλεκ	Luke 3:35; 1 Chr 1:19, 25	Division; part; separate
⑥ Eber / Ἔβερ	Luke 3:35; 1 Chr 1:18–19, 25	From beyond or across
⑦ Shelah / Σαλά	Luke 3:35; 1 Chr 1:18, 24	Sent; sprout; outstretching

(10) From Cainan to Enoch		
① Cainan[17] / Καϊνάν	Luke 3:36	Acquired (unexpectedly); a (great) possession
② Arphaxad / Ἀρφαξάδ	Luke 3:36; 1 Chr 1:17, 24	Boundary
③ Shem / Σήμ	Luke 3:36; 1 Chr 1:4, 24	Name, renown, fame
④ Noah / Νῶε	Luke 3:36; 1Chr 1:4	Rest, comfort
⑤ Lamech / Λάμεχ	Luke 3:36; 1Chr 1:4	Powerful one
⑥ Methuselah / Μαθουσαλά	Luke 3:37; 1Chr 1:3	When he dies, judgment; man of dart (javelin)
⑦ Enoch / Ἐνώχ	Luke 3:37; 1Chr 1:3	Dedicated, begin or initiated, teacher
(11) From Jared to God		
① Jared / Ἰαρέδ	Luke 3:37; 1Chr 1:2	Descent, to go or come down
② Mahalaleel / Μαλελεήλ	Luke 3:37; 1Chr 1:2	Praise of God, God be praised
③ Cainan / Καϊνάν	Luke 3:37; 1Chr 1:2	Acquired (unexpectedly); a (great) possession
④ Enosh / Ἐνώς	Luke 3:38; 1Chr 1:1	Man; mortal frailty
⑤ Seth / Σήθ	Luke 3:38; 1Chr 1:1	Substitute; granted; appointed one; foundation or grounds
⑥ Adam / Ἀδάμ	Luke 3:38; 1Chr 1:1	Man; mankind; human
⑦ God / θεός	Luke 3:38	The one and only true God; the Triune God

* The names were written according to NASB.

* Reference literatures on the meanings of the 77 people in the genealogy of Luke Chapter 3:

- Zodhiates, Spiros, *The Complete Word Study Dictionary: New Testament*. Chattanooga: AMG Publishers, 1994.
- Balz, Horst and Gerhard Schneider, *Exegetical Dictionary of the New Testament*. Grand Rapids: Eerdmans, 1990.
- Richard D. Hess, *Studies in the Personal Names of Genesis 1–11*. Neukirchen-Vluyn: Verlag Butzon & Bercker Kevelaer, 1993.
- Disciples Publishing House, ed. *The Oxford Bible Interpreter*, Vol. 106, Luke 1-8. Seoul: Disciples Publishing House, 2006.
- Compilation Committee for Christian Encyclopedia, ed, *Christian Encyclopedia*. Seoul: Christian Publishers, 1989–1992.

Until now we have seen that the genealogy in the Gospel of Luke lists 77 individuals in all, beginning with Jesus Christ and ascending all the way to God. Although the life journeys of these people are not detailed in the Bible, the fact that their names have been included in the genealogy of Jesus Christ is in itself a most glorious achievement.

(2) The administration of redemption in the genealogy of Luke 3

The genealogy in the Gospel of Luke contains the great administration of redemption.

First, this genealogy traces the origin of Jesus Christ all the way up to Adam.[18] Jesus Christ is intimately joined with all human beings who have existed and will exist from the beginning of time to its end. This reaffirms that it was for the salvation of fallen Adam's descendants that Jesus came to this world.

The first man, Adam, was clearly the son of God created in His image, but was unable to fulfill his duty because of disobedience. However, the one and only Son of God, Jesus Christ, came into this world as the last Adam (1 Cor 15:45), who redeemed all mankind and opened up the path for eternal salvation through obedience (Rom 5:12–21). Therefore, this genealogy reveals that God's own Son Jesus Christ, the representation of Adam, became the new beginning.[19]

The history of sin and death that began with Adam has transformed into the history of life through the second Adam, Jesus Christ. The eternal life of Jesus Christ has been given to all of God's elect. Jesus Christ is the root and basis of our faith and life. This is a mysterious truth which teaches us that all things that come through Jesus Christ are from God and that all things will be restored back to God through Jesus Christ as well.

Second, the fact that the genealogy begins with Jesus Christ and ends with God confirms Jesus Christ's divine origin (Luke 3:38).[20] The Son of God came into this world in order to save fallen mankind. If Jesus' genealogy ended with the first man Adam, we would have still remained distant and separated from God. However, Jesus Christ the mediator (John 14:6; Gal 3:19–20; 1 Tim 2:5; Heb 8:6; 9:15) embraced all of humanity and reconciled us to God (Eph 2:15–16; Col 1:21–22). We, who once were distant from God, have now been brought near through the blood of Jesus Christ (Eph 2:13).

In relation to this, let us direct our attention to where the genealogy is placed in the Gospel of Luke. The genealogy is recorded right after

Jesus' baptism. Because Jesus was sinless, He had no need to be baptized; however, He adamantly insisted that John the Baptist baptize Him. The reason for this was to fulfill "all righteousness" which was necessary for the redemption of mankind (Matt 3:15). Even though Jesus was sinless, He was baptized of His own accord as a sinner to participate in the "baptism of repentance" on behalf of all mankind (Mark 1:4; John 8:46; Rom 8:3–4; 2 Cor 5:21; Phil 2:8; Heb 2:14; 4:15; 7:26; 1 Pet 2:22; 1 Jn 3:5).

When Jesus came up out of the water during His baptism, a voice from heaven was heard saying, "You are My beloved Son, in You I am well-pleased." This was a clear testimony that Jesus Christ is the Son of God (Mark 1:11; John 1:29–34). The Gospel of Luke testifies to Jesus' sonship through this baptismal event. Immediately after this, in order to reaffirm this fact, the linear ascending genealogy was recorded.

Third, the genealogy demonstrates that Jesus Christ came as the seed of the woman to fulfill the covenant of salvation of mankind completely. Regarding this, Luke 3:23 states, "as was supposed, the son of Joseph." The people knew Jesus as "the son of Joseph," and "the son of a carpenter" (Matt 13:55). Yet, He was born of Mary and conceived by the Holy Spirit, which affirms His messianic role as the seed of the woman.

The redemptive significance of Luke's genealogy is its affirmation of Jesus Christ's coming according to the covenants as "the only begotten God who is in the bosom of the Father" (John 1:18) and "in very nature God" (Phil 2:6, NIV).

The infinite and eternal One put on a mortal form and died on the cross as the atoning sacrifice for the sins of mankind. God, being sinless and just, cannot condone nor overlook sin. Therefore, He made Jesus Christ pay the price of sin committed by mankind since the fall of Adam.

As such, the genealogy in the Gospel of Luke is filled with the amazing message that God, who is greater than all, is in a relationship with humanity whose lives are relatively insignificant and undeserving of His lovingkindness. The One whose face shines with the light of glory that is seven times brighter than the sun became our Immanuel (Isa 30:26; Matt 17:2), the sinner's closest friend (Matt 1:23). This shows us the sublime and magnificent value of the saints who have been chosen in Christ before the foundation of the world. Moreover, it reveals to us the burning love and redemptive zeal that God has toward His elect.

CHAPTER 6

Three Periods That Appear in the Genealogy of Jesus Christ

The generations in Jesus Christ's genealogy can be analyzed according to the three divisions set forth in Matt 1:17. The first period from Abraham to David is 14 generations; the second period from David to the deportation to Babylon is 14 generations; and the third period from after the deportation to Babylon to Jesus Christ is 14 generations. The first and second periods are divided by the life of "King David," and the second and third periods are divided by the "deportation to Babylon."

> **Matthew 1:17** Therefore all the generations from Abraham to David are fourteen generations; and from David to the deportation to Babylon fourteen generations; and from the deportation to Babylon to the time of Christ fourteen generations.

1. First Period—14 Generations from Abraham to David

This is the period of promise—the time from the beginning of Israel's history, which started with the Abrahamic covenant, up to the establishment of the Unified Kingdom of David.

> [1] Abraham → [2] Isaac → [3] Jacob → [4] Judah → [5] Perez
> [6] Hezron → [7] Ram → [8] Amminadab → [9] Nahshon → [10] Salmon
> [11] Boaz → [12] Obed → [13] Jesse → [14] King David

The names of the 14 generations of the first period in Matthew's genealogy are the same as the names listed in the genealogy of 1 Chronicles (1 Chr 1:27–34; 2:1–15; Ruth 4:18–22). They are also the same in the genealogy in the Gospel of Luke (Luke 3:31–34). The only difference noted among the names that appear in the genealogies are "Ram" (Matt

1:3–4), who also is called "Arni" in Luke according to some translations (Luke 3:33), and "David the king" (Matt 1:6), who is mentioned simply as "David" in Luke (Luke 3:31).

(1) Structure of the chronology (1,163 years in total)

The first period extends from Abraham's birth until King David's reign in Hebron. David reigned for 7 years and 6 months in Hebron and 33 years in Jerusalem (2 Sam 5:4–5; 1 Kgs 2:11; 1 Chr 3:4–5; 29:27). In this book, we consider that the first period of the genealogy in Matthew 1 ended when David ended his reign in Hebron, and the second period started with David's reign in Jerusalem. The reason for this is that the second period begins with the words, "David was the father of Solomon by Bathsheba who had been the wife of Uriah" (Matt 1:6). This affair with Bathsheba (2 Sam 11) took place after David's reign in Hebron and during the early part of his reign in Jerusalem (2 Sam 5:13–14; 1 Chr 3:4–5).

Abraham's birth was in the year 2166 BC and David's reign in Jerusalem started in the year 1003 BC. Thus, the total span of the first period is 1,163 years long. This period can be divided broadly into five sections and we will look into the details in Part 3 of this book.

① **Abraham—Isaac—Jacob—Judah—Perez—Hezron** (Matt 1:2–3)
From Abraham's birth (2166 BC) to the time Jacob took 70 of his family members into Egypt (1876 BC)—around 290 years

② **Hezron—Ram—Amminadab—Nahshon** (Matt 1:3–4)
430 years of slavery in Egypt

③ **Nahshon—Salmon** (Matt 1:4–5)
40 years of the wilderness journey after the Exodus and 16 years of the Canaan conquest for a total of 56 years

④ **Salmon—Boaz—Obed—Jesse** (Matt 1:5)
The time of the judges—340 years

⑤ **Jesse—David** (Matt 1:5–6)
47 years and 6 months includes King Saul's reign of 40 years and David's reign of 7 years and 6 months in Hebron

(2) The three women listed in the first period: Tamar, Rahab and Ruth

Matt 1:3 "Judah was the father of Perez and Zerah by **Tamar**."
Matt 1:5a "Salmon was the father of Boaz by **Rahab**."
Matt 1:5b "Boaz was the father of Obed by **Ruth**."

Unlike the genealogy in the Gospel of Luke, the genealogy in the Gospel of Matthew includes five women—Tamar, Rahab, Ruth, Uriah's wife and Mary. In Jewish tradition, women were never included in the genealogies; therefore, having these women's names listed is a peculiarity unique to Jesus' genealogy. Furthermore, the names of such famous matriarchs of faith like Sarah, Rebekah and Rachel, were not included in Jesus' genealogy; rather, the names of women who were lowly and disdained by society—women whose names were stained by sins—were included.

Through the three women included in the first period of Jesus' genealogy, we can understand that the scope of salvation has been expanded to include all Gentiles as well. In other words, God's redemptive activity is not limited to the people of Israel but is open to all nations and people (Rom 1:14–16; 3:22; 10:11–13). The gospel of Jesus Christ transcends race, gender and distinctions of class so that there is no discrimination in redemption whether for Greek or Jew (1 Cor 1:24; 12:13; Gal 3:28).

Colossians 3:11 a renewal in which there is no distinction between Greek and Jew, circumcised and uncircumcised, barbarian, Scythian, slave and freeman, but Christ is all, and in all.

The fact that unclean women have been included in the genealogy in the Gospel of Matthew shows us Jesus' selfless humility to save mankind. Jesus was sinless (Heb 4:15), knew no sin (2 Cor 5:21) and did not originally have a body of sin (Rom 6:6) like other humans. However, God condemned sin (Rom 8:3b) in the body of Jesus Christ the only begotten Son and made Him to be like a sinner (Phil 2:7). This is the profound mystery of substitutionary atonement for our salvation and the principle by which we have been justified (Rom 4:25).

Jesus could have kept His genealogy undefiled. However, in taking on the form of a servant to save sinners, He did not mind being called a descendant of women who were stained with lawlessness, adultery and even incest. Through this genealogy, we are able to discover that God's love is greater, wider and deeper than the universe. We can feel a deep gratitude for the sacrificial love of Jesus who endlessly humbled Himself even though He is God. The Word of the beginning came in the form of man, having his name listed among sinners in a human genealogy. Jesus' genealogy is filled with evidence that attests of God's *agape* love for sinners; Jesus Christ humbled Himself completely to the point of becoming a mockery among people in the genealogy (Ps 22:6–7).

(3) David—the only person in Matthew's genealogy who is counted twice

As the person who concludes the first period and begins the second, David is the only person who is counted twice (Matt 1:17). David is highlighted because he concludes one period and begins another. Also, among the many kings who are mentioned in the genealogy, only David is given the title "king" (Matt 1:6). It is not a coincidence that the genealogy is structured in groups of 14 generations because 14 is the sum of the numerical values represented by the letters in David's Hebrew name (דָּוִד).[21]

Clearly, the central figure of the genealogy in Matthew 1 in introducing Jesus Christ is David, and the genealogy illustrates the fact that Jesus Christ is the Son of David.[22] David, as someone prefiguring Jesus Christ, became the central figure in the genealogy of Matthew 1. This shows that Jesus Christ would come not only to fulfill the things of the past, but also to open up a new era as the central figure of redemptive history, thereby expanding the meaning of the administration of redemption.

The promise of the eternally established kingdom, which was to come through a son in the Davidic covenant, is not the kingdom that would be built by David's physical descendants; the promise ultimately points to the kingdom of God that would be established through Jesus Christ (Luke 1:31–33, 69; Rev 22:16).

2. Second Period—14 Generations of Kings from David to the Deportation to Babylon

The second period is one of disgrace and humiliation, listing the names of kings until eventually the Davidic line lost its kingship and the Israelites are tragically taken as captives into Babylon. Nevertheless, God did not forget the covenant that He made with David and continued to direct the flow of redemptive history with His sovereign grace and mercy.

1 David →	2 Solomon →	3 Rehoboam →	4 Abijah → 5 Asa
6 Jehoshaphat →	7 Joram →	8 Uzziah →	9 Jotham → 10 Ahaz
11 Hezekiah →	12 Manasseh →	13 Amon →	14 Josiah

The names listed in the second period of the genealogy in Matthew 1 are very similar to the names listed in the genealogy in 1 Chronicles (1 Chr 3:5–16). However, when comparing 1 Chronicles 3:11–12 to Matthew 1:8, we see that three kings between Joram and Uzziah (Azariah)—Ahaziah, Joash, and Amaziah—have been omitted in Matthew's genealogy. Including Athaliah, who reigned over the kingdom after her son Ahaziah had died, four kings are omitted in Matthew's record of the genealogy (2 Kgs 11:1–3; 2 Chr 22:10–12).

(1) The structure of the chronology (total of 406 years)

After David reigned in Hebron, he began his reign in Jerusalem in 1003 BC. Babylon's second invasion of Jerusalem occurred in the same year as Jeconiah's accession to the throne, in the 12th month of 598 BC according to the solar calendar. Jerusalem fell on the 16th day of the 3rd month in 597 BC when Jeconiah was taken captive to Babylon (2 Kgs 24:8–12; 2 Chr 36:9–10). Based on this historical data, we can deduce that the captivity to Babylon took place in 597 BC. Thus, the total duration of the second period is approximately 406 years from 1003 BC to 597 BC (See pp. 299–301, Ref. 1).

---

① **King David – Solomon** (Matt 1:6)
73 years which includes David's 33-year reign in Jerusalem and Solomon's reign of 40 years

---

② **Rehoboam—Abijah—Asa—Jehoshaphat—Joram—Uzziah—Jotham—Ahaz—Hezekiah—Manasseh—Amon—Josiah** (Matt 1:7–10)
332 years of the divided Kingdom

---

(2) The woman listed in the second period of the genealogy—Uriah's wife.

Matt 1:6b "David was the father of Solomon, whose mother had been Uriah's wife" (NIV)

With regard to Uriah's wife, many of the major English translations say, "…her who (that) had been the wife of Uriah" without mentioning the name "Bathsheba" (exceptions: NASB and NLT). The fact that the genealogy says, "Uriah's wife" instead of the name "Bathsheba" is very significant. The specific reasons for this will be discussed in more detail in the forthcoming books in The History of Redemption series, but it is certain that Uriah's faith is being emphasized.

It is truly significant that the second period of the genealogy, which includes the deportation to Babylon, begins with Uriah's wife whom David took for himself. While troubled Gentile women such as Tamar, Rahab and Ruth helped continue the lineage from Abraham through David, David's sin of taking Uriah's wife marked the beginning of the decline of David's royal line, and there has been no peace in the land since. It happened just as God said through Nathan the prophet: "Now therefore, the sword shall never depart from your house, because you have despised Me and have taken the wife of Uriah the Hittite to be your wife" (2 Sam 12:10). The consequence of David's sin of adultery was the destruction of the Temple in Jerusalem, the collapse of the nation and the Israelites' deportation to Babylon.

3. Third Period—14 Generations from after the Deportation to Babylon to Jesus Christ

The third period was the time of earnest yearning for restoration from the hardship and disgrace suffered during the 70 years of Babylonian captivity. It was also a time of eager expectation for the Messiah because the Israelites became despondent by gentile nations' constant attack when they returned from captivity and began to rebuild the temple.

1 Jeconiah	→ 2 Shealtiel	→ 3 Zerubbabel	→ 4 Abihud	→ 5 Eliakim
6 Azor	→ 7 Zadok	→ 8 Achim	→ 9 Eliud	→ 10 Eleazar
11 Matthan	→ 12 Jacob	→ 13 Joseph (Mary's husband)	→ 14 Jesus Christ	

(1) The structure of the chronology (total of 593 years)

The time span of the 14 generations from the exile into Babylon (597 BC) until the birth of Jesus Christ (4 BC) is approximately 593 years. Of the persons recorded in the third period—besides Shealtiel and Zerubbabel—Abihud, Eliakim, Azor, Zadok, Achim, Eliud, Eleazar, Matthan and Jacob have nothing recorded about them in the Bible. An in-depth look into these figures will be explored in the forthcoming books in The History of Redemption series.

① **Jeconiah—Shealtiel—Zerubbabel** (Matt 1:12)
This was the time from Jeconiah's deportation in 597 BC until the first return from captivity with Zerubbabel (as the central figure) and the Temple reconstruction in 516 BC (Ezra 6:15; Hag 1:1–2, 14–15).

① **Abihud—Joseph** (Matt 1:13–16)
This was a time of spiritual darkness that extended from near the time of the reconstruction of the Temple in 516 BC until the birth of Jesus Christ (4 BC).

(2) The remnants who prepared the way of the coming of Jesus Christ

When Israel was taken as captives into Babylon, it seemed as though faith had been totally wiped out, but God had left "remnants" to continue a godly line of life.

These were the "stumps" who were to continue God's administration of redemption. One of the Hebrew words for *remnants* is שְׁאָר (*shā'ar*). This word appears in the Bible about 260 times and means "worthless" and "small in number" (Deut 4:27; Jer 8:3). It refers to the remnant that was weak and small in number, yet did not disappear. They remained because they had received a special kind of grace and love from God (Rom 11:5).

We must remember that God's work of redemption does not happen through a large multitude but through a small number of godly offspring who fear God and obey His Word (Mal 2:15).

Until now, we have performed a cursory examination of the genealogy of Jesus Christ, which is divided into three periods. Jesus Christ's genealogy accurately depicts the entire shameful history of Israel's rebellion and disobedience which resulted from their continuous disbelief. This shows us how God's administration of redemption continues regardless of human beings' shortcomings and frailties. Moreover, it gives us human beings, who are weak and full of mistakes, an abundance of comfort and courage. The genealogy of Jesus Christ in Matthew 1 is a great stepping stone of hope which enables us to look only unto Jesus even in despair from sin and unbelief. This genealogy is also a great proclamation of the gospel, which brings us ultimate victory.

CHAPTER 7

The Number of Generations Omitted and the Names of the People Recorded

The genealogy of Jesus Christ is recorded in the very first chapter of the New Testament because the persons recorded in it were the conduits for God's administration of redemption through which the Messiah, Jesus Christ, was able to come into this world. Jesus' genealogy not only reveals the legitimacy of His physical descent, but it also shows us the line of faith that continued until Jesus Christ the incarnate God was able to come into the world. The genealogy in the Gospel of Matthew does not record every consecutive generation; there are many generations omitted in the genealogy.

This genealogy explains that Jesus Christ is the descendant of Abraham and David in order to testify that He is the Messiah. However, we must clearly understand that Jesus' genealogy is continued by the people of faith who held fast to God's covenants. Of course, there were some wicked people listed among the generations in the genealogy. However, we must not overlook the fact that God used those people as a means of fulfilling His administration of redemption despite the sins and failures of mankind.

1. The Number of Generations Omitted from the 430 Years of Slavery in Egypt

Judah's grandson, Hezron, was included among the 70 family members of Jacob at the time of their entrance into Egypt (Gen 46:12) and was a figure who lived at the beginning of the 430 years of slavery in Egypt. Also, Amminadab's son Nahshon being introduced as a leader of the tribe of Judah during the wilderness journey (Num 2:3; 10:14) allows us to deduce that this same Nahshon was from the last generation of slavery in Egypt. The harlot Rahab lived during the beginning of the conquest of Canaan right after the Israelites' entry into the Promised Land in 1406

BC (Josh 2:1). Therefore, Salmon, who married Rahab, must have been part of the second generation who was born in the wilderness, while his father Nahshon was of the last generation of Israelites who lived in slavery in Egypt.

Hence, only four generations—Hezron, Ram, Amminadab and Nahshon (Matt 1:3–4)—from the 430-year period of the slavery in Egypt are recorded in Jesus Christ's genealogy. If we take into account that there were ten generations in the corresponding time period from Ephraim to Joshua, we can see that many generations were omitted from this same time period in Jesus' genealogy (1 Chr 7:20–27).

2. The Number of Generations Omitted from the Period after Settling in Canaan until King David

The year the Israelites entered Canaan was 1406 BC and the year that David appeared in history was 1010 BC. However, in Jesus' genealogy, only four people—Salmon, Boaz, Obed and Jesse (Matt 1:5–6)—excluding David, are recorded in the 396-year time span.

As discussed, Salmon and Rahab lived during the time when the Canaan conquest began, and Boaz and Ruth lived in the final years during the time of the judges (Ruth 1:1; 4:21–22). In other words, there is more than a 300-year span between Salmon and Boaz. Here, we encounter a shocking fact: after Joshua, the leader of the conquest, and his generation had passed away, the people of the judges' era, which was a time of spiritual darkness, were almost entirely removed from Jesus' genealogy. By deleting the people of the time of the judges from the genealogy in Matthew 1, God clearly reaffirms the testimony of the Bible regarding the state of the spiritual darkness during the era of the judges (Judg 2:7–10; cf. Josh 24:31).

Those generations of people whose faith and devotion to God had dissipated were entirely removed from Jesus' genealogy.

3. The Number of Generations Omitted from the Period of the Kings in Judah

In the genealogy of Jesus Christ, there are 14 generations recorded from David to Josiah (Matt 1:6–11). Notably, when we compare that to the genealogy in 1 Chronicles, we see that three generations—Ahaziah, Joash and Amaziah—were omitted (1 Chr 3:11–12). All three are related in some way to the atrocious northern king, Ahab, and his wife, Jezebel (2 Kgs 8:26). Ahab and Jezebel's daughter, Athaliah, was the person who tried to stop God's work of redemption by wiping out the royal seed completely through which the Messiah would come (2 Kgs 11:1; 2 Chr 22:10). The three kings, who were related to Athaliah, were removed from the genealogy for committing wicked acts. This fulfilled God's prophecy through Elijah in 1 Kings 21:21 which said that God would bring about a disaster on Ahab and his household so that all the men of Ahab's household would be wiped out.

Furthermore, three more generations were omitted from Jesus Christ's genealogy around the time of the exile into Babylon (Matt 1:11–12; 2 Chr 36:1, 5, 11): Jehoahaz (2 Kgs 23:31; 2 Chr 36:1–2), Jehoiakim (2 Kgs 23:36; 2 Chr 36:5), and Zedekiah (2 Kgs 24:18; 2 Chr 36:11). The omission of these kings will be discussed in further detail in the next book of The History of Redemption series.

The genealogy of Jesus Christ in Matthew 1 goes through many twists and turns with many generations being cut off, then being reconnected, and cut off again. By considering these people and generations, we can better understand that it was not a simple task for God to send Jesus Christ into this world to save His chosen people.

4. The Names of the People Recorded in the Genealogy

Because many names have been omitted from Jesus' genealogy, the importance of the names that are included in it is highlighted. Aside from Joseph, all the figures recorded in Jesus' genealogy are Old Testament personages; therefore, we can say that the genealogy of Jesus Christ is a summary of the Old Testament's long history. It would not be an overstatement to say that these people existed through Jesus Christ and that they existed in order to reveal Jesus Christ (John 1:3; 5:39; Luke 24:27, 44). Thus, the individuals included in the genealogy are lamps illuminating our journey of faith. A detailed study of the accounts of these people through an examination of their names and achievements will be a very meaningful venture. The names are especially meaningful because they are more than just titles to differentiate one person from another.

First, a name signifies one's true nature and actions. Only when we know the person's name, can we correctly understand his nature and actions (Gen 25:26; 1 Sam 25:25). In that sense, the Hebrew people would always ask for someone's name first when they wish to know about a certain individual (Exod 3:13; Judg 13:17).

Second, a name reflects the hopes and expectations of the parents and the circumstances of the times. Parents do not name their children randomly. An offspring's name contains not only the faith and life of the parents, but also their hopes and expectations for their child and even more than that, it contains a broad summary of the circumstances of the times (Ruth 4:14–17).

Third, a name contains the plan of redemption. Biblical names bear special meanings. All Scripture is written through the inspiration of God (2 Tim 3:16), and these people who were inspired by the Holy Spirit wrote and spoke the things given to them by God (1 Pet 1:21). Therefore, of all the people since Adam who have come and gone in this world, the persons listed in the genealogy of Jesus Christ have names that bear special redemptive historical significance.

This book will seek to gain a better understanding of God's redemptive work that is found in the names and lives of the people in the genealogy of Jesus Christ. The study of the meanings and etymology[23] of their names will give deeper insight to God's administration, which is the foundation of the history of redemption.

Now, we will examine the 14 generations from Abraham to David, which is the first of the three periods of 42 generations in Jesus' genealogy. The second and third periods in the genealogy will be examined in the fourth and fifth books of The History of Redemption series.

We will obtain a general overview of the history that is related to the genealogy of Jesus Christ. We will even discuss the periods that are excluded from the genealogy, such as the time of the judges, Saul's reign, and the chronicles of the northern kingdom of Israel.

I sincerely pray and hope that many godly and faithful children of God will be inspired to continue the holy lineage of faith by understanding the administration of redemption that is contained in the genealogy of Jesus Christ.

עמלק

מדבר צין הוא קדש

ים המלח

מדבר סיני

מדבר פארן

מדבר שור

ארץ פלשתים

עיר כרמל

שבט

באר שבע

שבט שמעון

אכב נשן

פתם

שרה

צען

אלבסנדרי

לוח המסעות במדבר
אשר על פי ה' יסעו ועל פי ה' יחנו

רט' הרהגדגד	טו' רחמה	א' רעמסס
ל' יטבתה	טז' רמןפרץ	ב' סכת
לא' עברנה	יז' לבנה	ג' אתם
לב' עציןגבר	יח' רסה	ד' פיהחירת
לג' מדברצין	יט' קהלתה	ה' מרה
לד' הרההר	ך' הרספר	ו' אילם
לה' צלמנה	כא' חרדה	ז' ים סוף
לו' פונן	כב' מקהלת	ח' מדברסין
לז' אבת	כג' תחת	ט' דפקה
לח' דיבןגד	כד' תרח	יו' אלוש
לט' עלמןדבלתה	כה' מתקה	יא' רפידם
מ' הרי עברים	כו' חשמנה	יב' מדברסיני
מא' ערבתמואב	כד' מסרות	יג' קברתהתאו
	רח' בגי יעקן	יד' חצרות

PART THREE

The Genealogy of Jesus Christ: The History of the First Period

14 Generations from Abraham to David

1 Abraham → 2 Isaac → 3 Jacob → 4 Judah

→ 5 Perez → 6 Hezron → 7 Ram → 8 Amminadab

→ 9 Nahshon → 10 Salmon → 11 Boaz → 12 Obed

→ 13 Jesse → 14 King David

The first 14 generations in the genealogy of Jesus Christ begin with Abraham and end with David (Matt 1:2, 6, 17). These two names are the most notable and respected among the Jews. The first 14 generations share the following characteristics:

First, the first 14 generations of Jesus Christ's genealogy show the progressive development of Israel's history. Abraham is the beginning of the Jewish nation. Hence, Jews referred to Abraham as "Abraham our father" (Luke 1:73; John 8:53; Acts 7:2; Rom 4:12; Jas 2:21). David was the one who formally established the monarchical system in Israel. Thus, the first 14 generations in Jesus Christ's genealogy embody the progression from the beginning of Israel's history to the foundation of its kingdom.

Second, the first 14 generations of Jesus Christ's genealogy show that Jesus Christ is the Messiah. The genealogy recorded in the Gospel of Matthew testifies that Jesus is the son of David as well as the son of Abraham (Matt 1:1). The Jews considered Abraham and David the most important of all their ancestors and were proud to be their descendants. God promised the Messiah to these two people (Gen 12:3; 22:17–18; 2 Sam 7:12–13). Therefore, by proclaiming that Jesus Christ is actually the long-awaited Son who was promised to Abraham and David, Matthew is testifying that Jesus Christ is the Messiah.

Third, the first 14 generations of Jesus Christ's genealogy show that Jesus Christ is the Savior of the world. Among the first 14 generations in Jesus Christ's genealogy are three women—Tamar, Rahab, and Ruth. It is ground-breaking to have women, especially Gentiles, listed in the genealogy of Jesus Christ because women were customarily not supposed to be recorded in genealogies. This teaches us that Jesus Christ is the Savior, not just for the Jews, but also for all the Gentiles; He is the Savior of the entire world.[24]

David is mentioned twice in Jesus Christ's genealogy—once in the first period and again in the second period. In this book, we divide the reign of David into two parts: (1) the 7 years and 6 months of David's reign in Hebron is part of the first period of 14 generations in the genealogy; and (2) the 33 years of David's reign in Jerusalem is included in the second period of 14 generations.

The first period in Jesus Christ's genealogy, from Abraham to David's reign in Hebron, lasted about 1,163 years from the time Abraham was born in 2166 BC to David's reign in Hebron which ended in 1003 BC. Part 3 of this book will discuss the history of the first 14 generations from Abraham to David in the genealogy. Then Part 4 and Part 5 will examine the time period of the judges and the history of Saul and David.

CHAPTER 8

The First Generation

> **Abraham** – אַבְרָהָם / Ἀβραάμ
>
> Father of a multitude, father of many nations

Order
The first person in the genealogy of Jesus Christ (Matt 1:1–2; 1 Chr 1:27)

Background
His father was Terah and his son was Isaac (Matt 1:2; Luke 3:34). Isaac's older brother Ishmael was born by Hagar the Egyptian woman, 14 years before Isaac (Gen 16:1–16).

Key Point
Abraham is the first person listed in the genealogy of Jesus Christ. He became the father of the Jews and the father of faith (John 8:53; Rom 4:1, 16, 18; Gal 3:7, 29).

Abraham's original name was Abram. In Hebrew, the name אַבְרָם (*'abrām*) means "exalted father" and he was renamed Abraham at the age of 99 (Gen 17:5).

The name אַבְרָהָם (*'abrāhām*) is a compound word of אָב (*'āv*) and רָהָם (*rāhām*). אָב (*'āv*) means "father" or "forefather" and though the meaning of רָהָם (*rāhām*) is unclear, we infer from an Aramaic word *ruham*, which means "multitude," that the name *Abraham* means "father of a multitude" or "father of many nations."

1. Abraham Had Isaac, the Promised Son

(1) The Calling of Abraham

Abraham received a calling from God while he was living in Ur of the Chaldeans in Mesopotamia, "Depart from your country and your relatives, and come into the land that I will show you" (Acts 7:2–4).

When Abraham was 75 years old and living in Haran, God spoke to him again saying, "Go forth from your country, and from your relatives and from your father's house, to the land which I will show you." Abraham departed from Haran in obedience and came to the land of Canaan (Gen 12:1–5). At that time, God promised Abraham that He would make him a "great nation" (Gen 12:2). This promise was a great hope and blessing to Abraham who had no son.

(2) The birth of Ishmael

Abraham waited ten years since he received the promise of the "great nation," but was still not given a child. So, Abraham took Sarah's advice and had the "child of the flesh" through Hagar, an Egyptian maidservant, when he was 86 years old (Gen 16:16; Rom 9:6–8).

When Abraham considered making his servant Eliezer of Damascus his heir, God clearly promised him, "but one who shall come forth from your own body, he shall be your heir" (Gen 15:4). However, Abraham and Sarah foolishly tried to fulfill God's Word through Hagar the maidservant. This son Ishmael that Abraham had through Hagar eventually became the seed of discord in the household and the cause of strife between nations (Gen 16:4).

(3) The birth of Isaac

God said three times that "Sarah shall have a son" (Gen 17:16; 18:10; 14) when Abraham (age 99) and Sarah (age 89) were about to give up because it was nearly impossible for them to have a child. Abraham fell on his face and laughed in his heart (Gen 17:17) at this utterly unbelievable message. Sarah, standing at the tent door, also laughed to herself when she heard it (Gen 18:12–13).

Having seen and heard all of their laughing and inner thoughts, God rebuked them, "Is anything too difficult for the LORD?" (Gen 18:14), and said that the promise will be fulfilled "at the appointed time." Just as promised, God gave Isaac to Abraham at the age of 100 (Gen 21:1–5).

Matthew 1:2 states, "To Abraham was born Isaac." Here, the verb *born* is γεννάω (*gennaō*) in Greek. This verb was also rendered as "Abraham became the father of Isaac" after he received the covenant of circumcision in Acts 7:8. Γεννάω (*gennaō*) is distinguished from τίκτω (*tiktō*) which is used to describe women giving birth to a child (Matt 1:23; Luke 2:7).

The word γεννάω (*gennaō*) is generally used to describe the situation that occurs when an heir (i.e., the one to succeed and continue the heritage) is born to the father of a family. The fact that this word was used as many as 39 times in the active voice within the genealogy of Jesus Christ (Matt 1:1–17) indicates that His genealogy is not just about succeeding the blood lineage; it is also a covenantal genealogy that is continued by heirs of the covenant. This explains why Isaac was listed in the genealogy when Ishmael is supposed to be the firstborn of Abraham according to the order of birth (Rom 9:7–8).

2. Abraham Became the Father of Faith

(1) Abraham the father of the Jews

Jews called Abraham, "Abraham our father" (Luke 1:73; John 8:53; Acts 7:2; Rom 4:12; Jas 2:21). To the Israelites, God referred to Abraham as "your father Abraham" (Josh 24:3; Isa 51:2), and Jesus also said, "your father Abraham" (John 8:56). The Apostle Paul specifically wrote, "Our forefather according to the flesh" (Rom 4:1).

However, the Bible states that Jewish lineage alone will not make one a true descendant of Abraham (Rom 2:28–29). John the Baptist also rebuked the Pharisees and scribes in his day, saying, "Do not suppose that you can say to yourselves, 'We have Abraham for our father'" (Matt 3:9; Luke 3:8; cf. John 8:39–44).

(2) Abraham the father of faith

When Abraham had no heir, God told Abraham, "....one who shall come forth from your own body, he shall be your heir," and led him outside and said, "Now look toward the heavens, and count the stars, if you are able to count them...so shall your descendants be" (Gen 15:4–5). Abraham believed, and God reckoned it to him as "righteousness" (Gen 15:6). Here, Abraham demonstrated the means of salvation through justification by faith, not by works (Rom 4:9–11). Thus, Romans 4:16 states, "Abraham, who is the father of us all," and Romans 4:17–18 states, "a father of many nations." Likewise, the Bible testifies a remarkable truth that even a Gentile can become a descendant of Abraham and receive the same blessings as Abraham as long as he believes in the gospel of Christ (Gal 3:7–9). This truth is also proclaimed through the genealogy of Jesus Christ in Matthew 1. Since Jesus Christ is Abraham's descendant (Matt 1:1), anyone who belongs to Jesus Christ can become Abraham's descendant, whether Jew or Gentile (Gal 3:29).

Hence, the fact that Jesus Christ is Abraham's descendant testifies that Jesus came as the Savior not only for the Jews, but for all of God's chosen people, including the Gentiles.[25] Therefore, in this perspective, Abraham is the "father of many nations."

Through repeated covenants with Abraham, God promised that the Messiah will come as Abraham's descendant. In Genesis 22:17–18 God said, "Indeed I will greatly bless you, and I will greatly multiply your seed as the stars of the heavens, and as the sand, which is on the seashore; and your seed shall possess the gate of their enemies. And in your seed all the nations of the earth shall be blessed, because you have obeyed My voice." Here, the word *your seed*, which appears three times, is the singular form of זֶרַע (*zera* ʿ; seed, descendant), and refers to Jesus Christ who would later come as a descendant of Abraham. The genealogy in Matthew 1 reveals that Jesus Christ is the descendant of Abraham, and therefore proves that Jesus Christ is the Messiah, the fulfiller of that covenant.

3. Abraham's Bosom Was Portrayed as Paradise

There was a certain rich man, who habitually dressed in purple and fine linen, gaily living in splendor every day (Luke 16:19). However, this rich man died and went down to Hades, where he was in extreme torment in the flames of fire. His suffering was so severe that he even entreated a favor from "Father Abraham" to allow him a little water from the tip of a finger to cool his tongue (Luke 16:23–24).

On the other hand, there was a certain poor man named Lazarus who laid at the rich man's gate and was covered with sores, longing to be fed with the crumbs that fell from the rich man's table. Lazarus is Λάζαρος (*Lazaros*) in Greek, which means "God's help" or "God who helps." The rich man died and went to Hades, but Lazarus died and was carried away by the angels into "Abraham's bosom" (i.e., paradise; Luke 16:22–23). Paradise is παράδεισος (*paradeisos*) in Greek, meaning "the kingdom of heaven," the place of eternal joy and happiness. The Greek word ᾅδης (*hadēs*) refers to "hell," the place of eternal punishment. The Bible depicts "paradise" as "Abraham's bosom"[26] because he is the father of all believers and represents all those who will go to the "paradise" (Luke 19:9). Since Abraham's bosom is portrayed as the dwelling place for the saved (Matt

8:11; Luke 16:22–23), he became the central figure in paradise wherein all the believers' spirits would surely enter.

4. Abraham Received the Honorable Title, "Friend of God"

James 2:23 states, "and the Scripture was fulfilled which says, 'And Abraham believed God, and it was reckoned to him as righteousness,' and he was called the friend of God." Abraham was a "friend of God" (2 Chr 20:7; Isa 41:8).

Here, the word *friend* is φίλος (*philos*) in Greek, which implies that Abraham was in an intimate relationship with God. God reveals His covenant to those who are close enough to Him to be called His friend (Ps 25:14). God also informed Abraham about the destruction of the city of Sodom ahead of time (Gen 18:17). John 15:15 also states, "But I have called you friends, for all things that I have heard from My Father I have made known to you." To become Jesus' friend, one must do what Jesus commands—even if it means laying down his own life for Jesus (John 15:13–14). Because life is the most precious thing in this world, it is also the most difficult thing to give up. Abraham demonstrated the faith worthy of being called "God's friend" by obeying the command to sacrifice his only beloved son Isaac, who was as dear to him as his own life. James 2:21–23 links Abraham's work of offering Isaac on the altar to becoming "the friend of God."

Certainly, it must not have been easy to obey God's command to sacrifice Isaac on the altar. Isaac was the promised son whom Abraham had finally received at the age of 100 (Gen 21:5). It took 25 long years after God gave him the promise, "I will make you a great nation," when Abraham was 75 years old (Gen 12:2). Abraham and Sarah's affection for Isaac must have been extraordinary because Isaac was born to them when it was utterly impossible for them to conceive a child for they were 100 and 90 years old respectively, and Sarah was well past childbearing age.

It was this beloved son, Isaac, whom God had commanded Abraham to sacrifice as a burnt offering (Gen 22:2). A burnt offering is a sacrifice of an animal, which is slaughtered, cut into pieces, and sliced open in the belly. Its blood is sprinkled around on the altar, its entrails and legs are washed and burnt up on the altar. How could anyone give up his own child as a burnt offering? Abraham must have stayed awake all night in agonizing darkness. Nevertheless, Abraham did not delay at all in obeying the

Word when he received God's command (Ps 119:60). He rose up early in the morning, and without any discussion with his wife Sarah, saddled his donkey, took two of his young men, split wood for the burnt offering, and left for a mountain in Moriah with his son Isaac as God had instructed him.

During the three-day journey to the land of Moriah from Beersheba (Gen 22:4), Abraham must have been troubled and overcome with distress and anxiety. His heart was probably covered with pitch black darkness, engulfed with anguish and all kinds of agonizing thoughts such as "Do I really need to sacrifice Isaac? Could it be that I received the wrong revelation? How would I become a great nation as God promised if Isaac dies? Should I turn back?" Nonetheless, Abraham did not utter a single word as he climbed to the top of the mountain.

Leaving his two men at the base of the mountain, Abraham laid the wood for the burnt offering on Isaac his son and carried the fire and the knife in his hands (Gen 22:5–6). As they walked together, Isaac asked, "Behold, the fire and the wood, but where is the lamb for the burnt offering?" (Gen 22:7). Like a piercing dagger, this question must have cut right through Abraham's heart. Nonetheless, Abraham answered, "God will provide for Himself the lamb for the burnt offering, my son" (Gen 22:8), and silently went up to the place where God had told him to go.

On the mountain, Abraham built the altar, arranged the wood, bound and laid his son Isaac on top of the wood on the altar. Then, he took the knife to slay his son. In Genesis 22:10, the word *to slay* is שָׁחַט (šāḥaṭ) in Hebrew, meaning "to kill," "to behead an animal," or "to slaughter." Having severed his bond and love for his only son Isaac, Abraham was about to kill him with the knife. At the moment Abraham stretched out his hand to slay Isaac, he heard the voice, "Abraham, Abraham!" Abraham answered, "Here I am" (Gen 22:11), demonstrating his strong will and unwavering determination to obey. The angel of the Lord told him, "Do not stretch out your hand against the lad, and do nothing to him; for now I know that you fear God, since you have not withheld your son, your only son, from Me" (Gen 22:12).

Abraham's obedience demonstrates that only those who fear God to the extent of laying down their own precious lives and completely obeying the Word of God can be acknowledged as a "friend of God." Like Abraham, let us also go up to the top of the mountain, to the "place of which God had told [us]," with the faith to lay down our own lives and the determination to offer up even that which is the most precious to us! God will bestow upon us today the glorious epithet, "You are my friend."

Although Abraham did not know where he was going, he obeyed God's Word and left Ur of the Chaldeans. Then, he left the comforts of his settlement in Haran, a commercially thriving city. He continued to obey God's Word in his life. We will also receive and enjoy the same blessings as Abraham if we follow and obey God's Word in every moment of our lives (Gen 12:4; Gal 3:9; Heb 11:8).

CHAPTER 9

The Second Generation

> **Isaac** – יִצְחָק / Ἰσαάκ
>
> He laughs

Order
The second person in the genealogy of Jesus Christ (Matt 1:2; 1 Chr 1:28, 34)

Background
His father was Abraham and his mother was Sarah. His son who is recorded in the genealogy of Jesus Christ is Jacob (Matt 1:2; Luke 3:34).
Isaac's older brother Ishmael was born by Hagar the Egyptian woman, 14 years before Isaac (Gen 16:1–16).

Key Point
Isaac is the promised son Sarah bore to Abraham when he was 100 years old (Gen 21:1–5). Isaac became the father of Esau and Jacob, and Jacob entered in the genealogy of Jesus Christ.

The name Isaac is יִצְחָק (*yiṣḥāq*) in Hebrew, and Ἰσαάκ (*Isaak*) in Greek. The word יִצְחָק stems from צָחַק (*ṣāḥaq*), which means "to laugh," "jest," "play," or "mock." This name was given because Abraham did not believe in God's promise that "a child will be born to a man one hundred years old," and fell on his face, laughing in his heart (Gen 17:17–19).

1. Isaac Was the Promised Child

Abraham had two sons. The first was Ishmael, a child of the flesh whom Hagar bore when Abraham was 86 years old. The second was Isaac whom Sarah bore when Abraham was 100 years old. Isaac was the child of the promise whom God gave through Sarah at the fullness of the time according to His Word (Gen 17:18–21; 18:10, 14; 21:1–5).

Isaac was the child of the promise, not by man's good deed, but entirely by God's sovereign election as Romans 9:7–8 states,

> Neither are they all children because they are Abraham's descendants, but: "through Isaac your descendants will be named." That is, it is not the children of the flesh who are the children of God, but the children of the promise who are regarded as descendants.

Even after having received God's promise, Abraham did not completely believe. He fell on his face and laughed in his heart (Gen 17:17–21). The fact that his son was named *Isaac*, meaning "he laughs," was to make Abraham realize that he was not perfect. This name *Isaac* should also remind us to examine ourselves whether we truly have faith in God's promises (2 Cor 13:5).

2. Isaac Had Absolute Obedience

It is evident that Isaac had already grown up by this time because he carried the wood for the burnt offering up to the mountain (Gen 22:6) when God commanded Abraham to sacrifice Isaac as a burnt offering (Gen 22:1–2).

Thinking that it was strange not to have the sacrifice for the offering as he was carrying up the wood for the burnt offering, Isaac asked, "Behold, the fire and the wood, but where is the lamb for the burnt offering?" (Gen 22:7). Abraham could not tell him plainly, "My son, you are the sacrifice." Instead, he answered, "My son, God will provide for Himself the lamb for the burnt offering" (Gen 22:8).

Upon arriving at the place that God had told him, Abraham bound Isaac and laid him on the altar on top of the wood (Gen 22:9). The word *bound* used here is עָקַד ('āqad) in Hebrew, which is an expression used for the act of forcefully tying down the limbs of a sacrificial animal. When Abraham forcefully laid Isaac on the altar, Isaac could have very well resisted his father for he was in the prime of his youth. Instead, Isaac silently obeyed his father (Gen 22:9–10), demonstrating complete faith and absolute obedience to God.

The image of Isaac carrying the wood for the burnt offering up to the mountain in Moriah and becoming the offering sacrifice (Gen 22:6) foreshadows Jesus Christ carrying the cross up the hill of Golgotha and becoming the ultimate sacrifice of atonement for all of mankind in obedience (Matt 20:28; John 1:29). The prophet Isaiah described this sacrifice,

"He was oppressed and He was afflicted, yet He did not open His mouth; like a lamb that is led to slaughter, and like a sheep that is silent before its shearers, so He did not open His mouth" (Isa 53:7).

Having seen Abraham's faith and Isaac's obedience, God said, "Do not stretch out your hand against the lad," and provided a ram caught in the thicket by his horns to be sacrificed in place of Isaac (Gen 22:13–14). Hence, Abraham called the place, "Jehovah Jireh," which means "The LORD will provide" (Gen 22:14). Like Isaac, he who absolutely obeys will surely be saved from death and receive the blessing of "Jehovah Jireh."

3. Isaac Blessed Jacob with the Blessing of the Firstborn

Isaac was married to Rebekah at the age of 40 and was childless for 20 years. However, God answered Isaac's prayer and gave him twins, Esau and Jacob, when he was 60 years old (Gen 25:20–26).

The genealogy of Jesus Christ records the younger son Jacob, not the firstborn son Esau, as Isaac's successor. Such change in the order of the firstborn was unprecedented in common genealogical recordings of Israel. This reveals that God, in His sovereignty, had elected Jacob's line as the path for the coming of Jesus Christ.

At first, Isaac "unknowingly" blessed Jacob, thinking that he was blessing Esau. Soon after Jacob had received the blessings of the firstborn and left, Esau came in. Isaac "trembled violently" when he realized that he had blessed Jacob instead of Esau (Gen 27:33). He was trembling, not because he thought that he had made a mistake in blessing Jacob, but out of "holy fear" in realizing that he could have almost blessed Esau out of ignorance. It struck him that he could have acted against God's redemptive plan and sovereign providence.[27]

Consequently, by faith, Isaac refused Esau's persistent plea to give him the blessings of the firstborn as well (Gen 27:33, 37–40). In regard to this, Hebrews 11:20 states, "By faith Isaac blessed Jacob and Esau, even regarding things to come." True faith is putting God's plans and providence as priority over all worldly attachments.

Isaac probably thought of how he was named "he laughs," and believed that nothing is impossible for God's Word (Gen 18:14), resulting in determination that he would live a life of absolute obedience to God's Word. Isaac's willingness to obey when Abraham tried to offer him as a sacrifice is the model of absolute obedience (Gen 22:9–10).

Hebrews 5:8–9 states, "Although He was a Son, He learned obedience from the things which He suffered. And having been made perfect, He became to all those who obey Him the source of eternal salvation." Jesus was made perfect by learning obedience, as well as becoming the source of eternal salvation to all those who obey Him. By thoroughly learning the obedience of Jesus Christ, we must also be a part of Jesus Christ's work of eternal salvation and play a crucial role in the history of redemption.

CHAPTER 10

The Third Generation

> **Jacob – יַעֲקֹב / Ἰακώβ**
>
> The one who takes by the heel, supplanter

Order
The third person in the genealogy of Jesus Christ (Matt 1:2; 1 Chr 1:34)

Background
His father was Isaac and his mother was Rebekah. He had 12 sons including Judah (Matt 1:2; Luke 3:34).

Key Point
Although Jacob was the younger son, he became the firstborn by God's sovereign election (Gen 27:26–40; Rom 9:10–13), and became a direct ancestor of Jesus Christ according to the genealogy.

Jacob is יַעֲקֹב (ya'ăqōb) in Hebrew and Ἰακώβ (Iakōb) in Greek. יַעֲקֹב is derived from עָקַב ('āqab), which means "supplant" or "take by the heel." Thus, the name means "supplanter" or "the one who takes by the heel."

1. Jacob Received the Blessing of the Firstborn

Esau was actually the firstborn, but the one who received the birthright and the blessings was Jacob.

Abraham became the father of Isaac at the age of 100, and Isaac became the father of Jacob at the age of 60. Since Abraham lived to the age of 175, three generations—Abraham, Isaac, and Jacob—dwelled in tents together for 15 years (Heb 11:9). While living with Isaac and Jacob, Abraham probably taught and passed down God's covenant onto them. Jacob, who liked to dwell in tents (Gen 25:27), received detailed instructions in the faith through his grandfather Abraham and his mother Rebekah. Naturally, he sought after the blessings of the firstborn.

When Esau returned from the field famished and asked for the lentil stew that Jacob had made, the first thing Jacob wanted from his brother Esau in exchange for the stew was the birthright. It is evident that Jacob had direly yearned to attain the birthright. However, Esau "despised" his birthright (Gen 25:31, 34). After obtaining the birthright, Jacob even took away the blessings of the firstborn from Esau by going to their father Isaac before Esau did when Isaac was about to bless his brother Esau with the blessing of the firstborn (Gen 27:36).

While all of these events appear to be the result of Jacob's ambition, God's sovereign election and administration in the history of redemption was behind it all to establish Jacob as a direct ancestor of Jesus Christ. Later on, the Apostle Paul said, "So then it does not depend on the man who wills or the man who runs, but on God who has mercy" (Rom 9:16), clearly proving that the election of Jacob was by God's sovereignty.

2. Jacob Became the Foundation for the Establishment of the Nation of Israel

Jacob fled to his uncle Laban's house at the age of 76 because Esau wanted to kill Jacob for taking away his blessing of the firstborn (Gen 27:41). There, at the house of his uncle Laban, Jacob served for seven years and first received Leah as wife for his work. Then, seven days later, he took his beloved Rachel as his wife under the condition that he works seven more years (Gen 29:18, 27). Therefore, Jacob was 83 years old when he got married (1923 BC), which was 43 years after Esau got married (Gen 26:34).[28]

During his 20-year stay at his uncle Laban's house (Gen 31:41), he had 11 sons and one daughter by Leah, Rachel, Bilhah, and Zilpah (Gen 29:31–30:24). At the age of 90, he became the father of his eleventh son Joseph whose mother was Rachel (Gen 30:22–24). Thereafter he served six more years tending Laban's flock (Gen 30:25–31; 31:38–41). The twelfth son Benjamin was born to Jacob later through Rachel. The 12 sons of Jacob became ancestors of the 12 tribes of Israel, thus becoming the foundation for the establishment of the nation of Israel.

Jacob returned to the land of Canaan at the age of 96 in 1910 BC. Then, at the age of 130, he led his 70 family members into the land of Egypt (Gen 47:9). He lived in Egypt until the age of 147 and died there (Gen 47:28).

3. Jacob Blessed His 12 Sons by Faith

Before his death, Jacob prophesied regarding his 12 sons: "what shall befall [them] in the days to come" (Gen 49:1) and "the blessings appropriate to everyone" (Gen 49:28). As the inheritor of the covenant, however, Jacob blessed his sons according to the redemptive historical administration, not according to the order of their birth. Concerning this, Hebrews 11:21 states that it was "by faith" that Jacob blessed his sons and worshiped God as he was dying.

First, he did not give his firstborn Reuben the blessings of the firstborn. Reuben was the firstborn according to the order of birth, but had defiled his father's bed by sleeping with Bilhah, his father's concubine (Gen 35:22). Genesis 49:3–4 states, "Reuben, you are my firstborn; my might and the beginning of my strength, preeminent in dignity and preeminent in power. Uncontrolled as water, you shall not have preeminence, because you went up to your father's bed; then you defiled it—he went up to my couch."

Second, he granted the birthright to his fourth son, Judah. Jacob blessed Judah, so that his brothers would praise him and bow down to him (Gen 49:8). This was the prophecy that Judah will be the firstborn. This prophecy was first fulfilled through the royal family of David, who was from the line of Judah (2 Sam 5:1–2). But, it was fulfilled in its entirety when Jesus came as the descendant of Judah (Mic 5:2; Matt 1:2).

Third, he blessed his eleventh son, Joseph, with the blessing of the one distinguished among his brothers. Genesis 49:26 prophesied that Joseph would be "the one who was separate from his brothers" (KJV). Moses spoke of him in Deuteronomy 33:16 as "distinguished among his brothers" (NASB).[29] 1 Chronicles 5:1 states, "For Reuben was the firstborn, but because he defiled his father's bed, his birthright was given to the sons of Joseph the son of Israel; so that he is not enrolled in the genealogy according to the birthright." This implies that Joseph, too, received the birthright (cf. Gen 48:5–6; Ezek 47:13).[30]

The following translation of the passage (1 Chr 5:1) in the New Living Translation Bible (NLT) clearly explains why Joseph received the birthright:

> The oldest son of Israel was Reuben. But since he dishonored his father by sleeping with one of his father's concubines, his birthright was given to the sons of his brother Joseph. For this reason, Reuben is not listed in the genealogical records as the firstborn son.

When Jacob was born, he came out with his hand holding onto the heel of his twin brother Esau, who came out first (Gen 25:26). As indicated by the meaning of his name, Jacob later became a "supplanter" in the place of the firstborn and thus became a part of Jesus Christ's genealogy as Isaac's firstborn and a direct ancestor of Jesus Christ.

Jacob is the immediate forefather of the nation of Israel. His 12 sons formed the 12 tribes of Israel, the assembly of the covenant. Jacob's new name, *Israel*, became the name of the nation (Gen 32:28). However, this was not by Jacob's own doing, but by God's sovereign work in paving the path for Jesus Christ's coming through Jacob (Rom 9:10–13).

Jacob longed for the birthright and the blessings of the firstborn that his brother Esau had. That is why, as his name implies, he became the "supplanter" in the place of the firstborn. Jacob's heart and mind were focused solely on attaining the birthright and its blessings. Likewise, we must put our hopes on Jesus Christ and the blessings He brings, eternal life and the inheritance of God's kingdom. On these, we must fix our hearts, pour out our devotion, and exert all of our strength and unceasing efforts (Matt 11:12).

CHAPTER 11

The Fourth Generation

Judah – יְהוּדָה / Ἰούδας

To praise

Order
The fourth in the genealogy of Jesus Christ (Matt 1:2–3; 1 Chr 2:1–4)

Background
His father was Jacob and his mother was Leah. He had five sons and among the five, Perez was recorded in the genealogy of Jesus (Matt 1:2–3; Luke 3:33; 1 Chr 2:3–4).

Key Point
As the fourth son among the 12 sons of Jacob, Judah became a direct ancestor of Jesus Christ.

Judah is יְהוּדָה (yĕhûdâ) in Hebrew, and Ἰούδας (Ioudas) in Greek. יְהוּדָה, meaning "praised." This word is derived from יָדָה (yādâ), which means "to confess," "to praise," "to give thanks," "to shoot," or "to throw." It was entirely by God's sovereign election that Judah, among the 12 brothers, became a direct ancestor of Jesus Christ.

1. Judah, along with His Brothers, Sold Joseph to the Ishmaelites

When Jacob sent 17-year-old Joseph on an errand to bring back a report on the welfare of his brothers, he came to Shechem and then, went after his brothers all the way to Dothan (Gen 37:14, 17). However, his brothers stripped him of his varicolored tunic and threw him down into a pit in order to kill him (Gen 37:23–24). At that moment, Judah suggested that they sell him rather than kill him. Thus, they sold Joseph to the Ishmaelites and they took Joseph down to Egypt (Gen 37:26–28).

Stricken with guilt, Judah later went to Adullam in Canaan (Gen 38:1). There, Judah married a daughter of a certain Canaanite whose name was Shua. Judah was probably around 20 years old at the time. Genesis 38:2 states, "And Judah saw there a daughter of a certain Canaanite whose name was Shua; and he took her and went in to her." The Hebrew verbs for "saw," "took," and "went in to her" in this passage are all in the qal, waw consecutive, imperfect form and all imply that Judah saw her through the eyes of the flesh, liked her, and immediately married her. Because Judah took a Gentile woman simply for her physical appearance and thus failed to keep the purity of his faith, he brought tragedy upon his household. Abraham had previously informed Isaac not to take a wife from the daughters of the Canaanites (Gen 24:3). Therefore, Judah's act of taking a daughter from the Canaanites as his wife was a terrible mistake.

2. Judah Lost His First Son Er and His Second Son Onan

Judah became the father of Er, Onan, and Shelah by the daughter of Shua. For his firstborn Er, he took Tamar as his daughter-in-law (Gen 38:6). This must have been at least 15 years after Joseph was sold to Egypt since Er, Judah's firstborn, was already old enough to be married.

Nonetheless, Er was evil in the sight of the Lord and God "took his life" (Gen 38:7). The same expression (i.e., "took his life") was used successively for the death of the second son, Onan (Gen 38:10). Hence, it is possible that Er, too, may have died because of a sexual sin similar to Onan's.

When Er died, his younger brother Onan had to take Tamar, Er's widow, as his wife in accordance with the levirate marriage law (Deut 25:5–6). However, Onan wasted his seed on the ground when he went in to his brother's wife because he did not want to have any offspring with his sister-in-law only to have the child under his brother's name in the genealogy (Gen 38:9–10). Here, the word *waste* is שָׁחַת (*šāḥat*) in Hebrew, meaning "to destroy" or "to corrupt." In this context, it signifies the act of "emitting the semen outside the body and destroying its life."

> **Genesis 38:9** But Onan knew that the offspring would not be his; so whenever he lay with his brother's wife, he spilled his semen on the ground to keep from producing offspring for his brother. (NIV)

According to this translation, Onan did this repeatedly. God could not watch his wicked deed any longer, and He finally took his life.

Judah wanted to acquire an offspring through Onan after his firstborn Er had died because he most likely wished to continue the genealogy of God's covenant that had been passed down from Abraham, Isaac and Jacob. When the two sons both died, however, Judah gave that up and did not give his third son Shelah to Tamar in fear that Shelah might also die like his brothers (Gen 38:11). Despite the fact that his two sons had died suddenly because of their own wickedness, Judah placed the blame on Tamar for their deaths and sent her to her father's house to maintain her faithfulness (Gen 38:11). Because of his worldly concerns, Judah foolishly committed the error of discontinuing the lineage of God's descendants.

3. Judah Became the Father of Perez by Tamar, His Daughter-in-law

Tamar was told to return to her father's house and wait until Shelah grew up. So, Tamar went and waited. However, Judah did not give her to Shelah as his wife even after he had grown up (Gen 38:14). In response to this, Tamar did something that seemed totally inappropriate. She disguised herself as a harlot to entice her father-in-law on the road to Timnah, slept with him, and conceived twins—Perez and Zerah.

About three months later, when Judah heard that his daughter-in-law was pregnant, he wanted to burn her (Gen 38:24). Judah proved himself to be most detestable by pretending to be pure before his daughter-in-law and condemning her without hesitation—even wanting to let her be burned—though he himself had slept with "a harlot." After Tamar showed Judah the pledge—his signet ring, cords, and staff—that she received from him, Judah finally realized that Tamar had conceived with his seed. Then, Judah confessed, "She is more righteous than I, inasmuch as I did not give her to my son Shelah" (Gen 38:25–26).

Judah realized his own error as he witnessed Tamar's godly zeal to continue the covenantal lineage. Judah never had relations with Tamar again. This shows that he recognized his wrongdoing and repented of it (Gen 38:26).

From an ethical standpoint, Tamar's act was undoubtedly immoral. Nonetheless, it was not to satisfy her fleshly desires or to avenge her father-in-law that she had covered herself with a veil and sat by the much traveled gateway of Enaim[31] on the road to Timnah (Gen 38:14). Her decisive act—to continue God's holy lineage that was passed down through Abraham, Isaac, Jacob and Judah even at the risk of being accused as an adulterer and put to death—was a demonstration of her faith. Moreover, Tamar's detailed plan to request from Judah his signet ring, cords, and staff further shows her confirmation of faith (Gen 38:18).

The name *Tamar* is תָּמָר (*tāmār*), meaning "palm tree" or "pillar." It is derived from an unused root that means to be "erect." As a woman who had erected the falling household of Judah through her sacrificial faith, Tamar was indeed a woman of faith who stood tall like a palm tree and strong like a pillar.

The coming generations acknowledged that Tamar's act was in faith, and thus praised Ruth, a Moabite woman, saying, "may your house be like the house of Perez whom Tamar bore to Judah, through the offspring which the LORD shall give you by this young woman" (Ruth 4:12). God must have also highly esteemed Tamar's faith for she is recorded in Jesus Christ's genealogy, "to Judah were born Perez and Zerah by Tamar" (Matt 1:3).

Prior to the death of his father Jacob, Judah heard the prophecy that the Messiah would come as his descendant (Gen 49:8–12). At that moment, Judah must have reflected upon God's amazing providence in passing down His promised covenant through Tamar. He must have been astounded when he realized how terribly wrong he was to let his fleshly thoughts nearly cut off his lineage through which the Messiah would come. Judah most likely lived the remainder of his life with sincerity, praising God's marvelous providence in redemptive history.

CHAPTER 12

The Fifth Generation

Perez – פֶּרֶץ / Φαρές

Breach, forcefully broken out

Order
The fifth person in the genealogy of Jesus Christ (Matt 1:3; 1 Chr 2:4–5)

Background
His father was Judah, his mother was Tamar, and his son was Hezron (Ruth 4:18; Matt 1:3; Luke 3:33).

Key Point
Judah became the father of twins, Perez and Zerah, by Tamar (Gen 38:27–30). By coming out of Tamar's womb first, Perez received the blessing of being recorded as a direct ancestor of Jesus Christ.

The name *Perez* is פֶּרֶץ (*pereṣ*) in Hebrew and Φαρες (*Pharés*) in Greek. It is derived from the Hebrew verb פָּרַץ (*pāraṣ*), meaning "to break (through, down, over)" or "to burst." Thus, *Perez* means "breach," "a breakthrough," and "a bursting forth."

1. Perez Attained the Birthright in the Womb

Tamar was able to conceive twins after having relations just once with Judah. Giving a son to continue the holy lineage that leads to Jesus Christ was God's special providence.

However, an odd event occurred as Tamar was giving birth to the twins. One put out his hand first, so the midwife tied a scarlet thread on that hand. Then, the child drew his hand back inside the womb and the other child came out first. The midwife said, "What a breach you have made for yourself!" So he was named Perez (Gen 38:29). Then the child with the scarlet thread came out and he was named Zerah (Gen 38:28–30). The name *Zerah* is זֶרַח (*zerah*) in Hebrew and means "rising," "coming forth," "dawning," and "shining." This name was given to him because of his act of putting his hand out first.

The exclamation in Genesis 38:29, "What a breach you have made for yourself!" refers to the child without the scarlet thread, who pushed the other child with the scarlet thread out of his way and burst out of Tamar's body. This is how Perez became the firstborn and received the unimaginable blessing of having Jesus Christ come through his line.

We can apply the relationship between Perez and Zerah to the history of redemption in various ways. God gave the scarlet gospel of the cross to the Jews first. They were the firstborn according to the order in which the gospel was given. Nevertheless, they repudiated this gospel and judged themselves unworthy of eternal life (Acts 13:46), thereby rejecting God's purpose for themselves (Luke 7:30). However, the Gentiles received the gospel that the Jews had rejected, thus enjoying the blessing of becoming the firstborn of the gospel although they were originally the second born. What a pity it was for the Jews to have Jesus Christ, the treasure of eternal life, right before them and miss Him like the blind who cannot see and the deaf who cannot hear (Matt 13:13–17).

2. Perez Became the Father of Hezron

After becoming Judah's successor to be recorded in the genealogy of the Messiah, Perez became the father of two sons, Hezron and Hamul. Of the two sons, Hezron became the successor in the genealogy of the Messiah and a direct ancestor of Jesus Christ (1 Chr 2:5; Matt 1:3).

On the contrary, Perez's younger brother Zerah became the father of a shameful lineage from which Achan, the troubler of Israel, was born. During the conquest of Canaan, the Israelites destroyed the city of Jericho and attacked the city of Ai, but failed miserably because of Achan. Regarding this, 1 Chronicles 2:7 states, "The son of Carmi was Achar, the troubler of Israel, who violated the ban." Achar is the same as Achan, and he was the one who brought trouble upon all Israel. To find out who violated the ban, all the tribes were told to come forth and the Lord selected the tribe of Judah. Then, the family of Judah was brought near, and the Lord took the family of the Zerahites; and from the family of the Zerahites, the clan of Zabdi was taken. When his household came forward man by man, Achan was taken (Josh 7:16–18).

Although Perez was a child of an incestuous relationship, he was able to enter the genealogy of Jesus Christ because God's providence for redemption depends on His sovereignty, not on human lineage, background, or logic. Just as Perez pushed aside Zerah in the womb to become the firstborn, we also need to make a resolute decision to run the race in faith to become the firstborn of faith (1 Cor 9:24–26).

CHAPTER 13

The Sixth Generation

Hezron – חֶצְרוֹן / Ἑσρώμ

Surrounded by walls, fence

Order

The sixth person in the genealogy of Jesus Christ (Matt 1:3; 1 Chr 2:5)

Background

His father was Perez and his son was Ram as recorded in the genealogy (Ruth 4:18; Matt 1:3; Luke 3:33).

Key Point

Hezron had five sons: the first son was Jerahmeel (1 Chr 2:9, 25), the second was Ram (1 Chr 2:9), the third was Chelubai (a.k.a. Caleb; 1 Chr 2:9, 18), the fourth was Segub (1 Chr 2:21), and the fifth was Ashhur (1 Chr 2:24).

The name *Hezron* is חֶצְרוֹן, (*ḥeṣrôn*) in Hebrew and Ἑσρώμ (*Hesrom*) in Greek. Its assumed root is חָצַר (*ḥāṣar*), meaning "to enclose," "to secure a territory," or "to fence."

1. Hezron Was the Father of Five Sons by His Two Wives

Hezron became the father of Jerahmeel, Ram and Chelubai (Caleb) through his first wife (1 Chr 2:9). He also became the father of Segub and Ashhur by his second wife, Abijah, the daughter of Machir (1 Chr 2:24), at the age of 60 (1 Chr 2:21, 24). Specifically, Ashhur was born after Hezron's death, so his name means "dim" or "black," which seems to depict Abijah's gloomy circumstance of giving birth to a child after losing her husband.

On the other hand, the etymologies of the names of Hezron's other sons seem to be more positive than the name of Ashhur. Presuming that Hezron named his sons, it may be a possible indication that Hezron may have lived his life with a longing desire for the lovingkindness of God Most High.

The first son's name *Jerahmeel* is יְרַחְמְאֵל (*yĕraḥmĕʾēl*) in Hebrew, meaning "may God have compassion." The second son's name *Ram* is רָם (*rām*) in Hebrew and means "height" or "high place." The third son's name *Chelubai* is כְּלוּבָי (*kĕlûbāy*) in Hebrew, and is written as כָּלֵב (*kālēb*) in 1 Chronicles 2:18. The name *Caleb* means "dog," and he is not the same person as the Caleb who went to spy out the land of Canaan with Joshua and gave a report by faith. The fourth son's name *Segub* is שְׂגוּב (*sĕgûb*) in Hebrew. Its root is שָׂגַב (*sāgab*), which means "(inaccessibly) high" or "exalted."

2. Hezron's Family Grew Immensely by God's Sovereign Grace

The second chapter of 1 Chronicles records about the tribe of Judah in most detail amongst the 12 tribes of Israel, and more specifically, about the clan of Hezron (1 Chr 2:9–55) amongst Perez's descendants (1 Chr 2:5). The list of Hezron's descendants are listed in 1 Chronicles 2 in the following order: first, the sons of Ram, Hezron's second son, (1 Chr 2:10–17); the sons of Chelubai (Caleb), his third son, (1 Chr 2:18–20); the sons of Segub and Ashhur, whom Hezron's second wife bore (1 Chr 2:21–24); the sons of Jerahmeel, his firstborn (1 Chr 2:25–41); then again the sons of Mesha, the firstborn of Chelubai (Caleb); the sons by Caleb's two concubines (i.e., Ephah and Maacha; 1 Chr 2:42–49); and the sons of Chelubai (Caleb) by his other wife Ephrathah (1 Chr 2:19, 50–55).

The author of Chronicles first recorded all the shameful and despairing events that occurred in the family of Judah in detail before introducing Hezron's enormous family (1 Chr 2:3–4). Also recorded is the tragedy of how the generations were cut off three times because there were no sons among the descendants of Jerahmeel, Hezron's firstborn (1 Chr 2:30, 32, 34). Discontinuance in the lineage signifies that their inheritance would be forfeited, which was a disgrace to the household (Num 36:2–4). Hence, no one would have expected prosperity for the tribe of Judah that had been stained with such humiliation and shame. Yet, God greatly blessed the tribe of Judah, especially Hezron's family, and bestowed amazing prosperity on them, allowing redemptive historical administration to progress through them.

The second chapter of 1 Chronicles not only shows the prosperity of Hezron's family, but also a remarkable achievement from among his descendants—that there were families of scribes from the line of Salma, the son of Hezron (1 Chr 2:50–55). As interpreters of the law and teachers of the people, scribes held a very important position both socially and politically (2 Sam 8:17; 1 Kgs 4:3; 2 Kgs 12:10; Jer 36:12). It was Hezron's family that produced descendants who held crucial roles as guardians of the law.

The scribes were all "Kenites who came from Hammath, the father of the house of Rechab" (1 Chr 2:55). The house of Rechab had great zeal for God (2 Kgs 10:15–24). In particular, Jonadab (also called Jehonadab) the son of Rechab kept his household from transgressing and preserved their holiness (Jer 35:1–19) for which he later received the blessings of God's promise, "Jonadab the son of Rechab shall not lack a man to stand before Me always" (Jer 35:19).

The families of scribes were also called "the Kenites" (1 Chr 2:55). Moses' father-in-law, Reuel the Midianite, was a Kenite (Exod 3:1; Judg 1:16). Specifically, Hobab, the son of Reuel, became a generous guide for the Israelites during their march in the wilderness by Moses' earnest request (Num 10:29–32). Remembering his deed, God protected the Kenites who lived among the Amalekites by allowing them to leave before He destroyed the Amalekites during King Saul's reign (1 Sam 15:6). The Kenites, who were formerly Gentiles, were included into Hezron's clan within the tribe of Judah because they accepted faith in the Lord, and they fulfilled the duty as "the families of scribes."

The descendants of Hezron prospered and grew into an enormous family because God's sovereign grace had surrounded the household like a protective fence, as indicated by the meaning of the name *Hezron*. As the glorious family entrusted with the crucial work of guarding and transmitting God's covenant, Hezron's lineage became superior to the rest of the clans.

3. Hezron Was Buried in Caleb-ephrathah in the Land of Canaan

Hezron died in Caleb-ephrathah (1 Chr 2:24). This place called אֶפְרָתָה (*'eprātâ*) was the former name of Bethlehem (Gen 48:7; Ruth 1:2; 1 Sam 17:12; Mic 5:2). This reveals that Hezron, one of Jacob's 70 family members who entered Egypt (Gen 46:12), did not die in Egypt but in Canaan although it was prior to the time of the Exodus. There is no record of how Hezron moved to Canaan and lived there until his death. However, as a descendant of Abraham, Isaac, Jacob and Judah, it appears that he believed in God's repeated promise to the Israelites that He would give Canaan as their inheritance (Gen 12:7; 15:18; 28:4, 13), and thus came out of Egypt and settled down in Canaan.

All human beings on earth are weary foreigners who have left their homes and are temporarily sojourning in a foreign place (Lev 25:23; 1 Chr 29:14–15; Job 8:9; 14:2; Ps 102:11; 109:23; 144:4). However, we are sojourners with the hope of eternal life through Jesus Christ. Our true home is the everlasting kingdom of heaven, "My Father's house," and "a building from God" where there are many dwelling places (John 14:2; 2 Cor 5:1). The end for those who live without knowing "My Father's house" which should be their final destination and eternal dwelling place, is futile no matter how hard they labor or how extravagant their lives may be on this earth. Abraham, Isaac, and Jacob dwelled in tents as sojourners on this earth and looked toward the eternal city while holding fast onto the Word of the covenant (Heb 11:8–16). Likewise, I hope and pray that we may all seek the heavenly inheritance that is imperishable, undefiled, and does not fade away and gain the final victory in our sojourning lives on this earth.

CHAPTER 14

The Seventh Generation

Ram (Aram) or Arni – רָם / Ἀράμ

Exalted, high

Order

The seventh person in the genealogy of Jesus (Matt 1:4; 1 Chr 2:9–10)

Background

His father was Hezron and his son was Amminadab as recorded in the genealogy (Ruth 4:19; Matt 1:4), and he is also recorded as Judah's great grandson (Luke 3:33).

Key Point

Although he was the second born, he was included in the genealogy of Jesus Christ. His older brother was Jerahmeel, and his younger brothers were Chelubai, Segub, and Ashhur (1 Chr 2:9, 21, 24).

Ram is רָם (*rām*) in Hebrew and Ἀράμ (*Aram*) in Greek. The name *Ram* is derived from רוּם (*rûm*), which means "high," "exalt," and "raise." Hence, the name *Ram* means "high."[32] From the same root, רָמָה (*rāmâ*) means "high place." Ram is also called *Arni* (Ἀρνί) in Luke 3:33 and this name also means "high place."[33]

1. Ram Was Recorded in the Genealogy of Jesus Christ Although He Was the Second Born

Hezron, Ram's father, had three sons through his first wife. Jerahmeel was the first son and Ram was the second son. 1 Chronicles 2:9 states, "Now the sons of Hezron, who were born to him were Jerahmeel, Ram, and Chelubai." Ram, although he was the second son, received the blessing of being included in the line through which Jesus Christ came (1 Chr 2:9–12). How was Ram able to receive this blessing?

Ram's older brother Jerahmeel took another wife when he already had one. 1 Chronicles 2:26 states, "Jerahmeel had another wife, whose name was Atarah; she was the mother of Onam." In Hebrew, the name *Atarah* is עֲטָרָה (ʿăṭārâ), meaning "crown" or "coronet." Jerahmeel's act of taking another wife shows that he lacked godliness.

The second chapter of 1 Chronicles also records the fact that generations among the descendants of Jerahmeel were cut off three times: "Seled died without sons" (1 Chr 2:30), "Jether died without sons" (1 Chr 2:32), and "Sheshan had no sons, only daughters" (1 Chr 2:34). This was perhaps not entirely unrelated to the reason that Jerahmeel could not be recorded in the genealogy as the firstborn.

2. The Genealogy According to the Gospel of Luke Records Ram as "Arni"

Ram was recorded as the son of Hezron from the tribe of Judah, the son of Jacob, and became an ancestor of David (Ruth 4:19–22; 1 Chr 2:9–10) and Jesus (Matt 1:3–4). In the genealogy of Luke (Luke 3:33), he is recorded as "Arni" (ASV, NET, NJB, NLT, NRSV, RSV, etc.).

The genealogies from Abraham to Ram found in Matthew 1 and Luke 3 can be compared as depicted in the following chart:

Genealogy in Matthew	Abraham	Isaac	Jacob	Judah	Perez	Hezron	Ram
Genealogy in Luke	Abraham	Isaac	Jacob	Judah	Perez	Hezron	Arni

When comparing the 14 generations in the first period of Jesus Christ's genealogy, which appear in the first chapter of Matthew with the corresponding people in the third chapter of Luke, the only difference found is between Ram and Arni (Luke 3:33). It is natural to accept that Ram and Arni are two different names for the same person, with the name written differently. According to the Textus Receptus, *Arni* found in Luke 3:33 of some English translations is recorded as the same person as Ἀράμ (*Aram*) in Matthew.

Ram was the second born, and his older brother was Jerahmeel. It is interesting to note that Jerahmeel gave his first son the same name as his younger brother, Ram (1 Chr 2:25). Jerahmeel must have liked his brother Ram for him to name his son Ram also. From this, we can presume that Ram lived a life that was respected even by his own family.

The name *Ram* means "exalted," and his other name *Arni* means "high place." Although Ram was the second son, he was recorded in the genealogy of Jesus Christ by the sovereign work of God; and like the meaning of his name, he was highly exalted. God exalts those who humble themselves in the presence of the Lord (Jas 4:10), and He exalts those who humble themselves under the mighty hand of God at the proper time (1 Pet 5:6). When Jesus Christ humbled Himself by becoming obedient even to the point of death on the cross, God highly exalted Him, and bestowed on Him the name that is above every name (Phil 2:8–9).

CHAPTER 15

The Eighth Generation

> ## Amminadab (Aminadab) – עַמִּינָדָב / ʾΑμιναδάβ
> My noble kinsman

Order
The eighth person in the genealogy of Jesus Christ (Matt 1:4; 1 Chr 2:10)

Background
His father was Ram and his son was Nahshon as recorded in the genealogy (Ruth 4:19; Luke 3:33).

Key Point
Amminadab's daughter, Elisheba, married Aaron the high priest (Exod 6:23).

Amminadab is עַמִּינָדָב (ʿammînādāb) in Hebrew and ʾΑμιναδάβ (Aminadab) in Greek. The Hebrew name עַמִּינָדָב is a compound word of עַם (ʿām) and נָדִיב (nādîb), where עַם means "people" or "kinsman" and נָדִיב means "make willing" or "noble." Hence, the name עַמִּינָדָב means "my kinsman is noble."[34]

1. Amminadab Is Related to the House of Aaron the High Priest

Amminadab's[35] daughter, Elisheba, was married to Aaron the high priest. Exodus 6:23 states, "And Aaron married Elisheba, the daughter of Amminadab, the sister of Nahshon, and she bore him Nadab and Abihu, Eleazar and Ithamar."

As Moses' older brother, Aaron was the most essential leader to guide the Israelites through their wilderness journey into Canaan (Exod 6:20, 26). Given that Amminadab's family married into the family of Aaron the high priest, it can be deduced that the family must also have been a godly household involved in the leadership role.

The name Elisheba is אֱלִישֶׁבַע (*'ĕlîšeba'*) in Hebrew, which means "My God has sworn" or "God is an oath." The four sons born unto Elisheba and Aaron were "Nadab, Abihu, Eleazar and Ithamar" (Exod 6:23). Nadab and Abihu offered before the Lord a strange fire which the Lord had not commanded them. Then, fire came out from the presence of the Lord and consumed them, and they died while they were without sons (Lev 10:1–2; Num 3:4; 26:60–61). Therefore, Eleazar and Ithamar succeeded Aaron in serving as priests (Num 3:4), and their household served God throughout the generations (Num 20:25–28; Deut 10:6; Josh 14:1).

2. The Account of Amminadab's Time Shows that Some Generations Were Omitted in the Genealogy of Jesus Christ

In 1876 BC, Jacob led his family of 70 members into Egypt. The list of Jacob's family who moved to Egypt includes Judah and his son Perez, and even Perez's son Hezron. Genesis 46:12 states, "And the sons of Judah: Er and Onan and Shelah and Perez and Zerah (but Er and Onan died in the land of Canaan). And the sons of Perez were Hezron and Hamul." Nahshon is described as Amminadab's son in the genealogy of Jesus Christ according to Matthew and is also listed among the tribal leaders of Israel in the wilderness after the exodus (Num 1:7; 2:3; 10:14). Now, considering that their time of slavery in Egypt was 430 years, it cannot be right that there were only four generations—Hezron, Ram, Amminadab, and Nahshon—over such a long period of time. Hence, we can conclude that the genealogy of Jesus Christ is not an exhaustive list of every person, but a selective list from the perspective of redemptive history.

Matthew Chapter 1 Genealogy	Abraham	Isaac	Jacob	Judah	Perez	Hezron	Ram	Amminadab	Nahshon
			Entered Egypt			430 years in Egypt			40 years in the wilderness

The name *Amminadab* means "My kinsman is noble." God considered His covenanted people exceptionally precious among all the peoples of the earth. God said, "you shall be My own possession among all the peoples" (Exod 19:5). The word *possession* is סְגֻלָּה (*sĕlūllâ*) in Hebrew, which signifies "a valued personal property," and "a property for which the owner has special affection." This illustrates that God has esteemed His people as His most precious unique possession, and that He cherishes and protects them.

Believers are God's most precious treasures, valuable possessions that He cherishes and protects (Deut 26:18; 1 Pet 2:9). In the presence of God's immense love that elects and cherishes the worthless beings like us, the only thing that we can do is faithfully offer up our gratitude and our lives.

CHAPTER 16

The Ninth Generation

> **Nahshon** – נַחְשׁוֹן / Ναασσών
>
> Know from experience, diligently observe, that which foretells

Order
The ninth person in the genealogy of Jesus Christ (Matt 1:4; 1 Chr 2:10)

Background
His father was recorded as Amminadab and his son as Salmon (Ruth 4:20; Matt 1:4; Luke 3:32).
He is the older brother of Elisheba, the wife of Aaron the high priest (Exod 6:23).

Key Point
He was the leader of the tribe of Judah during the years in the wilderness (Num 1:7; 2:3; 10:14). He was the representative of the soldiers 20 years or older in the tribe of Judah.

Nahshon is נַחְשׁוֹן (*naḥšôn*) in Hebrew and Ναασσών (*Naassōn*) in Greek. This Hebrew name is derived from the word נָחַשׁ (*nāḥaš*), which means "learn by experience," "diligently observe," "divine," or "practice divination or fortune telling."

1. Nahshon Was the Leader of the Tribe of Judah in the Wilderness

The Israelites journeyed from Rameses on the fifteenth day of the first month in the first year of the Exodus and arrived at the Wilderness of Sinai in the third month (Num 33:3; Exod 19:1). While they remained there for about one year, they received the Ten Commandments and the pattern of the tabernacle. Then, on the first day of the second month in the second year, they took a census of men who were 20 years old and older, all who were able to go to war (Num 1:1–3).

When numbering the soldiers, Moses ordered the head of each tribe to come forward to take the census (Num 1:2–4; 16–18). Nahshon was chosen as the leader from the tribe of Judah (Num 1:7, 16). Another way of saying "leader" is *head* (Num 1:4, 16), which is רֹאשׁ (*r'ōš*) in Hebrew, meaning "head" or "chief." At that time, soldiers from the tribe of Judah who were 20 years old and older were 74,600 in total (Num 1:27). Nahshon was chosen as a leader from a large number of people (Num 1:17). From the fact that Nahshon was designated as a leader before Moses and Aaron, it is evident that Nahshon was a man of exemplary faith, worthy to represent the 74,600 people from the tribe of Judah.

2. Nahshon Was the First in Presenting an Offering

On the first day of the first month, in the second year of the Exodus, the tabernacle was completed. Upon its completion, Moses performed the ritual of consecration by anointing the tabernacle and all of its furnishings and utensils. At this time, the leaders from the tribes brought to God 6 covered carts and 12 oxen, a cart for every two of the leaders and an ox for each one (Num 7:1–3).

Then, the leaders also offered the dedication offering for the altar. The leaders presented their offering, one each day, for 12 days. Among the 12 tribes, the first one to present the offering was Nahshon from the tribe of Judah. Numbers 7:12 clearly states, "Now the one who presented his offering on the first day was Nahshon the son of Amminadab, of the tribe of Judah." Nahshon was blessed to be the first leader to present an offering on behalf of his tribe, the tribe of Judah.

3. Nahshon Went on Ahead in the Wilderness March

The Israelites marched in four divisions according to their armies in the wilderness. The first division was composed of the tribes of Judah in the lead, Issachar, and Zebulun; the second division was composed of the tribes of Reuben in the lead, Simeon and Gad; the third division was composed of the tribes of Ephraim in the lead, Manasseh, and Benjamin; and the fourth division was composed of the tribes of Dan in the lead, Asher, and Naphtali (Num 10:14–28).

Numbers 10:14 states, "The standard of the camp of the sons of Judah, according to their armies, set out first, with Nahshon the son of Amminadab, over its army." The New Living Translation of the same verse states, "Judah's troops led the way. They marched behind their banner, and their leader was Nahshon son of Amminadab." Nahshon, who led the tribe of Judah, was marching on ahead of all 12 tribes. This shows that Nahshon was a man of remarkable leadership and that people recognized his dedication.

The act of walking on ahead of people entails an imperative responsibility of pioneering and sacrificing for the rest. When Jesus Christ made His entry into Jerusalem to fulfill His great mission of redemption on the cross, He walked on ahead of the disciples (Mark 10:32; Luke 19:28).

Moreover, those who walk on ahead, as the meaning of the name *Nahshon* implies, need to have a superior ability to observe, seeing what others cannot see, and understanding what others cannot understand, like the seers and the prophets in the Old Testament times. I sincerely hope that we may diligently search the Bible deeply and witness God's administration of redemption hidden in the Scriptures, so that we may become leaders in the work of establishing God's kingdom (Isa 34:16).

CHAPTER 17

The Tenth Generation

Salmon – שַׂלְמוֹן / Σαλμών

Garment, coat, cloak

Order
The tenth person in the genealogy of Jesus Christ (Matt 1:4–5; 1 Chr 2:11)

Background
His father was Nahshon and his son was Boaz as recorded in the genealogy (Ruth 4:20–21; Matt 1:4–5; Luke 3:32).

Key Point
When Joshua sent two men to spy out the city of Jericho, Rahab the harlot—whom Salmon later married—hid them.

Salmon is שַׂלְמוֹן (śālmôn) in Hebrew and Σαλμών (Salmōn) in Greek. It is derived from a slightly variant form of the Hebrew word שַׂלְמָה (śālmâ), which is a general term for clothes and used as "garment," "coat," and "cloak."

1. Salmon Married Rahab the Harlot

Matthew 1:5 states, "And to Salmon was born Boaz by Rahab." Rahab in this verse refers to Rahab the harlot in the second chapter of the book of Joshua.

When the Israelites completed the 40-year wilderness journey and camped at Shittim in the plains of Moab, Joshua secretly sent two spies to view the Canaanite land and the city of Jericho (Josh 2:1). These two men lodged at the house of a harlot whose name was Rahab.

Then, the king of Jericho heard that men from the sons of Israel came to search out the land of Jericho and sent word to Rahab saying, "Bring out the men who have entered your house" (Josh 2:2–3). However, Rahab hid the men in the stalks of flax on the roof and sent away the soldiers of Jericho by telling them that the two men had already come and gone (Josh 2:4–6). She hid the men of God despite the danger of being put to death if the truth were exposed.

The city of Jericho was the first gateway into the land of Canaan since it was located on the pathway that leads from the plains of Moab on the east of the Jordan to the land of Canaan. Jericho was strategically a very important city because the Israelites would not have been able to enter Canaan without conquering it. The city was known to have an impregnable fortress whose outer wall measured about 6 feet (1.8 m) thick, 30 feet (9.2 m) high, and was spaced 15 feet (4.5 m) wide from its inner wall.

With the help of Rahab, the two spies were able to obtain all the information regarding the city of Jericho, which greatly aided them in fully occupying the city after the walls fell. Rahab played an integral role in the divine history of redemption by not only saving the two spies, but also making a critical contribution in conquering the city of Jericho.

According to the ethical standards of the world, Rahab's deed could be considered despicable, for it was an act of betraying her own country and people. However, she had both a penetrating insight into divine redemptive history and a firm faith in God. She confessed, "I know that the LORD has given you the land" (Josh 2:9). She felt convicted that God would allow Israel to conquer Canaan and believed that trying to stop it would only be an act of standing against God's providence.

It is truly remarkable that an unclean woman from a gentile city of Jericho could firmly confess her faith with regard to the promise of Canaan, which God continuously made with Abraham and his descendants (Gen 15:7; 17:8; 26:3; 28:13; 35:12; 50:24; Exod 6:8; 23:28–30; Num 33:52–53; 34:1–12; Deut 6:18; Josh 1:15). It was by faith that Rahab peacefully welcomed the two spies (Heb 11:31).

Rahab said in Joshua 2:10 that the Lord dried up the water of the Red Sea, and she confessed in Joshua 2:11, "The LORD your God is God in heaven above and on earth beneath." She was confessing that the God of Israel is the one and only God who created and governs the entire universe. Rahab possessed not only a keen insight and thorough understanding of God's redemptive history, but also an assured faith in God. Just as her name Rahab (רָחָב) implies "wide," "big," and "broad," she was a woman with a generous heart, a broad perspective, and great faith.

Because she was convinced that only God was able to save her and her family from death, she beseeched the two spies to swear by God and give her a pledge of truth (Josh 2:12–13). They answered her, "Tie this cord of scarlet thread in the window and gather to yourself into the house your father and your mother and your brothers and all your father's household." Rahab obeyed and tied the scarlet thread in the window and gathered all her family (Josh 2:18–21). Just as promised, Joshua spared Rahab and all those whom she had in her household when he destroyed the entire city of Jericho with fire (Josh 6:23–25).

The scarlet thread tied in the window was a sign of salvation like the Passover lamb's blood that the Israelites put on the doorposts and the lintel of their houses to evade death at the time of the exodus (Exod 12:7, 13). Hence, it signifies the blood of Jesus Christ—that paid for the sin of all mankind—delivered us from death and gave us eternal life (Eph 1:7; 1 Pet 1:18–19).

Regarding Rahab's faith, James 2:25 states, "And in the same way was not Rahab the harlot also justified by works, when she received the messengers and sent them out by another way?" According to this statement, Rahab clearly was "justified." That the account of Rahab's act of faith in hiding the spies immediately follows the account of Abraham's act of faith in offering Isaac is very noteworthy (Jas 2:21–25). The Bible clearly points out that even Rahab, a lowly gentile harlot, was a possessor of faith great enough to receive justification by God just as men like Abraham were justified by faith.

It was indeed this woman, Rahab the harlot, whom Salmon married. Although Rahab was only a Canaanite woman and a lowly harlot, she received the greatest blessing of being written in the genealogy of Jesus Christ along with her husband Salmon through faith.

2. Salmon Had a Generous Heart

Salmon married Rahab the harlot (Josh 2:1). The New Testament also records her as "Rahab the harlot" (Heb 11:31; Jas 2:25). The Hebrew word for *harlot* is זָנָה (zānâ), meaning "to commit adultery" or "to play harlot." This word does not merely refer to an innkeeper, but to a prostitute who makes a living by selling her body.

If Salmon were narrow-minded, he would not have married Rahab, even if she had converted to a believer of the Lord because of the fact that she was a harlot. Nevertheless, like his name Salmon, he covered up her shameful past as with a garment or a cloak.

Do we not also have many wrongdoings and transgressions we wish to cover up? The good news is that Jesus Christ has not only covered the multitude of our sins with His precious blood on the cross, but also considered us righteous (Ps 103:12; Rom 3:24–28; 4:24–25; 1 Cor 6:11; Titus 3:7).

We who are created anew through righteousness and holiness of the truth are clothed in the blood of Jesus Christ.

> **Revelation 7:13–14** Then one of the elders answered, saying to me, "These who are clothed in the white robes, who are they, and from where have they come?" I said to him, "My lord, you know." And he said to me, "these are the ones who come out of the great tribulation, and they have washed their robes and made them white in the blood of the Lamb."

What is needed for those clothed in the robe of Jesus Christ's precious blood is a generous heart and love that can cover up other people's flaws. God's greatest commandment is "You shall love the LORD your God with all your heart, and with all your soul, and with all your mind" (Matt 22:37–38), and the second is "You shall love your neighbor as yourself" (Matt 22:39). This commandment, "You shall love your neighbor as yourself," can be considered the royal law (Gal 5:14; Jas 2:8) because it would be a lie to say that we love God, whom we cannot see, if we cannot even love our brothers, whom we can see (1 Jn 4:20–21).

Love covers a multitude of sins (1 Pet 4:8). Rather than exposing the flaws of others, I pray that we will all become people of great faith like Salmon, who can cover and embrace others with a generous heart and love.

CHAPTER 18

The Eleventh Generation

Boaz – בֹּעַז / Βοός

Quickness, swiftness, strength

Order

The eleventh person in the genealogy of Jesus Christ (Matt 1:5; 1 Chr 2:11–12)

Background

His father was recorded as Salmon, his son as Obed (Ruth 4:17, 21–22).

Key Point

Ruth, who married Boaz, was originally a Moabitess, but followed the faith of Naomi, her mother-in-law, and became part of the nation of Israel.

Boaz is בֹּעַז (bo'az) in Hebrew, meaning "keenness" or "fleetness," and Βοός (Booz) in Greek. Ruth 2:1 portrays him as "a man of great wealth." Here, "a man of great wealth" is an expression used for a powerful, influential, and prosperous man.

1. Boaz Lived During the Period of the Judges

Boaz lived in the period of the judges that went through cycles of depravity resulting from idolatry, intermarriage with Gentiles, and all kinds of sin because "every man did what was right in his own eyes" (Judg 2:11–15, 17:6, 21:25, Ruth 1:1).

When a great famine struck Bethlehem, a relative of Boaz, Elimelech (אֱלִימֶלֶךְ: my God is king) and his wife Naomi (נָעֳמִי: my delight) and their sons, Mahlon and Chilion, left the Promised Land and moved to the foreign land of Moab. The famine in Bethlehem was God's wrath toward sin. The names of the two sons born to Elimelech and Naomi seem to depict how severe that wrath was. The name *Mahlon* (מַחְלוֹן) means "sick," and *Chilion* (כִּלְיוֹן) means "pining."

After Naomi's husband, Elimelech, died in Moab, Naomi took two Moabite women as her daughters-in-law, Orpah (עָרְפָּה: neck, back) and Ruth (רוּת: friendship).

After dwelling in Moab for about ten years, her two sons, Mahlon and Chilion, died suddenly (Ruth 1:5). After that, Naomi heard that "the LORD had visited His people by giving them bread" (Ruth 1:6), and she and her two daughters–in-law set out to return to her homeland. However, Naomi tried to send them back. Of the two daughters-in-law, Orpah left, but Ruth clung to Naomi to the end.

When Naomi had come to Bethlehem, the women said, "Is this Naomi?" (Ruth 1:19). However, Naomi said to them, "Do not call me Naomi; call me Mara" (Ruth 1:20). The name *Mara* (מָרָא) means "bitter" or "bitterness," depicting the great affliction Naomi had faced in Moab. Naomi understood that her affliction had been given by the Almighty God, and thus confessed, "The LORD has testified against me, and the Almighty has afflicted me" (Ruth 1:21). In the midst of such affliction in Naomi's household, God chose Ruth, a woman of great faith, and led her to meet Boaz, thereby allowing her to enter into the genealogy of Jesus Christ.

2. Boaz Was a Mighty Man of Wealth, Yet a Man of Humility

Boaz had great wealth and was very influential in that region, yet he was also a virtuous man of humility who unreservedly associated with those under him and showed kindness and mercy to the needy.

Even though he was the landlord, he personally went out to the field to greet the reapers first (Ruth 2:4), ate with them (Ruth 2:14), and slept on the threshing floor (Ruth 3:7). He was truly a simple man who did not boast in his authority. Also, Boaz had compassion for Ruth, who was gleaning, and offered her bread (Ruth 2:14). He kindly showed his benevolence to her by commanding his young men to let grain from the bundles purposely fall for her so that she could glean as much as possible.

Boaz appears as a Jesus-like figure. Jesus, who had abandoned His glorious throne in heaven and had come down to the earth, always showed His care for each one of the least (Matt 18:10, 14; 25:40, 45); He thoroughly emptied and lowered Himself to become the sinners' friend (Phil 2:6–8; Matt 11:18–19; Mark 2:15).

Ruth was descended from the Moabites whom God cursed, "No Ammonite or Moabite shall enter the assembly of the LORD…" (Deut 23:3). She had lost her husband during a most difficult time due to extreme famine and had to live a shunned life in a foreign land. Like Ruth, we were under the bondage of eternal death and totally alienated from the possibility of becoming a part of the chosen people, deserving of no rights, power, or even acknowledgment (Rom 3:23; 6:23). However, all the glory, wealth and happiness that the prominent man Boaz had became Ruth's when they married. We, too, have freely received all the wealth, glory, and happiness of Jesus Christ, the most powerful One, by coming under His wings (Luke 13:34) and becoming His bride (Rev 19:7–8). There is no greater happiness on this earth!

3. Boaz Acted Swiftly in Becoming the Kinsman-redeemer

As a close relative of Naomi and Ruth, Boaz had the obligation and right to redeem, based on the duties of the goel (Ruth 2:20; 3:2). The duties of the goel is a Jewish law that gave the right to the nearest kin to redeem and repurchase, as well as to avenge blood when one dies. The word *goel* is the participle of the Hebrew word גָּאַל (*gāʾal*), which means "to redeem," "do the part of a relative," or "redeem a kinsman."[36] This duty foreshadows the redemptive work of Jesus Christ who delivered us from Satan's hand with the cost of His own blood.

The same duty also fell upon the nearest kinsman to liberate his brother who, being poor, had been forced into slavery because of his debt (Lev 25:47–55). Also, when a fellow countryman becomes so poor that he has to sell his property, the land was to be restored to him when his nearest kinsman comes and buys back what his relative had sold (Lev 25:23–28). One important aspect of the duties of goel was that it transferred upon the closest relative the duty to marry the childless widow of his deceased brother in order to sustain his family line.

In order to give Ruth in marriage to Boaz, who she thought was the nearest kinsman-redeemer, Naomi instructed Ruth to go to the threshing floor where Boaz slept, uncover his feet and lie down, and do whatever he tells her to do (Ruth 3:1–5). Ruth followed Naomi's instructions and requested Boaz to accept her proposal in marriage by saying, "Spread your covering over your maid, for you are a close relative" (Ruth 3:9).

Boaz said that he would accept Ruth's proposal and make sure that she is redeemed. However, since there was a relative closer to her than he, Boaz promised to redeem her if that relative refused to redeem her (Ruth 3:12–14). Boaz immediately went up to the gate and took ten men of the elders and discussed the matter with the relative closer to Ruth than he. At first, the closer relative readily agreed to redeem Naomi's land, but when he heard from Boaz that Ruth must be acquired in order to raise up the name of the deceased on his inheritance, he instantly gave it up for he was afraid that it might jeopardize his own inheritance (Ruth 4:1–6). Therefore, Boaz obtained the right as kinsman-redeemer, and married Ruth (Ruth 4:7–13).

Boaz acted swiftly, like the meaning of his name, in obeying God's command to become kinsman-redeemer. The word *swift* means "quick" or "prompt." The prophet Daniel, who lived during the years of the Babylonian captivity, was filled with God's spirit and had an extraordinary mind (translated as "keen," "extraordinary," "excellent," or "exceptional" in Dan 5:12; 6:3). As a result, he remained faithful without any fault or blame, and the commissioners and satraps could find no ground of accusation against him (Dan 6:4). Only those who act swiftly to obey God's will can live consecrated lives in their words and deeds (Eph 1:4; 5:27; Phil 1:10; 2:15; Col 1:22; 1 Thes 3:13; 5:23; 1 Tim 6:14; 2 Pet 3:14; Jude 1:24).

Boaz's swift obedience of faithfully fulfilling the duty of a kinsman-redeemer foreshadowed Jesus Christ who promptly obeyed the Father's predestined will to save sinners every step of the way and bore the cross to fulfill the duty of the true kinsman-redeemer. As a result of Jesus' obedience, we have been freed from Satan's powers and are now heirs of God's Kingdom.

4. Boaz Became the Father of Obed by Ruth

It was not by coincidence that Ruth went and gleaned in the field of Boaz, who was a relative of her father-in-law Elimelech, that she met him there (Ruth 2:3), married him, had Obed, and was recorded in the genealogy of Jesus Christ (Ruth 4:13; Matt 1:5). This was all part of God's blessed providence in order to fulfill His good will in the divine administration of redemption.

We must not overlook Ruth's amazing faith displayed in this account. When Naomi urged Ruth to stay behind in Moab, Ruth replied and confessed her faith in Naomi's God, "Your people shall be my people, and your God, my God" (Ruth 1:16). While the Moabites could never enter the assembly of the Lord (Deut 23:3), Ruth's faith transcended such a law. Her faith did not end there; she even confessed that nothing other than death would separate her from Naomi, her mother-in-law (Ruth 1:17). She considered following her mother-in-law more important than her own life.

Compared to Moab, where Ruth's parents and relatives had been a comfort to her for her entire life, the land of Israel provided her no support. It was especially tough to adjust in Israel because of the severe hostility toward foreigners. Ruth's departure from Moab to Israel could be compared to Abraham's departure from his country, his relatives, and his father's house to follow the Word of God (Gen 12:1–4).

As soon as Boaz married Ruth, God gave them a son named *Obed*. Ruth had no son during the ten years of her marriage with Mahlon, Naomi's son (Ruth 1:4–5; 4:10). Yet, she gave birth to a son immediately after marrying Boaz because God enabled her to conceive (Ruth 4:13; Matt 1:5). This son Obed was the grandfather of David (Ruth 4:17, 22). Thus, Boaz and Ruth also received the glorious blessing of becoming the ancestors to the great king David and to Jesus Christ (Matt 1:5). The blessing which the people pronounced upon Boaz, "and may you achieve wealth in Ephrathah and become famous in Bethlehem" (Ruth 4:11), was fulfilled.

God prepared the way for Jesus Christ finally through Boaz and the Moabite woman Ruth even in the midst of the dark period of the judges, which was interspersed with unending transgressions (Matt 1:5).

Although Ruth was a Gentile and, moreover, a Moabite woman who could never enter the assembly of the Lord (Deut 23:3), she became a member of the tribe of Judah through Boaz. Ruth came to receive protection under God's wings, and Boaz took her in under his own wings (Ruth 2:12).

Jesus Christ, foreshadowed by Boaz, the prominent man of wealth, is the Savior not only for the Israelites, but also for the Gentiles, and He is the healer who knows and heals the pains of all outcasts (Ps 34:18; 51:17; 147:3; Isa 57:15; 61:1; 66:2). Jesus Christ is the one and only Savior who can deliver us from our sins, death, and all kinds of curses (John 14:6;

Acts 4:12; cf. 1 Cor 1:30; Matt 20:28; 1 Pet 1:18–19). Therefore, let us commit all that we are to Jesus Christ and trust Him (Ps 37:5; 55:22; Pro 16:3; 1 Pet 5:7).

Jesus makes us lie down in green pastures and leads us beside quiet waters (Ps 23:2), keeps us from hunger or thirst (Isa 49:10; Rev 7:16), and hides us under the shadow of His wings as our resting place to escape from the heat (Ps 17:8; 36:7; 57:1; 63:7; 91:1; 121:6; Isa 4:5–6). Moreover, He tenderly embraces us when we wander about without a place to go, wipes every tear from our eyes (Rev 7:17), and at last, leads us to His everlasting tabernacle (Rev 21:3; Ezek 37:27).

CHAPTER 19

The Twelfth Generation

Obed – עוֹבֵד / Ἰωβήδ

Serve, servant

Order
The twelfth person in the genealogy of Jesus Christ (Matt 1:5; 1 Chr 2:12)

Background
His father was Boaz and his son was Jesse (Ruth 4:21; Matt 1:5; Luke 3:32).

Key Point
Naomi nurtured her grandson Obed, whose name the neighbor women provided, and who later became the father of Jesse, King David's father (Ruth 4:17).

The name *Obed* is עוֹבֵד (*'ôbēd*) in Hebrew and Ἰωβήδ (*Iobēd*) in Greek, meaning "serving," "worshipper," and "servant." It is an active participle of עָבַד (*'ābad*), which means "to work," "to serve," "to labor," and "to serve another by labor."

1. Obed Was Named Because He Was Known to Be "A Son Born to Naomi"

Obed was born to Boaz when Boaz married Ruth the Moabitess and carried out his duty to redeem his kinsman. Ruth 4:13 states, "So Boaz took Ruth, and she became his wife, and he went in to her. And the LORD enabled her to conceive, and she gave birth to a son." Women in the neighborhood praised God for giving Boaz and Ruth a son and prayed, "May his name become famous in Israel" (Ruth 4:14). Later, Obed actually became famous for it was written, "He is the father of Jesse, the father of

David" (Ruth 4:17). His name became even more famous when his name was included in the genealogy of Jesus Christ.

However, the name *Obed* was the name given by the neighbor women. Ruth 4:17 states, "And the neighbor women gave him a name, saying, 'A son has been born to Naomi!' So they named him Obed. He is the father of Jesse, the father of David." Although Obed was Ruth's son, the statement, "a son has been born to Naomi," implies that Naomi was the cause of Obed's birth and that she would be his nurse in the future. We must not forget people like Naomi, who laid the foundation of our faith and life, as long as we are alive on this earth (Eph 2:20–22). The name נָעֳמִי (nā'ŏmî) means "my delight." Had it not been for the labor and dedication of people of faith like Naomi, we would not have had the blessings and delight that we enjoy today.

2. Obed Supported Naomi

Ruth 4:16 states, "Then Naomi took the child and laid him in her lap, and became his nurse." Here, the word *nurse* is אָמַן ('āman) in Hebrew, which is the root to the word *amen* that is used every time today's believers pray. The word אָמַן ('āman) means "to support," "to be faithful," and "to nourish." Hence, the word illustrates how Naomi devotedly brought up Obed as if he were her own son.

Obed was brought up with Naomi's love, and it is likely that he later honored and supported Naomi with great devotion. That is why the neighbor women spoke to Naomi regarding Obed, "May he also be to you a restorer of life and a sustainer of your old age" (Ruth 4:15). According to the New Living Translation, this same verse is translated as, "May he restore your youth and care for you in your old age." Because Naomi brought up her grandson Obed with great devotion, in her later years, she received great support from Obed. The word *sustainer* in Ruth 4:15 is כּוּל (kûl) in Hebrew, which means "to sustain" and "to provide." In the piel form (a form of emphasis), this verb conveys that Obed sustained Naomi by striving to provide all things and honoring her with all his strength.

Today, we must revere and serve God in thankfulness for His amazing grace that has nourished us (Deut 6:5; Matt 22:37–38; Eph 5:29). Moreover, we must also honor our parents, and love and cherish our neighbors as ourselves (Matt 19:19; 22:39). The whole Law and the Prophets depend on these two commandments (Matt 22:40). It is wrong to profess to believe in God and yet not look after one's neighbors. The Bible places special emphasis on serving and looking after the poor and the sick (Pro 14:21; 21:13; 28:27; Ps 41:1) with the promise that God will repay us for such good deeds since it is as if we are lending to the Lord (Pro 19:17; cf. Pro 11:24–25; Matt 25:40, 45). He who serves Christ with all his heart, and also serves his neighbors with all his might is, like Obed, acceptable to God and approved by men (Rom 14:18; Col 3:23).

CHAPTER 20

The Thirteenth Generation

Jesse – יִשַׁי / Ἰεσσαί

God exists, God lives

Order
The thirteenth person in the genealogy of Jesus Christ (Matt 1:5; 1 Chr 2:12)

Background
His father was Obed and his son was David (Ruth 4:22; Matt 1:5; Luke 3:32).

Key Point
Jesse had eight sons and two daughters, and David was the youngest son among them (1 Sam 16:10–12; 17:12; 1 Chr 2:13–16).[37]

The name *Jesse* is יִשַׁי (yišāy) in Hebrew and Ἰεσσαί (Iesssai) in Greek. יִשַׁי (yišāy) is in the identical form as יֵשׁ (yēš) and its root word means "existence" and "there is." Jesse is the grandson of Boaz and Ruth, the son of Obed, and the father of David (Ruth 4:21–22).

Because Jesse lived in Bethlehem, he was also called "Jesse the Bethlehemite" (1 Sam 16:1, 18; 17:12, 58).

1. David, Jesse's Youngest Son, Was Selected to Become King

God said that he would forsake Saul due to his sin and seek out for Himself a man after His own heart to hand over the throne to him (1 Sam 13:14; 16:1). The first reason for forsaking Saul was that he offered burnt offerings although he was not a priest (1 Sam 13:9–14). The second reason was that he disobeyed God's command to destroy the Amalekites completely (1 Sam 15:8–9, 22–23).

Now, God spoke to the prophet Samuel, "I will send you to Jesse the Bethlehemite, for I have selected a king for Myself among his sons" (1 Sam 16:1), and then He sent him to Jesse.

When Jesse and his seven sons came out to meet him, the prophet Samuel saw Eliab and marveled at his appearance and height of his stature. Certain that he would be the king, Samuel said, "Surely the LORD's anointed is before Him" (1 Sam 16:7). At that time, God said, "I have rejected him," because man looks at the outward appearance, but the LORD looks at the heart (1 Sam 16:7). Thus, Samuel realized that his standard of judgment was incorrect, and when Jesse had his next six sons pass before him, he probably no longer looked at their outward appearance, but rather searched the depth of their hearts with a prayerful spirit. As a result, Samuel said, "Neither has the LORD chosen this one (1 Sam 16:8–10)." How disappointed Jesse must have felt! But, even after Jesse showed all of his seven sons, he did not even think of showing David.[38] In response to Samuel's question, "Are these all the children?" Jesse answered, "There remains yet the youngest, and behold, he is tending the sheep (1 Sam 16:11)." It was as if he were saying, "There remains yet the youngest, but since he is a mere child who tends the sheep, would the LORD select him?" Even Jesse, the father, did not think David could possibly become king (Isa 55:8; 1 Cor 1:25). Truly, David became king entirely by the sovereign election of God, who sees the heart.

The prophet Samuel anointed David and "the Spirit of the LORD came mightily upon him from that day forward" (1 Sam 16:13).

2. Jesse Was the Closest Observer of All the Events Leading up to David's Enthronement

Starting from when his youngest son David was selected by God and anointed as king by the prophet Samuel (1 Sam 16:3–13), until his accession to the throne, Jesse was the closest witness to the entire course of God's providence.

First, Jesse received the notice from King Saul's messenger that his son David would become Saul's servant (1 Sam 16:19). This had come about because an evil spirit terrorized Saul, and his servants were seeking a man who was a skilled harpist. Then, one of the young men who heard of this recommended David, the son of Jesse (1 Sam 16:17–18). So, Jesse took a donkey loaded with bread, a jug of wine and a young goat, and sent them to Saul via David his son (1 Sam 16:20).

After seeing David and having great confidence in him, Saul made him his armor bearer and sent a message to Jesse, saying, "Let David now stand before me for he has found favor in my sight" (1 Sam 16:22). At that time, David commuted from home, where he tended his father's sheep, to the palace, where he attended to Saul (1 Sam 17:15).

Second, Jesse sent David on an errand to look into the welfare of his brothers who were in battle with the Philistines (1 Sam 17:17–18). At the time, Jesse did not fight in the battle because he was already well advanced in years, but his grown sons—Eliab, Abinadab, and Shammah (1 Sam 17:12–13)—were out in the battlefield. When David arrived at the valley of Elah, he heard Goliath the giant Philistine taunting the army of the living God and bravely approached him in the name of the God of the armies of Israel. The stone that David slung struck the forehead of the fully armed giant, Goliath, and he fell at once. Then, David cut off his head with Goliath's sword (1 Sam 17:47–51). Afterwards, King Saul inquired, "Whose son are you, young man?" and David answered, "I am the son of your servant Jesse the Bethlehemite" (1 Sam 17:58). On that day, Saul took him and did not let him return to his father's house (1 Sam 18:2).

Third, Jesse stayed with David during the years of his life of refuge. When David escaped to the cave of Adullam at the beginning of his flight of refuge, Jesse went down there to him (1 Sam 22:1).

After that, David briefly left his father and mother in the care of the king of Moab. 1 Samuel 22:4 states, "Then he left them [the parents] with the king of Moab; and they stayed with him all the time that David was in the stronghold." According to the original language, this means that David's parents stayed with the king of Moab only until David left the stronghold of Moab. This indicates that the parents departed together with David later when he was leaving the stronghold of Moab. Therefore, it becomes apparent that Jesse stayed with David throughout the years of David's refuge.

Jesse did not even consider David when the prophet Samuel came to select one among his sons to become king. Jesse must have been startled and probably could not believe what was happening when he watched the prophet Samuel anointing David, the son whom he thought was the least qualified to be king.

Jesse witnessed the anointing of his youngest son, whom he considered most insignificant. Shortly after, David received an unforeseen formal invitation from King Saul, by a young man's recommendation, to enter the king's palace. He also saw that David, when Jesse sent him to his brothers in the battlefield, struck down the Philistine giant, Goliath, and was praised by the people more highly than Saul their king. From then on, David acted more wisely than Saul's other servants especially during the frequent battles against the Philistines, and Jesse noticed that David's fame elevated rapidly, causing his name to be highly esteemed among the people and the king's servants (1 Sam 18:5, 16, 30).

Through these totally unexpected events, Jesse must have been astounded to witness God's Word that was spoken through the prophet Samuel being fulfilled completely. Further, as Jesse accompanied David during his life of refuge, he witnessed that God was with David, protecting his life in every perilous moment as King Saul sent out his army to kill David. Finally, after about ten years of a weary and tearful life of refuge, Jesse saw David enthroned as the king of the unified kingdom of Israel.

Having witnessed the course of David's life, Jesse probably realized that God is indeed the sovereign ruler whose providence is over the entire history of mankind and that every Word He speaks is fulfilled. Jesse learned that God really "lives"—like the meaning of His name—and that His Word is always living and active, being fulfilled as He has spoken even when men neglect, misunderstand, and doubt Him.

3. Jesse Was Referred to as an Ancestor of the Messiah

Isaiah 11:1 states, "Then a shoot will spring from the stem of Jesse, and a branch from his roots will bear fruit." This verse clarifies and explains the Messianic prophecies of Isaiah 7:14 and 9:6 more vividly.

First, the Messiah comes as "a shoot" and "a branch." A *shoot* in Isaiah 11:1 is חֹטֶר (*hōṭēr*) in Hebrew, meaning "branch" or "twig." A *branch* is נֵצֶר (*nēṣer*) in Hebrew, meaning "shoot" or "sprout." These two expressions symbolize the future coming of the Messiah who would seem very insignificant like a little shoot or branch. Indeed Jesus was born in a manger, in quite a pitiful state, as the son of a carpenter (Isa 53:2; Jer 23:5).

Second, the Messiah would come from "the stem of Jesse." Coming from the stem of Jesse as mentioned in Isaiah 11:1 signifies that Jesus would come as a descendant of Jesse. It was prophesied that Jesus would come as a descendant of Jesse rather than as a descendant of David in order to foretell the humble birth of Jesus Christ. This is because Jesse was merely a lowly shepherd who lived in a small town of Bethlehem. In fact, Jesus came as a son of a poor carpenter from Nazareth (Matt 13:55) and worked as a carpenter, a job which people considered lowly during that time (Mark 6:3).

The word *stem* is גֶּזַע (*gezā'*) in Hebrew, meaning "stump," "stem," and "cut down." It also means "a shoot from a stump." Here, the imagery of a shoot sprouting out from a stump of a felled tree that was left behind to wither depicts the coming of Jesus into the extremely impoverished state of the politics, economy, society, culture and religion of the time. Immediately before the incarnation of Jesus, the Israelite society under King Herod's tyranny was just like a tree that had been cut down at its base. Into such a gloomy world of total darkness where all hopes had vanished away, Jesus came as the light of life, the light of salvation (Luke 1:78–79; John 1:4–5; 8:12; 9:5).

Third, the Messiah comes from the "root of Jesse." Isaiah 11:1 states, "a branch from his roots will bear fruit." Here, the word *root* is שֹׁרֶשׁ (*šōreš*) in Hebrew, which means "root" or "origin." It is prophesied in Isaiah 11:10, "Then it will come about in that day that the nations will resort to the root of Jesse, who will stand as a signal for the peoples; and His resting place will be glorious." This verse implies that the nations would repent and return at the coming of the Messiah, so that His kingdom would be glorified. The Apostle Paul explained that this prophecy had been fulfilled in Jesus, proclaiming that Jesus Christ is the root of Jesse, the one and only hope for the nations (Rom 15:12).

Fourth, the Messiah's work of salvation would at last bear fruit. Isaiah 11:1 states, "Then a shoot will spring from the stem of Jesse, and a branch from his roots will bear fruit." Here, the phrase, *will bear fruit* is expressed in one word, פָּרָה (*pārâ*), which means "fruitful" or "abundant fruition"; since it is in the imperfect form, it indicates a continual abundance into the future. This is just like a small mustard seed that continues to grow and becomes a tree, so that the birds of the air come and nest in its branches (Matt 13:31–32).

Although Jesus came in a humble and fragile form like a tender shoot, His gospel will be witnessed to the ends of the earth, and eventually numerous souls will enter God's kingdom and live forever (Ezek 17:22–23).

Likewise, Jesse was greatly honored and blessed to have his name used to prophesy the coming of Jesus Christ. Jesse can attest to the fact that an insignificant person like himself can become the father of the highest ruler of a nation and experience the sovereign providence of the living God. Jesse means "He lives." We may find ourselves in situations of despair where everything has been cut off and fallen with only a stump remaining. Despite all this, when we possess the faith as small as a mustard seed and absolutely trust in the living God, we will always be able to rise again and ultimately receive the blessing of bearing great fruit (Matt 17:20).

CHAPTER 21

The Fourteenth Generation

David – דָּוִד / Δαυίδ

Beloved, friend

Order

The fourteenth person in the genealogy of Jesus Christ (Matt 1:5–6; 1 Chr 2:13–15)

Background

His father was Jesse and his son was Solomon (Matt 1:5–6; Luke 3:32; Ruth 4:17). He had seven older brothers and two older sisters (1 Chr 2:13–16).

Key Point

David ruled for 40 years (1010 BC – 970 BC); during the first seven and half years of his reign in Hebron, he had six sons (2 Sam 3:2–5; 1 Chr 3:1–9), and during the approximately 33 years of his reign in Jerusalem, he had 13 sons (2 Sam 5:13–16; 1 Chr 14:3–7). Besides these, he also had a son named Jerimoth (2 Chr 11:18).[39]

David is דָּוִד (*dāwid*) in Hebrew, and Δαυίδ (*Dauid*) in Greek, meaning "beloved," "friend," or "lover." This word shares the same root consonants as דּוֹד (*dôd*), which means "to boil" or "to love." As his name indicates, David was very much loved by God (Acts 13:22).

Behind David's faith was his godly mother. David described his mother as "Your handmaid" (Ps 86:16). Psalm 116:16 states, "O LORD, surely I am Your servant, I am Your servant, the son of Your handmaid, You have loosed my bonds." The word *handmaid* in this verse refers to his mother. In Hebrew, this word is אֲמָתֶךָ (*'ămatekā*), with a pronoun suffix added to אָמָה (*'āmâ*), which means "handmaid," "maidservant," and "female slave." This is an expression that was commonly used when a maidservant refers to herself (Ruth 3:9), and hence depicts how David's mother "always lowered herself before God and humbly served Him."

David describes his own mother as "Your handmaid" and himself as "Your servant" or "the son of Your handmaid." According to this, it is evident that it was from his mother that he inherited his faith to serve God in the manner of a servant. Although the name of David's mother is not mentioned in the Bible, it seems that she must have been a godly woman of a great faith who had much influence on David.

Having been raised under his mother's influence of faith, David became the person who appears most frequently in the genealogy of Jesus Christ (Matt 1:1, 6, 17). The first 14 generations of Jesus Christ's genealogy in Matthew 1 begin with Abraham and end with David. This book purposefully includes the time of David's reign in Hebron as part of the first 14 generations of the genealogy. The first period of 14 generations ends with "and to Jesse was born David the king," emphasizing that David was already a king (Matt 1:6).

1. David's Life of Refuge Calls to Mind the Suffering of Jesus Christ

Jesse's eighth son David was a shepherd who tended the flocks. Later, he was anointed as a king by the prophet Samuel (1 Sam 16:13). Then, he had to live a life of refuge relentlessly pursued by Saul.

The shame and suffering David faced typify the harsh suffering and humiliation that Jesus Christ would face for our sins.

David did not have a place to sleep as he was pursued by Saul. Frequently, David had to stay in either caves or the wilderness. This portrays how Jesus was put in a manger after He was born because there was no room in the inn (Luke 2:7), and how He was shunned in Nazareth, His hometown where He grew up (Luke 4:16–30; Matt 13:53–58; Mark 6:1–6), for He said, "The foxes have holes, and the birds of the air have nests, but the Son of Man has nowhere to lay His head" (Matt 8:20; Luke 9:58).

Faced with life-threatening situations, David confessed "My God, My God, why have You forsaken me? Far from my deliverance are the words of my groaning?" (Ps 22:1). This reminds us of Jesus' cry on the cross, "*Eli, Eli, lama sabachthani?* (My God, My God, why have You forsaken Me?)" (Matt 27:46; Mark 15:34).

David described his utterly exhausted state, which resulted from his severe suffering, as "I am poured out like water." He also described the excruciating pain in his body as "all my bones are out of joint" (Ps 22:14).

The expression, "out of joint," is פָּרַד (*pārad*) in Hebrew, meaning "to separate," "to divide," "to shatter," and "to break." Jesus, too, poured out His blood and water on the cross (John 19:34), and suffered as He was scourged all over the body until His bones fell out of joint (Matt 27:26; Mark 15:15).

David expressed his collapsing heart as, "My heart is like wax; it is melted within me" (Ps 22:14). The word wax is דּוֹנַג (*dônag*) and it refers to beeswax, which melts easily at a temperature of 122° Fahrenheit (50° Celsius). Therefore, David is describing the exceedingly frail state of his heart by the imagery of beeswax melting before fire in Psalm 22:14. Before the cross, Jesus expressed the intense suffering in His heart when He said, "My soul is deeply grieved, to the point of death" (Matt 26:38).

During his long years of refuge, David confessed "My tongue cleaves to my jaws" (Ps 22:15), which depicts suffering as if his body and soul were being consumed in fire. This reminds us of how Jesus was severely parched on the cross and cried out, "I am thirsty" (John 19:28).

David expressed his extreme mortification, "They divide my garments among them, and for my clothing they cast lots" (Ps 22:18). And these very words were fulfilled precisely when the Roman soldiers crucified Jesus, took His outer garments and made four parts, and cast lots for the tunic also (John 19:23–24).

Indeed, the suffering of David seems to depict the passion of Jesus Christ on the cross. Just as David made it through the time of refuge and finally became a king in Hebron, so, too, was Jesus resurrected from death and exalted onto the right hand of God's throne with the name which is above every name (Mark 16:19; Acts 2:31–33; Phil 2:9).

2. David Became the Passageway of the Messianic Covenant

After years of escaping from King Saul, David was at last anointed and became the king of Judah in Hebron (2 Sam 2:4).

But, among the kings that appear in the genealogy of Jesus Christ in the gospel of Matthew, David is the only one with the title "king." Matthew 1:6 states, "And to Jesse was born David the king." The title given to David, "the king," is the fulfillment of the prophecy that a king would come from the tribe of Judah and that it would not cease until the coming of Shiloh (Gen 49:10).

The "scepter" mentioned in Genesis 49:10 refers to a short staff that symbolizes royal power and "the scepter shall not depart from Judah" prophesies that kings will come through the lineage of the tribe of Judah. Also, Shiloh (שִׁילֹה) means "the one who gives rest" or "the one who brings peace," and thus refers to the Messiah. The verse, "until Shiloh comes," is a prophecy that the Messiah would ultimately come through the tribe of Judah. As a king from the tribe of Judah, David fulfilled the prophecy, "the scepter shall not depart from Judah," and thus confirmed the prophecy that the Messiah (Shiloh) would come as his descendant (2 Sam 7:12–13). In the end, David was a very crucial "king" with respect to the redemptive purpose for he fulfilled and confirmed this Messianic prophecy.

Through the first half of David's life prior to his reign in Hebron, we learned that God surely protects His beloved ones and exalts them to His place of glory even from under the shadow of despair and suffering, and from the times of extreme hardship and danger. Though hardships may come our way, let us firmly hold onto faith and the assured hope by fixing our eyes on the glory that is to be revealed. God will certainly strengthen us through His love so that we may overcome the present hardships, and He will finally allow us to become the central partakers of the great glory in the end as He has promised (Rom 8:18; 2 Cor 4:17–18; 1 Pet 1:6–7).

עמלק

מדבר צין הוא קדש

ים המלח

עתר
מקדה
עיר כרמל

שבט

קדש ברנע

מדבר פארן

מדבר סיני

מדבר שור

ארץ פלשתם

שמעון
שבט
באר שבע
יהודה
גת בית מועכה
אשקלון

ארץ גשן
פתם
שרה
אלכסנדרי
צען

לוח המסעות במדבר
אשר על פי ה׳ יסעו ועל פי ה׳ יחנו

א׳ רעמסס	טו׳ רתמה	וט׳ הרהגדגד
ב׳ סכת	טז׳ רמן פרץ	ל׳ יטבתה
ג׳ אתם	יז׳ לבנה	לא׳ עברונה
ד׳ פיהחירת	יח׳ רסה	לב׳ עציןגבר
ה׳ מרה	יט׳ קהלתה	לג׳ מדברצין
ו׳ אילם	כ׳ הרספר	לד׳ ההר ההר
ז׳ ים סוף	כא׳ חרדה	לה׳ צלמנה
ח׳ מדבר סין	כב׳ מקהלת	לו׳ פונן
ט׳ דפקה	כג׳ תחת	לז׳ אבת
יו׳ אלוש	כד׳ תרח	לח׳ דיבן גר
יא׳ רפידים	כה׳ מתקה	לט׳ עלמן דבל
יב׳ מדברסיני	כו׳ חשמנה	מ׳ הרי ענרים
יג׳ קברתהתאוה	כז׳ מסרות	מא׳ ערבתמואב
יד׳ חצרות	כח׳ בני יעקן	

PART FOUR

The History of the Judges

1 Othniel ➜ 2 Ehud ➜ 3 Shamgar ➜ 4 Deborah
➜ 5 Gideon ➜ 6 Tola ➜ 7 Jair ➜ 8 Jephthah
➜ 9 Ibzan ➜ 10 Elon ➜ 11 Abdon ➜ 12 Samson

Salmon, the tenth person in the first 14 generations in the genealogy of Jesus, married the harlot Rahab (Matt 1:5). Salmon was one of the two men whom Joshua had sent to spy out the land of Canaan and the city of Jericho (Josh 2:1). This proves that he lived during the time of the conquest of Canaan. In addition, Jesse, the thirteenth person in the genealogy, lived during the time of the prophet Samuel (1 Sam 16:1). Thus, we can see that among the first 14 generations in the genealogy of Jesus, the generations from Salmon (the tenth) to Jesse (the thirteenth), overlap with the time of the judges. This chapter focuses on the historical background of the first 14 generations in the genealogy of Jesus by examining the works of the judges who ruled Israel after the conquest of Canaan prior to the reign of the kings.

The 12 tribes of Israel who settled in Canaan diligently worshiped God while Joshua and the elders were alive for they witnessed God's great works during the 40 years in the wilderness and the conquest of Canaan. However, after the death of Joshua and the elders, another generation grew up who knew neither the Lord nor what He had done for Israel (Judg 2:10). Here, the word *to know* is יָדַע (*yāda*') in Hebrew and is used to describe the intimate relations between a husband and wife. Thus, it does not refer to plain knowledge but to knowledge obtained through experience.

This "another generation" may have vaguely heard about God's works, but they had no personal experience in their lives that compelled their hearts to believe. Judges 3:7 states, "And the sons of Israel did what was evil in the sight of the LORD, and forgot the LORD their God, and served the Baals and the Asheroth." Here, the word *forgot* is שָׁכַח (*šākaḥ*) in Hebrew and is the opposite of the word יָדַע (*yāda*') (Hos 2:13; 4:6; 13:4-6). This word שָׁכַח (*šākaḥ*) does not only signify merely forgetting something in one's mind, but the act of forgetting accompanied by the act of challenging God. This "another generation" who did not know God and forgot about God did what was evil in the sight of God and served other gods, especially the Baals and the Asheroth (Judg 2:7-13).

The 340-year period of the judges in Israel was truly a time of spiritual darkness during which the people did not know the Lord. Judges 21:25 summarizes this period well: "In those days there was no king in Israel; everyone did what was right in his own eyes" (Judg 17:6; 18:1; 19:1; Rom 1:28). This does not merely indicate a lack of a monarchical system to govern disarranged Israel. It means that the Israelites did not acknowledge God as their true king, and they rejected His rule. The Israelites, by rejecting God's rule, allowed corruption and confusion to seep in. As a result, they had to live with bitter suffering in the hands of gentile oppressors.

Even in the midst of people's continued disbelief and chaos, God continued to guide the nation of Israel, a mere union of 12 tribes, as His own chosen people. He nurtured them into a powerful nation so that He might display His power and mighty works among the nations through them. This was part of God's great plan to preserve the lineage of faith through which He would send the Messiah to this earth.

CHAPTER 22

Understanding the Judges

1. Definition of the Judges

Judges were appointed when Israel was still a union of 12 tribes before the establishment of a strong centralized governing body. The judges were rulers set in place when Israel cried out to God after enduring hardship from both inside and outside the nation (Judg 2:16; 3:9). During ordinary times, they judged and ruled according to the division of the tribes or according to regions. During times of war, they acted as leaders of the army.

The Hebrew word for *judges* is שֹׁפְטִים (*šōpěṭîm*) and means "those who mediate," "those who govern," and "those who are in charge of judging." This term comes from the Hebrew word שָׁפַט (*šāpaṭ*), meaning "to judge," "to mediate" and "to govern."

Judges 8:23 states, "But Gideon said to them, 'I will not rule over you, nor shall my son rule over you; the LORD shall rule over you.'" Thus, God is the one and only true ruler, and the judges were ruling agents on God's behalf. The spirit of God came down upon the judges when they were established. *Spirit* is רוּחַ (*rûaḥ*) in Hebrew and refers to the Holy Spirit.

Judges 3:10 states that the spirit of the Lord came down upon Othniel. Judges 6:34 states that the spirit of the Lord came upon Gideon. Judges 11:29 states that the spirit of the Lord came upon Jephthah. Judges 13:25 states that the spirit of the Lord began to stir Samson. In this manner, the beginning of the judges' work had divine origins. Thus, the Bible refers to the judges as "deliverers" on God's behalf (Judg 3:9, 15).

There are 12 judges in the Bible.

Othniel → Ehud → Shamgar → Deborah → Gideon → Tola → Jair →
Jephthah → Ibzan → Elon → Abdon → Samson

Of those 12, Othniel, Ehud, Deborah, Gideon, Jephthah, and Samson are classified as major judges; extensive and detailed narratives are given about their deeds. Shamgar, Tola, Jair, Ibzan, Elon and Abdon are classified as minor judges.

The short narratives of the minor judges specify who succeeded whom, with phrases such as "after him, came…" (Judg 3:31; 10:1, 3; 12:8, 11, 13). This shows that there was no break in God's plan for salvation throughout history. God showed continuous love and concern for His people by sending judges not only during times of national crisis, but even during peaceful times when there were no attacks from neighboring nations.

What was striking is that these judges were mostly ordinary people, considered flawed or less than ideal for the position. For example, Ehud was left-handed and his right hand was disabled (Judg 3:15), Shamgar was a farmer or a shepherd (Judg 3:31), and Deborah was a woman (Judg 4:4). Gideon was weak and the youngest male in his family (Judg 6:15), Jephthah was the son of a harlot who had been driven out by his father's sons to live among worthless fellows (Judg 11:1–3), and Samson was a morally corrupt man (Judg 14:1–3; 16:1). However, when God was with them and they were filled with the Holy Spirit, they became mightier than anyone else. They were the saviors of their times who rescued the people from the hands of their enemies.

God chose people with imperfections and weaknesses as judges to save Israel in order to show them that the true savior and ruler of Israel is not man, but God Himself. There is no savior other than God (Isa 43:11; 45:21). God's boundless compassion, mercy and love were more clearly demonstrated in the midst of man's unbelief and rebellion.

2. Characteristics of the Period of the Judges

The period of the judges was the darkest period in the history of Israel and was characterized by spiritual and moral corruption.

(1) The period of the judges was a period during which the people did evil in the sight of the Lord.

Judges 2:11 Then the sons of Israel did evil in the sight of the LORD, and served the Baals,

This evil manifested itself in various ways.

First, the Canaanites were not totally destroyed (Judg 1:19–36). God commanded Israel to utterly destroy the Canaanites. He warned Israel that if they did not obey, the Canaanites would teach Israel to do the detestable things that the Canaanites have done for their gods (Deut 20:16–18). God also warned them that if they do not drive them out, the Canaanites would become a snare and a trap for them and the Israelites would ultimately be driven out (Josh 23:13; Judg 2:3).

However, the Israelites disobeyed and did not totally drive out the Canaanites. Judges 1 repeatedly testifies to how the Israelites were not able to drive out the Canaanites: "But they could not drive out the inhabitants of the valley…" (Judg 1:19), "But the sons of Benjamin did not drive out the Jebusites…" (Judg 1:21), "So the Canaanites persisted in living in that land…" (Judg 1:27), "But they did not drive them out completely…" (Judg 1:28), "Ephraim did not drive out the Canaanites who were living…" (Judg 1:29), "So the Canaanites lived among them…" (Judg 1:30), "Nor did Asher drive out those living in…" (Judg 1:31), and "Neither did Naphtali drive out those living in Beth-shemesh…" (Judg 1:33).

Second, the Israelites worshipped idols. The Israelites ended up serving the Canaanite idols because they did not completely drive out the Canaanites. The sons of Israel served the Baals (Judg 2:11), Ashtaroth (Judg 2:13), and other various gods (Judg 2:17, 19; 3:6). Since the Israelites had fallen into idolatry, which God detests the most, the entire nation was doomed to suffer a period of darkness (Exod 20:3–5; Deut 5:7–9; 7:4).

Third, the Israelites intermarried with Gentiles. God warned the Israelites not to intermarry with Gentiles (Deut 7:3–4), but they ignored His Word and took the daughters of the Canaanites as their wives and gave their daughters to the sons of the Canaanites (Judg 3:6). This practice held true not only among the people but also among the judges who were established as leaders (Judg 12:9; 14:1; 16:1).

Fourth, the Israelites committed sins of immorality. According to the Webster's Revised Unabridged Dictionary, the word *immoral* means, "conflicting with generally or traditionally held moral principles." Sins of immorality were rampant during the period of the judges. The Levites were religious leaders, but they still took concubines for themselves (Lev 21:13–15; Judg 19:1). At the time, the Levites lived in 48 cities throughout the nation. As leaders, they led the way toward corruption instead of taking on the responsibility of being the salt and the light for the people.

The wicked men of Gibeah collectively violated and abused a Levite's concubine all night until morning. They let her go at the approach of dawn, but she died as a result (Judg 19:25–26). Then, the master of the concubine took a knife and cut the concubine into 12 pieces, limb by limb, and sent them throughout the territory of Israel (Judg 19:29).

The period of the judges was truly a time of wickedness, more so than the time of Sodom and Gomorrah. Sin was prevalent, and adultery and murder were casually committed. Extremely evil crimes that were simply unthinkable by God's own covenanted people were rampant (Judg 19:30). The prophet Hosea said of the corruption of his time, "They have gone deep in depravity as in the days of Gibeah" (Hos 9:9; 10:9).

(2) The period of the judges was a period of repeated evil.
The period of the judges was a period of repeated cycles of evil. There were repeated cycles of sin, punishment, repentance, salvation, forgetfulness, and sin again. The people committed the sin of disobeying God's Word and were punished by God. Through suffering punishment, they would at last repent and receive God's salvation, but with the passage of time, they would forget what had happened and would sin again. This wretched cycle of evil would repeat itself again and again, and it is repeated in the history of mankind. At the same time, it is part of our personal history today, the history of weak human beings.

The Israelites' *sin* was forgetting God and doing what was evil in God's sight by serving the Baals and the Asheroth (Judg 3:7).

God allowed the gentile nations to oppress the Israelites as their *punishment*. Consequently, Israel had to serve these nations and endure suffering in their hands because the Israelites had kindled God's anger against them (Judg 3:8).

The Israelites *repented* in their suffering and sought God and called out to Him (Judg 3:9).

God brought *salvation* upon the repentant people by sending judges to save them from the oppression of the Gentiles.

In times of peace, the Israelites *forgot* their God again (Judg 3:11).

Then, they *sinned again* by worshipping idols and doing what was evil in the sight of God (Judg 3:12).

As the cycle of evil repeated itself, corruption manifested itself in varied and intensified forms, and the people fell deeper and deeper into the pit. This cycle of evil contributed to mankind's corruption, total depravity and total spiritual inability. This total depravity and spiritual inability spread through to the basic characteristics and functions of mankind. It was inherited continuously throughout all mankind since the fall of Adam. Romans 5:12 states, "Therefore, just as through one man sin entered into the world, and death through sin, and so death spread to all men, because all sinned" (Rom 5:19).

Despite the deepening corruption and the perversion of faith, God sent judges to save the people as a foreshadowing of how He would send Jesus Christ to save people from Satan's oppression despite the ever continuing sinfulness of mankind. Just as the judges were saviors during their period (Judg 3:9, 15), Jesus Christ is the one and only eternal Savior of this corrupt world (Isa 43:11; Hos 13:4). There is no other path to salvation besides Jesus Christ (John 14:6; Acts 4:12).

CHAPTER 23

Chronology of the Period of the Judges

After the Israelites entered Canaan and were victorious in their conquest of the land, they buried Joseph's bones—which they had brought out with them from Egypt (Exod 13:19)—in Shechem in 1390 BC (Josh 24:32). Solomon ascended to the throne in 970 BC (1 Kgs 6:1). Since David ruled for about 40 years, David must have acceded the throne in 1010 BC (1 Kgs 2:11). Saul also reigned for 40 years, which means that he ascended the throne in 1050 BC (Acts 13:21).

A liberal calculation of the period of the judges would include the time of Eli and Samuel until the reign of Saul from 1390 BC to 1050 BC.[40] However, a conservative calculation of the period of the judges would include the end of the period as the end of the eight-year reign of Abdon, the last judge (Judg 12:13-15).

There are two reasons why some scholars calculate the period of the judges starting from the time of Eli and Samuel until the reign of Saul.

First, an official conclusion regarding Eli in 1 Samuel 4:18 states, "Thus he judged Israel forty years." This verse refers to Eli as judge.

Second, the work of salvation Samuel performed during his early years (1 Sam 1–7) was similar to the work of the judges, and Samuel himself also spoke of how he worked with the other judges as a savior (1 Sam 12:11).[41]

Even by a liberal estimate, the judges' period was no longer than 340 years (1390-1050 BC). Only when the judges' regnal years are calculated in consecutive order, the years total 410. Thus, this discrepancy of the total number of years of the judges' period proves that there was overlap between different judges' reigns.

Accordingly, the entire period of the judges cannot be calculated simply by adding up the regnal years of all the judges. The overlapping years in their times need to be taken into consideration. Not all judges ruled over the entire nation. At times, some reigned in different localized areas in the same time period. Hence, their times of reign overlapped with each other.

1. The Reigning Periods of Ehud and Shamgar Appear to Overlap[42]

If the reigns of Ehud and Shamgar did not overlap but were consecutive reigns, then it would be logical for the Bible to record that Shamgar reigned after Ehud and that Jabin, king of Canaan, oppressed Israel after the reign of Shamgar. However, Judges 3:31–4:3 does record Shamgar's works after Ehud, but there is no record of the years of his reign. It only records that Jabin's oppression took place after Ehud's reign. This shows that Shamgar's reign fell within the time of Ehud's reign and that Jabin's oppression began after Ehud's reign.

Chart: The Periods of Oppression and Peace During the Time of the Judges

Oppressors and Judges	Periods of Oppression / Peace	Verse Reference
Oppression by Cushan-rishathaim, king of Mesopotamia	8 years	Judg 3:8
Judge Othniel	40 years	Judg 3:11
Oppression by Eglon, the king of Moab	18 years	Judg 3:14
Judge Ehud	80 years	Judg 3:30
Judge Shamgar	?	Judg 3:31
Oppression by Jabin, king of Canaan	20 years	Judg 4:3
Judge Deborah	40 years	Judg 5:31
Oppression by Midian	7 years	Judg 6:1
Judge Gideon	40 years	Judg 8:28
Oppression by Abimelech	3 years	Judg 9:22
Judge Tola	23 years	Judg 10:2
Judge Jair	22 years	Judg 10:3
Oppression by Ammon	18 years	Judg 10:8
Judge Jephthah	6 years	Judg 12:7
Judge Ibzan	7 years	Judg 12:9
Judge Elon	10 years	Judg 12:11
Judge Abdon	8 years	Judg 12:14
Oppression by the Philistines	40 years	Judg 13:1
Judge Samson	20 years	Judg 15:20
Total Years without considering the overlapping periods	**410 years**	

2. The Reigning Periods of Tola and Jair Appear to Overlap[43]

> **Judges 10:1-3** (NKJ) After Abimelech there arose to save Israel Tola the son of Puah, the son of Dodo, a man of Issachar; and he dwelt in Shamir in the mountains of Ephraim. He judged Israel twenty-three years; and he died and was buried in Shamir. After him arose Jair, a Gileadite; and he judged Israel twenty-two years.

Looking at these verses, it is logical to conclude that the reigns of Tola and Jair overlap because there was no instance of foreign oppression, and the two judges ruled in totally different regions. Tola reigned mainly in Shamir (Judg 10:1), in the hill country of Ephraim, which was near Shechem, midway between the Jordan River and the Mediterranean Sea. However, Jair reigned mainly in Gilead (Judg 10:3), east of the Jordan River. Thus, there is a high probability that these two men judged at the same time but in separate regions, one to the west and one to the east of the Jordan River.

3. The Periods of Oppression by the Ammonites and the Philistines Appear to Overlap (Judg 10:7-8; 13:1)[44]

> **Judges 10:7–8** And the anger of the LORD burned against Israel, and He sold them into the hands of the Philistines, and into the hands of the sons of Ammon. And they afflicted and crushed the sons of Israel that year; for eighteen years they afflicted all the sons of Israel who were beyond the Jordan in Gilead in the land of the Amorites.

It states, "And the anger of the LORD burned against Israel, and He sold them into the hands of the Philistines, and into the hands of the sons of Ammon," so the oppression by the Philistines and affliction at the hands of the Ammonites must have begun at the same time. Judges 13:1 states, "Now the sons of Israel again did evil in the sight of the LORD, so that the LORD gave them into the hands of the Philistines forty years." Thus, the 18-year oppression by the Ammonites in the land east of the Jordan River must have begun at the same time as the 40-year oppression by the Philistines in the land west of the Jordan River. The judge Samson reigned during the first 20 years of the 40-year oppression by the Philistines (Judg 15:20).

Considering the overlapping reigns, the actual period of the judges was from 1390 BC until 1050 BC, no more than 340 years.[45]

CHAPTER 24

The Works of the Judges

> ## 1. Othniel – עָתְנִיאֵל / Γοθονιηλ
> God is strength, God moves forward

Background
He was the son of Kenaz from the tribe of Judah and the nephew of Caleb (Josh 15:17; Judg 1:13; 3:9).

Period of Activity
God punished Israel by the hands of Cushan-rishathaim, king of Mesopotamia, for eight years (Judg 3:8). Then, He established Othniel as judge, and gave peace for 40 years (Judg 3:11).

The name עָתְנִיאֵל (*ŏtnî'ēl*) is a compound word made up of עָתַק (*'ātaq*), meaning "to move" and "to advance forward," and אֵל (*'ēl*), meaning "God." Hence, the name means "God is strength" and "God moves forward." Othniel was the first judge and the one who saved Israel from the oppression of Cushan-rishathaim.

According to Joshua 15:17, Othniel was a son of Caleb's brother Kenaz and he became Caleb's son-in-law.

1. Othniel Was a Courageous Man

Caleb vowed to give his daughter, Achsah, to the one who attacked Debir and captured it (Josh 15:16; Judg 1:12). At the age of 85, Caleb was advanced in years (Josh 14:10), but he believed in God's promise, "I will give the land on which he had set foot" (Deut 1:36). In faith he embraced the challenge of conquering the rugged land of Hebron and received that land as his inheritance (Josh 14:13–14).

Debir's former name was Kiriath-sepher (Josh 15:16; Judg 1:11) and was strategically located about 20 km (12.5 mi) southwest of Hebron. When Joshua first conquered the land, the sons of Anak had been occupying it (Josh 11:21). The sons of Anak were able fighters in battle, great in stature and strong (Num 13:33), so no one would readily volunteer to fight them.

However, Othniel was the first person to volunteer, and he captured Debir (Josh 15:17; Judg 1:13). This Othniel, who was from the tribe of Judah, held onto God's Word, "Judah shall go up; behold, I have given the land into his hand" (Judg 1:2). Trusting in God's strength, he bravely advanced to seize the land that no one else had dared to attempt.

2. Achsah, Who Became Othniel's Wife, Fully Obeyed Her Father's Will

Caleb gave his daughter Achsah to Othniel, as he had vowed (Josh 15:17; Judg 1:13). Caleb's daughter was precious to him, and this was reflected in his vow to grant her to the man who conquered Debir. The Hebrew word for *Achsah*, עַכְסָה (*'aksâ*), means "anklet." An anklet, an ornament worn by the Israelite women, is a subtle piece of jewelry that can exude luster and quiet elegance. In accordance with her name, Achsah followed after the faith of her father, possessing noble faith and wisdom that allowed her to obey her parents without selfish pride.

She obeyed without protest her father's command to marry Othniel and to go to the land of the Negev (Judg 1:15). The land of the Negev refers to the regions of Debir, which Othniel had conquered. The Hebrew word for *Negev*, נֶגֶב (*negeb*), means "south" and "rough and parched land." The regions of Debir were dry and parched like the desert regions.

Not only was Achsah obedient, she was also a wise daughter. She persuaded her husband, Othniel, to ask her father for a field (Judg 1:14). The word *field* in Hebrew is שָׂדֶה (*sādeh*) and refers to flat land that can be farmed. She foresaw that if they were going to live in a dry and parched land, they would need a field to farm.

With this in mind, Achsah alighted from her donkey, and Caleb asked her, "What do you want?" However, the wise Achsah did not ask for a field straight away. She said to her father, "Give me a blessing, since you have given me the land of the Negev, give me also springs of water" (Judg 1:15).

The Hebrew words for *springs of water* are גֻּלֹּת מָיִם (*gūllōt māyim*) and are in the plural form, referring to many springs. Land with many springs is ideal for farming. Wise Achsah, by asking for the springs, naturally received good land. Caleb gave her the upper springs and the lower springs (Judg 1:15). These were a precious asset, because they provided water to both the higher and lower regions.

Just as Caleb gave both upper and lower springs to an obedient daughter when she made her wise request, God will also pour out various blessings in abundance to those who wholly obey without protesting even under unfavorable circumstances (Deut 30:9, 16; Jas 1:17).

3. Othniel Saved Israel from Cushan-rishathaim's Oppression

The Israelites did what was evil in the sight of God and served the Baals and the Asheroth. Thus, God sold them into the hands of Cushan-rishathaim, king of Mesopotamia, so that they were oppressed for eight years (Judg 3:7–8). When they cried out to God, He sent Othniel to save them from the hands of Cushan-rishathaim, and He gave them peace for 40 years (Judg 3:9–11). The word *cried* in Judges 3:9 is זָעַק (*zāʿaq*) in Hebrew and refers to "crying out for help in the midst of despair." After enduring eight years of oppression, the Israelites cried out sincerely to God, and He raised up a deliverer for them (Judg 3:9).

Later on in time, Sennacherib, king of Assyria, came with 185,000 soldiers and seized Jerusalem. At this time, King Hezekiah and Isaiah the prophet prayed and cried out to heaven (2 Chr 32:20). The word *cried* used in this verse is also זָעַק (*zāʿaq*), the same word used in Judges 3:9. God heard the cry of King Hezekiah and the prophet Isaiah and sent an angel who made corpses out of the 185,000 mighty soldiers overnight (2 Chr 32:21; 2 Kgs 19:35). Hebrews 11:33 states, "who by faith conquered kingdoms." In the same way, King Hezekiah's and Isaiah's prayer of faith gave them victory over a strong nation like Assyria.

Ultimately, prayer is the weapon that triggers God's powers (Mark 9:29; Jas 5:16). If we earnestly call out to God with repentance in times of suffering, God will draw near to us (Deut 4:7; Ps 34:18; Jas 4:8) and meet us (Deut 4:29; Jer 29:13). God answers the prayers of His chosen people and even takes away their deep-rooted rancor when they pray without ceasing and without despair (Luke 18:1–8).

Othniel was able to defeat Cushan-rishathaim because the spirit of the Lord was upon him (Judg 3:10). In order to fulfill the work of God, His Spirit has to come upon the person (Zech 4:6).

Missionary and evangelistic work expands only through God's power and through the strength received through the work of the Holy Spirit (Acts 1:8; cf. Acts 2:4; 4:31; 8:17; 10:44; 11:24; 13:2–4, 52). Acts 9:31 states, "So the church throughout all Judea and Galilee and Samaria enjoyed peace, being built up; and, going on in the fear of the LORD and in the comfort of the Holy Spirit, it continued to increase." Today, the power of the Holy Spirit is the source of energy for the advancement of God's plan for salvation.

2. Ehud – אֵהוּד / Αωδ

Tightly joined, united

Background

He was the son of Gera from the tribe of Benjamin (Judg 3:15). His sons were Naaman, Ahijah, and Gera (1 Chr 8:6–7). They were leaders of the inhabitants of Geba, one of the cities of the tribe of Benjamin (Josh 18:24).

Period of Activity

God punished Israel through Eglon, king of Moab, for 18 years (Judg 3:14). Then He raised Judge Ehud and gave them peace for 80 years (Judg 3:30).

After the time of the judge Othniel, the Israelites did evil in the sight of God and sinned again, inciting God to strengthen Eglon, king of Moab, to fight against Israel. Yet again, the Israelites cried out to God, and He raised Ehud as a deliverer (Judg 3:15).

Ehud is אֵהוּד (ʾēhûd) in Hebrew, and the name comes from the word אֹהַד (ʾōhad), which means "to unite." Thus, Ehud means "strong union," "union," "unity," and "consolidation."

1. God Used Ehud Despite His Weakness

Judges 3:15 states that Ehud was a left-handed man. The term *left-handed* in Hebrew is אִישׁ אִטֵּר יַד־יְמִינוֹ (ʾîš ʾiṭṭēr yad yĕmînô) and refers to a person whose right hand is dysfunctional, more than a person who is just naturally left-handed. Although Ehud was from the tribe of Benjamin, which means "son of the right hand," he had a significant disadvantage of not being able to use his right hand. However, God chose to use Ehud who could not use his right hand freely, over many others whose right hands were normal because Ehud was united with God.

God uses the weak who are united with Him to shame the strong who have turned their backs on Him (1 Cor 1:27). He chooses the people who are considered base and despised by the world in order to nullify the wise, the strong and the powerful in the world (1 Cor 1:28). When we wholly rely upon God, our weaknesses can become instruments through which God's powers can fully work (2 Cor 12:9–10).

2. God Strengthened Moab Against Israel

The Israelites forgot about their eight years of suffering and the bitter life under the oppression of Cushan-rishathaim, and once again did evil in the sight of God so that God strengthened Moab against Israel (Judg 3:12). The Hebrew word associated with the word "strengthened" is חָזַק (ḥāzaq) and means "to help" and "to hold." God, who had previously protected Israel, now held Moab with His mighty hand and strengthened them. The word חָזַק (ḥāzaq) signifies that not only did God give them military strength (1 Kgs 20:23), but also mental strength in order to give them courage. This means that God strengthened the Moabite king Eglon's military force and gave them mental strength so that they could fight against Israel. Once Eglon was strengthened, he made allies with the sons of Ammon and Amalek. Together, they defeated Israel and possessed the city of the palm trees (the city of Jericho, Deut 34:3; Judg 3:13).

Ammon and Moab had been cursed and thus became nations that could not enter the assembly of the Lord (Deut 23:3–6). Also, it was said of Amalek, "You shall blot out the memory of Amalek from under heaven" (Deut 25:19). Accordingly, the Israelites despised and looked down upon these nations most of all, but they lost their most prized land to them without even a chance to fight back. For 18 years the Israelites acted as slaves to these nations and were forced to endure the shame and suffering of having to offer tributes to them (Judg 3:14–15).

When His chosen people repeatedly took the rebellious path, God punished them by strengthening their enemies and allowing them to seize Israel's most prized possessions, so that His people would seek their God again.

3. Ehud Killed King Eglon of Moab and Saved Israel

Ehud was sent to deliver the tribute to the king of Moab (Judg 3:15). He sent all the king's people away, telling them that he had a secret message for the king. Then he went into the roof chamber where the king was sitting alone and killed him with a cubit-long (about 18 inches, or 46 cm) two-edged sword that he had strapped to his right thigh under his cloak (Judg 3:16–23).

Then Ehud blew his trumpet in the hill country of Ephraim and led the sons of Israel who followed him. Ehud said, "Pursue them, for the LORD has given your enemies the Moabites into your hands" (Judg 3:27–28). He showed great leadership during the deliverance of Israel.

First, Ehud was not a leader who gave orders from behind the battle lines; he led the people and went into battle himself. Judges 3:27 states, "and he was in front of them."

Second, Ehud did not take pleasure in his heroism after killing Eglon. Instead, he gathered the strength of the people to drive out the Moabites. When doing God's work, we need to work together as a group rather than trying to do everything on our own.

Ultimately, Ehud was able to strike down 10,000 Moabites at the fords of the Jordan River across from Moab, and he saved Israel from Moabite oppression (Judg 3:27–29). After this, Israel enjoyed peace for 80 years (Judg 3:30). Ehud's 80-year rule was the longest period of peace enjoyed during the time of the judges. By the special grace of God, the Israelites were able to live in peace and independence during this time. We are punished by God when we sin. If we come to an understanding through the punishment, repent, and continue in union with God once again, then we will be able to sustain a life of true peace (John 14:27; 15:5).

3. Shamgar – שַׁמְגַּר / Σαμεγαρ
Sword, God-given

Background
He was the son of Anath, but there are no clear records of the tribe he was from (Judg 3:31).

Period of Activity
There are no records about what was happening during the reign of Shamgar, since the Bible records only one line regarding Shamgar following Ehud. After that, the narrative goes straight to Deborah (Judg 4:1). From this we can infer that Shamgar must have died not too long after becoming a judge.

Shamgar was the third judge after Ehud (Judg 3:31). The origin of his name is uncertain, but Shamgar is שַׁמְגַּר (šamgar) in Hebrew and means "sword" and "God-given."[46] When Shamgar was born, his father Anath called him Shamgar most likely as a confession that he was a "God-given" son. The name *Anath* comes from the Hebrew word עֲנָת (ʿănāt), meaning "to answer" and "to respond." Hence, his name means "answer."

1. God Called Shamgar, an Ordinary Farmer

According to Judges 3:31, Shamgar struck down 600 Philistines with an oxgoad. An oxgoad is a thick and rounded stick about 8 feet (2.5m) in length. One end of this stick is pointed and used to spur on oxen while the other end is a small shovel used for farming purposes. This simple tool revealed God's power and became a weapon like a sword used to defeat the Gentiles.

God also used the staff in Moses' hand when He parted the Red Sea and performed the great work of leading the Israelites out of Egypt. Even a plain staff can become "the staff of God" (Exod 4:20; 17:9) and perform great miracles when it is used with God's power. Shamgar was an ordinary farmer, but God poured down His powers upon him, so that he became a great judge who was able to save God's people with an oxgoad.

2. Shamgar Saved Israel from the Oppression of the Philistines

With regard to the time period during which Shamgar lived, Judges 5:6 states, "In the days of Shamgar the son of Anath, in the days of Jael, the highways were deserted, and travelers went by roundabout ways."

The Hebrew word for *highways* is אֹרַח (*'ōraḥ*) and is in the plural form, referring to not just one highway but to all the highways throughout the land of Israel. These highways were usually used for travel and commerce, but the fact that they were deserted reveals that violence and pillage was rampant during these lawless times owing to the oppression of the Philistines.

Roundabout ways is עֲקַלְקַל (*'ăqalqāl*) in Hebrew and means "winding," "crooked," and "detour." This means that the people avoided the large highways and took winding paths where they were less likely to be seen by others. This is an indication that the Philistine oppression was unbearably brutal. It was under such circumstances that Shamgar saved Israel by killing 600 Philistines with an oxgoad.

The Philistines at this time resided on the coast of the Mediterranean Sea and were strong enough to plan an expansion toward the east. However, God poured down His powers upon Shamgar so that he was able to defeat them with an oxgoad. The secret to victory for the saints is not the quality of their weapons nor the number of their military forces; the key to victory is the power given by God (1 Sam 14:6; 17:47).

When it comes to God's work of salvation, our exceptional skills and special talents do not determine whether God will use us. This is the important lesson we learn from Shamgar's experience. God uses even people who were born blind to manifest His work (John 9:1–4).

On our own, we are incompetent and insignificant, but once we are in God's hands, we are able to perform great work through His power in order to glorify Him. Even a person who appears weak and dull-witted can be used as a sharp "sword" in God's hands for His great work when His Word bestows understanding and ability (Eph 6:17; Heb 4:12).

4. Deborah – דְּבוֹרָה / Δεββωρα

Honey bee, bee

Background

Deborah was the wife of Lappidoth (meaning "torch" or "lightning") from the tribe of Ephraim. She used to sit under the palm tree between Ramah and Bethel as the people came to her for judgment (Judg 4:5).

Period of Activity

The Israelites were abused for 20 years at the hands of Jabin, king of Hazor, and Sisera, the commander of his army (Judg 4:3). God raised Deborah, a female judge, and gave peace in the land for 40 years (Judg 5:31).

Deborah is דְּבוֹרָה (dĕbôrâ) in Hebrew and means "bee" or "honeybee" and comes from the word דָּבַר (dabār), which means "to speak" and "to command."

Looking at Deborah's life, she was as diligent as a bee and was able to carry out various duties. She possessed faith powerful like that of a bee's sting. With her great faith, she was able to defeat Israel's enemies (1 Jn 5:4–5). Lastly, she was able to bring to the Israelites victory as sweet as honey.

1. Deborah Was a Female Judge Who Arose When the Rulers Ceased in Israel (Judg 5:7)

The Israelites did evil in the sight of the Lord once again after the death of Ehud (Judg 4:1). As a result, God allowed Jabin the Canaanite king to severely oppress Israel for 20 years (Judg 4:3). The Hebrew word *oppression* is לָחַץ (lāḥṣ) and means "to bend," "to press," and "to pressure." This word is used in cases where a stronger party exploits the weaker party and thus indicates that the Israelites suffered under exploitation by Sisera. We can surmise from this word, used together with the word *severely*, חָזְקָה (hozě qâ), meaning "intense," that the Israelites gasped for breath each day from their weariness caused by the severe oppression and exploitation.

Before Othniel was raised as judge, the Israelites served Cushanrishathaim for eight years (Judg 3:8). Before Ehud, the Israelites served and paid tribute to Moab for 18 years (Judg 3:14). Now, before the emergence of Deborah as judge, the Israelites were oppressed and exploited severely for 20 years under Jabin the Canaanite king (Judg 4:3). The prolongation of their oppression indicates that idolatry and sins of Israel had increased, and that God's discipline became weightier accordingly. In her song, Deborah pointed out that the Israelites had been subject to attacks by foreign nations because of their idolatry (Judg 5:8).

Deborah received a command from God to save Israel when the Israelite cities had been devastated and were in a critical state following the long period of persecution and severe oppression at the hands of Jabin. Judges 5:7 states, "The peasantry ceased, they ceased in Israel, until I, Deborah, arose…." The Hebrew word for *peasantry* is פְּרָזוֹן (*pĕrāzôn*). This word can be rendered in two ways. First, it can be rendered as "village life" (NIV), "inhabitants of the villages" (KJV), and "people who live in open country" (HALOT). Second, it can be rendered as "warriors" or "mighty men" (NET, LXX).

Taking into account the two meanings of the word, the phrase "the peasantry ceased, they ceased" shows that the villages were desolated when Deborah arose as the judge. The people deserted the villages because they did not have fortresses and were open to invasion and attack. Furthermore, there was no capable leader to protect the people at this time.

After 20 years of severe oppression, the people cried out to the Lord in heaven (Judg 4:3), but there was no true leader to save the people. While men did not even have the courage to come forth, a resolute leader arose with an image of a strong mother who sets out to protect her child. Her name was Deborah and she was called "a mother in Israel" (Judg 5:7). Deborah's soul stirred up, and she firmly resolved to sacrifice herself to save the nation (Judg 5:12).

At the time, women were held in such low esteem that they were not even included in the census (Num 1:2). However, as the sole female judge, Deborah received complete support from the Israelites (Judg 4:8) and awoke the leaders of the time from their senselessness, arming them with faith. She also saved the nation by fulfilling the critical duty of commander-in-chief during the war against King Jabin and Sisera, his army commander.

Deborah commanded Barak to lead 10,000 soldiers to fight against King Jabin (Judg 4:6). The Israelite army consisted of 10,000 official soldiers and 40,000 volunteers who could help them (Judg 5:8).

On the other hand, Sisera, King Jabin's commander, advanced to war with 900 iron chariots (Judg 4:13). Chariots were carriages pulled by horses and were used during war, and these chariots were specially made with iron throughout and were used as tanks today. During the conquest of Canaan, the tribe of Judah was unable to drive out the inhabitants of the valley because they had iron chariots (Judg 1:19). Thus, iron chariots were weapons of great strength at the time.

Aside from the 900 iron chariots, Sisera gathered together all the men with him (Judg 4:13, 15). Considering that Jabin was able to severely abuse the Israelites for 20 years, his army must have been great in number. Israel's military, consisting of 10,000 men, were truly too feeble to face Jabin's military consisting of 900 iron chariots and all his men.

Deborah proclaimed that the words she spoke were the commands of the God of Israel, and to Barak she said, "Behold, the LORD, the God of Israel, has commanded…and I will give him into your hand" (Judg 4:6–7). Barak said that he would go only if Deborah went with him, so she went (Judg 4:8–10). She inspired confidence in Barak by courageously shouting, "Arise! For this is the day in which the LORD has given Sisera into your hands; behold, the LORD has gone out before you" (Judg 4:14).

2. Deborah Glorified God with a Song of Victory and Honored Those Who Meritoriously Served in Battle

Israel's military power was no match for King Jabin and Sisera's iron chariots; but through God's intervention and providence, Israel gained victory. Deborah sang a song of victory (Judg 5), and it contained the following two main themes.

(1) She praised God because victory came completely through God's help.

Although the Israelites and its leaders fought hard in the war, Deborah praised God and gave thanks to the God who had helped them gain victory (Judg 5:2–3).

God Himself came down in order to strike Sisera's mighty army (Judg 5:13 NKJV). Using Barak, God routed Sisera, his chariots and all of his men with the edge of the sword (Judg 4:15). The word *routed* is derived from the word הָמַם (*hamām*), which means "to break," "to step on," and "to confuse." This means that God confused Jabin and Sisera's army so that Barak could obtain victory. God sent torrential rain to create rapids in the Kishon River (Judg 5:4, 21), so that the deluge made all the land a large mud puddle with swamps to confound and mire the iron chariots, allowing Barak's 10,000 men to attack and annihilate them (Judg 4:14).

Seeing this, Sisera panicked, alighted from his chariot, and fled on foot (Judg 4:15). All of Sisera's men fell to the sword and there was not one left standing (Judg 4:16). Judges 5:20 states, "The stars fought from heaven, from their courses they fought against Sisera." The "stars" here refer to the heavenly beings or angels.[47] God sent His angels to destroy Sisera's army. Later, during King Hezekiah's time, when the Assyrian king, Sennacherib, attacked Israel with his great army, the 185,000 men in the Assyrian army were struck down instantly by the angel of the Lord (2 Kgs 19:35).

(2) Deborah sang a song to honor those who served in war.
Although Deborah was commander-in-chief during battle, she did not take credit for the victory. Instead, she praised the achievements of those who risked their lives; she sympathized with their predicaments and expressed gratitude toward them.

① **She honored Barak.**
Judges 5:12 states, "…Arise, Barak, and take away your captives, O son of Abinoam." The name *Barak* (בָּרָק) means "flash of lightning," and he was the son of Abinoam from the tribe of Naphtali (Judg 4:6, 12; 5:1, 12). Barak arose again in faith when the nation was in crisis. He commanded the field operations and helped Deborah who was commander-in-chief. He committed his life for his given mission, and Hebrews 11:32 records him as a man of faith.

② **She honored the nation and its people.**
In Judges 5:9, Deborah sang, "My heart goes out to the commanders of Israel, the volunteers among the people; bless the LORD!" Deborah did not snatch the glory of victory for herself. She was a true leader who shared the joy with the nation and its people (Judg 5:2).

③ **She honored Jael who killed Sisera.**
In Judges 5:24, she sang, "Most blessed of women is Jael, the wife of Heber the Kenite; Most blessed is she of women in the tent." Heber's wife, Jael,

was a Kenite, a Gentile. She had an amicable relationship ("there was peace"; Judg 4:17) with Jabin, the oppressor. However, when Sisera fell into deep sleep while hiding out in her tent, using a hammer she drove a tent peg into his temple and killed him (Judg 4:21). Although she used a cruel method to kill him, the act revealed God's justice. So Deborah praised her and sang, "Most blessed is she of women in the tent" (Judg 5:24).

④ **She honored the tribes that participated in the war.**
Although this was a war in which God was with them, not all the tribes took part in it as Deborah had commanded. Deborah said that not taking part in the war was equivalent to not coming to the help of the Lord (Judg 5:23). Judges 5:15–18 states that the tribes that did not take part in the war included the tribes of Reuben, Dan, Asher, and those who lived in Gilead (i.e., a region in the east of the Jordan River where the tribes of Gad and half-tribe of Manasseh lived). The tribe of Reuben assembled by the stream and exhaustively discussed whether they would take part in the war, but they used their livestock as an excuse not to participate (Judg 5:15–16).[48] Judges 5:17 indicates that the tribe of Dan stayed in their ships and that of Asher sat on the seashore. This was a rebuke against them for using their livelihoods as an excuse not to take part in the war.

On the other hand, the tribes of Ephraim, Benjamin, Zebulun, Issachar, and Naphtali all risked their lives and fought hard (Judg 5:14–15, 18). Deborah described these tribes as those who love the LORD and praised them, saying that they would be "like the rising of the sun in its might" (Judg 5:31a).

Today, there is a call for warriors of faith like Deborah and Heber's wife Jael to risk their lives in taking the lead to save the nation in times of crisis.

In a male-dominated society, Deborah became an unprecedented female leader and fulfilled her duties as judge well, saving a nation that had lived in misery from severe abuse for 20 years. Thus, the 40 years during which Deborah ruled over Israel were marked by undisturbed peace (Judg 5:31b). The Hebrew word for *undisturbed* is שָׁקַט (*šāqaṭ*) and means "to be calm," "to be tranquil," and "to be at peace." This does not refer to a quiet and leisurely state, but to the true rest that the Israelites enjoyed after receiving freedom from gentile oppression with the cessation of war through God's blessing (Josh 11:23; Jer 30:10).

God seeks people who listen to the Word with faith, preach the Word and act according to the Word, despite weaknesses that they may possess. The name *Deborah* means "honey bee" and is derived from the word דָּבַר (*dābar*). The significance of this word's meaning—"to speak"—cannot be neglected.

A single bee may be feeble, but a swarm of bees is powerful. The Israelites were able to defeat the seven tribes of Canaan, not by their own spears and swords, but by the hornets sent by God (Exod 23:28; Deut 7:20; Josh 24:12). The word *hornet* is צִרְעָה (*ṣirĕʿâ*) in Hebrew and refers to species similar to bees, but they have bigger bodies and are more aggressive. They also travel in swarms like bees.

Just as God sent hornets to destroy Israel's enemies, so too did He use Deborah, a solitary figure, to free Israel from Jabin's oppression and restore true peace. We must pray that many true leaders like Deborah will gather like swarming bees and come together to proclaim God's Word and lead the rest of the world by living exemplary lives of faith!

5. Gideon – גִּדְעוֹן / Γεδεων
Woodcutter, lumberjack, warrior

Background

Gideon was the youngest son of Joash the Abiezrite from the tribe of Manasseh (Judg 6:11, 15; Josh 17:2). Gideon had 71 sons including Abimelech (Judg 8:30–31) and was buried in Ophrah after his death (Judg 8:32).

Period of Activity

God punished the Israelites through the Midianites for seven years (Judg 6:1), and Gideon ruled in peace for 40 years (Judg 8:28).

God gave peace during Deborah's 40-year reign as judge (Judg 5:31). However, because the Israelites sinned in the sight of the Lord yet again, God handed them over to the Midianites for seven years (Judg 6:1). All the Israelites lived with anxiety (Judg 6:2-6). Because they could not rest with a sense of safety even in their own tents, they had to make for themselves dens, caves and strongholds (Judg 6:2). When harvest time drew near, the Midianites, the Amalekites and the sons of the east would come and plunder the fields, leaving nothing behind, even taking all the livestock (Judg 6:3–5). This situation continued for seven years until Israel's weakness was at its peak (Judg 6:6), and their outcry reached heaven (Judg 6:7). Gideon was the judge who saved Israel from the oppression of the Midianites. The Hebrew name Gideon, גִּדְעוֹן (*gidĕʿôn*) means "woodcutter," "lumberjack," and "warrior," and the name comes from the word גָּדַע (*gadāʿ*), which means "to cut a tree and make it fall."

1. Gideon Was Called as a Great Warrior

Gideon was called while he was threshing wheat in a winepress to keep it from the Midianites (Judg 6:11). Wheat was normally threshed on a threshing floor where there was good air circulation, but Gideon threshed it in a winepress at home for fear that it would be plundered by the Midianites. While Gideon was threshing the wheat, heavy-hearted and filled with concern for himself and his nation, the angel of the Lord appeared to him and said, "The LORD is with you, O valiant warrior" (Judg 6:12). Gideon was a weak and timid person who was threshing wheat in the winepress out of fear of the Midianites. Yet, God called him a "valiant warrior." This teaches us that no matter how feeble a person may be, if God is with the person, the person can be used as a valiant warrior for God's great work.

Gideon heard God's Word and responded, "O my lord, if the LORD is with us, why then has all this happened to us? And where are all His miracles which our fathers told us about, saying, 'Did not the LORD bring us up from Egypt?' But now the LORD has abandoned us and given us into the hand of Midian" (Judg 6:13). Although Israel's troubles were the result of the people's own disobedience and disbelief, Gideon complained that they were the result of God forsaking His promise to be with His people.

However, God turned to Gideon, who was protesting, and encouraged him saying, "Go in this your strength and deliver Israel from the hand of Midian" (Judg 6:14). Gideon replied, "O LORD, how shall I deliver Israel? Behold, my family is the least in Manasseh, and I am the youngest in my father's house" (Judg 6:15). To Gideon who knew his own weakness, God said, "Surely I will be with you, and you shall defeat Midian as one man" (Judg 6:16).

At that moment, Gideon also asked for a sign to prove that it was the Lord speaking to him, and he said that he would bring an offering to God (Judg 6:17–18). Gideon poured out broth over the offering as the angel of the Lord had commanded, and the angel of the Lord put out the end of the staff that was in his hand and touched the meat and the unleavened bread. Then, fire sprang up from the rock and consumed the meat and the unleavened bread. Then Gideon believed that the one who had appeared to him was an angel of the Lord, and he built an altar there and named it "Jehovah Shalom," which means "the LORD is Peace" (Judg 6:19–24). Although Gideon had complained against God and asked for signs because he did not fully believe in God's Word, God held onto Gideon until the end and made him a valiant warrior.

2. Gideon Carried Out a Religious Reformation

On the night that Gideon was called as judge, he obeyed God's command and took ten servants with him to pull down the altar of Baal and cut down the Asherah that was beside it (Judg 6:25–27). When the men of the city found out what had been done, they tried to kill Gideon (Judg 6:28–30). Joash, Gideon's father, criticized Baal's incompetence severely by saying that those who worship Baal would be punished by the living God (Judg 6:31). Then he renamed his son *Jerubbaal*, meaning "contend with Baal" (Judg 6:32). Later, the people removed the "baal" from the name and replaced it with "besheth" and called Gideon *Jerubbesheth*, meaning "shame will contend" (2 Sam 11:21).

Some time later, when the Midianites prepared for an attack, the Spirit of the Lord came upon Gideon, and he blew a trumpet and assembled the people for war against the Midianites (Judg 6:33–34). Then he asked God for a sign. God showed him two signs as he had requested. The first time, God showed him a sign where there was dew only on the fleece of wool while the ground remained dry. The second time, there was dew on the ground but the fleece remained dry. God tolerated the doubting Gideon and was patient with him until the end, showing His great love in order to save Israel (Judg 6:36–40).

3. Gideon Selected 300 Warriors

There were about 32,000 soldiers who had gathered by the time Gideon was about to go to war against the Midianites. This was an inferior number compared to the 135,000 soldiers that the Midianite army possessed (Judg 8:10). However, God said, "The people who are with you are too many…" (Judg 7:2) and commanded Gideon to decrease the number of his soldiers. God proclaimed that unless this was done, He would not give Midian into their hands (Judg 7:2). This was so that the Israelites would not boast against God saying, "My own power has delivered me" (Judg 7:2).

All the 32,000 men who had pitched tents near the spring of Harod were men who had volunteered to fight against Midian (Judg 7:1). However, God sent 31,700 men back to the tents and chose only 300 men (Judg 7:8).

There were two steps in the process by which God chose the 300 men.

First, God commanded that all the men who trembled with fear to turn back. God said, "Whoever is afraid and trembling, let him return and depart from Mount Gilead" (Judg 7:3) because He saw that the hearts of others would be fearful because of those who trembled (Deut 20:8). When God gave Moses regulations regarding the Lord's army, He also commanded the officers to say, "Who is the man that is afraid and faint-hearted? Let him depart and return to his house…" (Deut 20:8). At this time, 22,000 men out of the 32,000 men departed, and there were 10,000 men left (Judg 7:2–3).

Next, God commanded that all men who knelt to drink water be sent back. Hence, the remaining 10,000 were led to the water to drink. There, 9,700 of them knelt down and hurriedly drank the water (Judg 7:5). The Hebrew word for *kneel* used here is כָּרַע (*karāʿ*), and it does not merely refer to kneeling down but to kneeling down and bowing to the ground. The 9,700 men had knelt on their knees, stooped down toward the ground, and drank frantically with their faces buried in the water with both hands on the ground. In other words, they did not show any sign of alertness although they were in a situation where battle could have broken out at any time. However, the remaining 300 men put their hands to their mouths and lapped the water, looking out for the enemy as they drank. God sent the 9,700 men back home, and kept only the 300 men who lapped the water like dogs lap while they kept watch, prepared to engage in battle at any time (Judg 7:4–8).

This final group of 300 men devoted all their heart and strength in response to God's calling and stayed alert so that they might fulfill their duties (Luke 21:36). Those who are not alert and awake, and those who are not faithful to the fulfillment of their duties, cannot be used as God's warriors (2 Tim 2:26; 1 Pet 5:8; Rev 16:15).

4. Gideon Triumphed in Battle Using Trumpets and Torches

On the night that God chose the 300 men, He commanded Gideon saying, "Arise, go down against the camp, for I have given it into your hands" (Judg 7:9). However, God saw fear in Gideon's heart. He had a small army of 300 men, while his enemy was as numerous as locusts and as the sand on the seashore (Judg 7:12). In order to give Gideon confirmation that he would prevail, God commanded him to take his servant and go to the camp of the enemy and listen to what they were saying (Judg 7:10). God said, "…you will hear what they say; and afterward your hands will be strengthened that you may go down against the camp" (Judg 7:11).

Gideon took his servant Purah down to the enemy's camp as God had commanded. When Gideon came, a man was relating a dream to his friend saying, "Behold, I had a dream; a loaf of barley bread was tumbling into the camp of Midian, and it came to the tent and struck it so that it fell, and turned it upside down so that the tent lay flat" (Judg 7:13). Then his friend interpreted the dream saying, "This is nothing less than the sword of Gideon the son of Joash, a man of Israel; God has given Midian and all the camp into his hand" (Judg 7:14). Now, after listening to the Midianite soldier's dream and its interpretation, Gideon had the conviction that he would be victorious (Judg 7:15).

The "loaf of barley bread" which appears in the dream was food normally eaten by the poor people during those times, and it represented weak Gideon. The "tent" represented the tents of all the Midianites. God showed in advance how He would take weak Gideon and use him as His sword in order to drive out the whole Midianite army entirely.

At the beginning of the middle watch (between 10 p.m. and 11 p.m.), Gideon and 100 men who were with him saw that it was time for the Midianites to change guards (Judg 7:19). Thus, they blew the trumpets and smashed the pitchers that were in their hands. The rest of the men that were behind them also blew trumpets and broke pitchers and cried out, "A sword for the LORD and for Gideon!" (Judg 7:20).

The 300 men divided into companies of 100 and circled the enemy's camp to besiege it. "Each stood in his place around the camp" (Judg 7:21) and continued to blow trumpets. Holding their torches and standing steadfast, they cried out loudly.

The sound of 300 trumpets and pitchers shattering resonated throughout the valley near the hill of Moreh. Also, the fiery torches flared and lit up the camp like daylight. Normally, one or two people would blow the war trumpet from one direction. However, 300 men blew their trumpets together from all sides, and the Midianite army thought that they were completely surrounded by an enormous army and fell into a state of great fear and confusion.

Judges 7:21 describes this scene, "and each stood in his place around the camp; and all the army ran, crying out as they fled." The enemy was so frightened that they cried out and fled in a great hurry. They were in such a state of chaos that they killed one another with their swords and thus destroyed themselves (Judg 7:22). Judges 7:22 states, "…the LORD set the sword of one against another even throughout the whole army." Because Gideon's men had truly obeyed God's commands, God set the sword of judgment in the enemy's camp and destroyed them.

Gideon sent messengers to assemble the Israelites to pursue the Midianite army that had fled, and he went before them and guarded the Jordan River (Judg 7:24). The people of Ephraim captured two Midianite leaders. They caught Oreb and killed him at the rock of Oreb, and Zeeb at the winepress and brought their heads to Gideon (Judg 7:25; 8:3; Ps 83:11; Isa 10:26).

Gideon and the 300 men relentlessly pursued the two Midianite kings, Zebah and Zalmunna, across the Jordan River (Judg 8:4). The 135,000 men of the Midianite army fell into a state of confusion and killed one another with their swords. They were pursued by Gideon's 300 men (Judg 7:22), and all 120,000 men died. The 15,000 men who had survived were with the two kings, Zebah and Zalmunna, in Karkor (Judg 8:10–12). Judges 8:11 states that the remaining 15,000 men were "unsuspecting." The Hebrew word for *unsuspecting* is בֶּטַח (*beṭāḥ*) and means "safety." Thus, the 15,000 men had put their guard down, thinking that there was no chance for Gideon and his 300 men to pursue them so far. Consequently, they had not properly fortified themselves.

Gideon raided the 15,000 men and captured Zebah and Zalmunna. He destroyed the army of 15,000, which was 50 times as many as the 300 of his army (Judg 8:12). This was the fulfillment of God's Word, "Surely I will be with you, and you shall defeat Midian as one man" (Judg 6:16). Objectively speaking, it is impossible for an army of 300 men to kill 120,000 men and pursue the remaining 15,000 to defeat them as well. What was the secret to their victory?

First, they relied completely upon God. It is impossible for 300 men to defeat 135,000 men, but even more so when they are not even armed with the most advanced weapons. Gideon's men were armed with trumpets and torches, but they were victorious because they relied completely upon God. More specifically, relying on God means following the person whom God has established as leader. God worked through Gideon in the war against Midian, so the key to victory was obeying Gideon's commands. The expressions, "For the LORD and for Gideon" (Judg 7:18) and "A sword for the LORD and for Gideon" (Judg 7:20) meant that God was working with Gideon, a man of God.

When Moab, Ammon and the inhabitants of Mount Seir gathered against King Jehoshaphat of the southern kingdom of Judah to attack him, Jehoshaphat proclaimed, "Listen to me, O Judah and inhabitants of Jerusalem, put your trust in the LORD your God, and you will be established. Put your trust in His prophets and succeed." He obtained a great victory through God's help (2 Chr 20:20).

Second, the 300 warriors obeyed in unity. The 300 men were divided into three companies, and each person held torches in their left hands and trumpets in their right hands (Judg 7:16, 20). At that point, Gideon emphasized twice, "Look at me, and do likewise. And behold, when I come to the outskirts of the camp, do as I do" (Judg 7:17). They would have failed if even one man out of the 300 had disobeyed and done as he had wanted.

The 300 men followed Gideon and acted as one. This was the key to their victory. The three companies blew their trumpets at the same time and then broke their pitchers. They held torches in their left hands and trumpets in their right hands and shouted so that the Midianite army killed one another with their swords. Then they fled, giving Gideon a miraculous victory (Judg 7:19–23).

The pitchers that they broke and the torches that were hidden inside them represent the awesome glory of God manifested through feeble men who are as fragile as pitchers (2 Cor 4:7; Col 2:3). When our egos are broken down just as the pitchers were broken and the work is allowed to progress according to God's ways, the mighty power of Jesus Christ will be revealed and we will gain victory.

5. Gideon's 300 Warriors Were Exhausted, but Continued to Pursue to the End and Completed Their Mission

The war against Midian started at the beginning of the middle watch (Judg 7:19), and Gideon and his 300 men pursued the fleeing Midianite soldiers from the valley near the hill of Moreh (Judg 7:1) to Beth-shittah toward Zererah, as far as the edge of Abel-meholah, by Tabbath (Judg 7:22).

It was a difficult and exhausting war, but Judges 8:4 states, "Then Gideon and the 300 men who were with him came to the Jordan and crossed over, weary yet pursuing." The word *weary* is עָיֵף (*'āyēp*) in Hebrew and means "exhausted," "without strength," "fatigued," and "thirsty." This word is used when one uses energy beyond what one possesses so that one is physically pushed to the limit and exhausted (Gen 25:29–30; 2 Sam 16:14; 17:29). Gideon's small army of 300 men was fighting against a great army of 135,000 men, and they were certainly exhausted (Judg 8:10).

The word *pursuing* in Judges 8:4 is רָדַף (*rādap*) in Hebrew and means "to follow," "to pursue," and "to hunt." It refers to the act of pursuing closely so as to not lose the object of the pursuit (the goal). The 300 men precisely obeyed God's command by following Gideon closely so that they did not lose sight of his every deed and action. The word *pursuing* is in the participial form of the verb and means that the 300 warriors continuously followed Gideon without ceasing.

There were times during the war with Midian when Gideon's 300 men were so tired that they wanted to stop and give up from exhaustion. There were probably times when they felt that they had pursued the Midianites enough and wanted to quit. At times, they may have thought that Gideon was asking too much of them. Yet the men continued to follow Gideon to the end. Although they appeared as though they would faint, they mustered enough energy to get up and continue the pursuit. The warriors probably encouraged their companions, who were wearied and could not go on anymore, and lifted them up again, saying, "Have strength, O great man!" Ultimately, they completely destroyed all 135,000 men in the Midianite army and fulfilled their duty to save their nation (Judg 8:12).

Gideon's men became even more drained by the jealousy and contentions against them from among the tribe of Ephraim who boasted of their achievements and status (Judg 8:1). The men of Ephraim were greatly disgruntled that they were excluded from the war from the start. To this Gideon responded, "Is not the gleaning of the grapes of Ephraim better than the vintage of Abiezer?" (Judg 8:2). The phrase "gleaning of the grapes" refers to the lower quality grapes that are gathered after the main harvest, and the "vintage" refers to the first harvest of grapes which takes place in July. Abiezer is the name of a clan within the tribe of Manasseh to which Gideon belonged. The vintage is normally higher in quality than the gleaning of the grapes, but here Gideon tells the men of Ephraim that their grapes are so superb in quality that the gleaning of their grapes is better than Abiezer's vintage.

Here, Gideon highly praised the men of Ephraim, saying that their military achievements at the end of the war were greater than what Gideon's men had done since the start of the war. With a humble and mature faith, Gideon praised the achievements of the men of Ephraim and quelled their discontent as well as the strife among the tribes.

Even more than this incident, the cold treatment and reproach from their own people further aggravated the 300 men who were already tired. During their pursuit of Zebah and Zalmunna, the 300 men had to cross the Jordan River and were so exhausted that they asked for some bread for the army. Not only did the men of Succoth and Penuel refuse to give them bread, but also they mocked the army (Judg 8:5–9). The men, however, did not let the mocking bring them down. Instead, they pursued the two kings with the intention of completely destroying the Midianite power. Finally, Gideon's army killed the two kings and suppressed the Midianites, thus saving their nation.

People who fulfill the duties God has entrusted to them are people who follow through to the end despite exhaustion (Heb 10:37–39; Rev 14:4). We must not give up halfway before God's will is fulfilled. Although there may be unimaginable amount of misunderstandings, tribulations, persecutions, and scorn that add to fatigue, those who follow to the end without despair will experience miraculous victory and salvation (Matt 10:22; 24:13; Luke 21:19; Gal 6:9).

In truth, Gideon had achieved an enormous victory by striking down the Midianite army which was comparable to a giant tree. God's salvation does not depend on whether or not there are a great number of people (1 Sam 14:6). God displayed His greatness through Gideon, a person who was as insignificant as a loaf of barley and as fragile as a clay pot.

Because God strengthened Gideon's feeble hands (Judg 7:11), his 300 men were able to defeat an army that was 450 times larger as if they were striking one man. Through God's work, the least became a thousand and the smallest, a mighty nation (Isa 60:22). In our lives of faith, there are times when we look at our surroundings, and our hearts become discouraged and weakened. However, instead of despairing, we must look upon God who provides mighty strength to the weak (Ps 63:2; Isa 40:31; 2 Cor 12:9–10).

Today, God's right hand upholds and helps those who rise up in faith to fulfill the duties God has entrusted to them (Isa 41:10–13; Ps 63:8; 73:23; 139:10). I pray that we may rely on God completely, cast away all doubts, and overcome all obstacles as we march forward to the great victory in the end. Although we may encounter an enemy formidable like a giant tree, I pray that we may cut it down with the sword of the Lord and discover the overflowing joy of victory.

6. Tola – תּוֹלָע / Θωλα

Worm, maggot

Background
Tola was the son of Puah and the grandson of Dodo from the tribe of Issachar. He became judge "after Abimelech" (Judg 10:1).

Period of Activity
He became a judge and saved Israel and ruled for 23 years (Judg 10:2).

Gideon had made a golden ephod with 1,700 shekels of gold earrings that he collected from the spoils of the people. However, that ephod became a snare for Gideon and his household (Judg 8:24–27). Gideon also had many wives and a concubine in Shechem who bore him Abimelech, but this also became a snare for him (Judg 8:29–31).

After Gideon's death, the Israelites betrayed God yet again and worshipped the Baals (Judg 8:33–35). Abimelech, Gideon's son, sought to make himself king and tried to kill all of his 70 brothers. He managed to kill 69 brothers, but Gideon's youngest son, Jotham, escaped by hiding. However, a certain woman threw an upper millstone on Abimelech's head and crushed his skull. Abimelech then asked his armor bearer to kill him and died by his armor bearer's sword, ending his life tragically (Judg 9:18, 53–56). It was at this time that God established Tola as judge. The name *Tola* is תּוֹלָע (*tôlāʿ*) in Hebrew and means "worm" and "maggot." It comes from the word יָלַע (*yālaʿ*), which means "to speak without thinking," "to speak hastily," and "to swallow."

1. Tola Saved Israel

The only written record of Tola in the Bible appears in Judges 10:1–2. Judges 10:1 (NKJ) states, "After Abimelech there arose to save Israel Tola the son of Puah, the son of Dodo, a man of Issachar; and he dwelt in Shamir in the mountains of Ephraim." The word *arose* is in the waw consecutive form of the Hebrew word קוּם (*qûm*). This word is used to signify rising up resolutely in order to accomplish a certain deed. Tola felt righteous indignation because of Abimelech's tyranny; and after Abimelech's death, he arose with strength and a sense of duty to carry out God's righteousness in Israel. The word *save* is in the hiphil stem of יָשַׁע (*yāsa'*) and means "was made to save." This means that God, by His sovereign work, saved the Israelites from oppression. He worked through Tola to save Israel.

2. Tola Was Buried in Shamir in the Land of Ephraim

Tola was from the tribe of Issachar located in the northern part of Israel (Judg 10:1). However, Tola reigned as judge in the land of the tribe of Ephraim located in the middle part of Canaan. It is notable that he was not buried in his own homeland when he died, but in Shamir in the land of Ephraim (Judg 10:2). Gideon (Judg 8:32), Jephthah (Judg 12:7), Ibzan (Judg 12:10), Elon (Judg 12:12), Abdon (Judg 12:15) and even Samson were all buried in their homelands (Judg 16:31). However, Tola left his homeland and reigned in Shamir, where God had sent him, for 23 years and did not leave until the last day of his life. The word *lived* in Judges 10:1 is in the active participial form of the Hebrew word יָשַׁב (*yāsab*) and means that he lived there continuously, not just temporarily for a time. The name *Shamir* (שָׁמִיר; thorns, adamant, flint) is derived from the word שָׁמַר (*sāmar*), which means "to keep" and "to guard."

Those who love God are faithful in keeping and guarding their place of duty, but those who love the world will abandon their place in the end. Demas was the Apostle Paul's fellow worker (Col 4:14; Phlm 1:24), but Paul said, "Demas, having loved this present world, has deserted me and gone to Thessalonica" (2 Tim 4:10). The word *loved* is an aorist active participle of the Greek word ἀγαπάω (*agapaō*), and it means that Demas loved the world to the extent that he would lay down his life for it.

Tola's bones were buried in the place of his duty where God had sent him. This is a great lesson for many ministers today who easily forsake their place of calling and their sheep for the sake of their own comfort, benefit, and, for the reason of money (greater income).

The name *Tola* means "worm" and "maggot." He probably regarded himself as lowly and helpless as a worm or a maggot, and humbly relied on God's help (Job 25:6; Isa 41:14). Only those who rely on God and His help every moment of their life, realizing their own weakness, can fulfill their calling to the end (Ps 121:1–2, 146:3–5).

Those who do not expect a reward for fulfilling their calling, but regard it as their eternal inheritance, and are continuously faithful with all their lives will surely receive the crown of life (Rev 2:10).

7. Jair – יָאִיר / Ιαϊρ
Enlightener, the one who shines light

Background
Jair was a Gileadite and is presumed to have been from the tribe of Manasseh (Judg 10:3).

Period of Activity
He is recorded as judge after Tola and he served for 22 years (Judg 10:3).

Jair the Gileadite is recorded as judge after Tola (Judg 10:2–3). It is presumed that his period of reign as judge overlapped with Tola's period of reign, because, while Tola ruled in Shamir of Ephraim, Jair ruled in Gilead, east of the Jordan River. Considering that their places of service were different and that there was no Gentile oppression at the time, it is certain that the two judges ruled at the same time but in different places.

Jair arose as judge around the same time as Judge Tola who was discussed earlier (Judg 10:1, 3). Here, the word *arose* is קוּם (*qûm*) in Hebrew and means "to boldly arise in a determined manner in order to accomplish a certain deed". The Hebrew word for *Jair* is יָאִיר (*yāʾîr*) and means "enlightener," "the one who enlightens" and "the one who shines light." It comes from the word אוֹר (*ʾôr*), which means "to shine light," "to brighten" and "to shine." The word *enlightener* signifies one who instructs or imparts knowledge to another person who has little knowledge or is ignorant and tied down by convention. Jair rose up with a sense of calling and, for 22 years, he instructed and enlightened the people.

1. Jair Judged Israel for 22 Years in Peace

God usually raised judges when the Israelites cried out to Him during their suffering and oppression by the Gentiles which was a result of their evil deeds. However, during Jair's time there is no mention of evil deeds committed in the sight of God or of gentile oppression. Thus, we know that Jair's 22-year reign was a time of peace.

From the meaning of Jair's name we can make a cautious deduction about the reason for the continuous peace. Like the meaning of his name, "enlightener" and "one who shines light," Jair probably enlightened the people who were darkened by sin by teaching them the Word of light and making a great effort to keep them away from sinning in the sight of God (Ps 119:11).

The Word of God enlightens simple people so that they can move from darkness into the light (Ps 119:130). All the darkness in us is cast away when God lights the lamp of our souls with His Word (Ps 18:28).

2. Jair Enjoyed Riches and Honor, and Even His Descendants Received Blessings

Jair had 30 sons and they rode on 30 donkeys and, even at young ages, they possessed 30 cities in the land of Gilead (Judg 10:4). These cities are called Havvoth-jair, and they got their name when Jair, the son of Manasseh, took the towns in Gilead just before entry into Canaan (Num 32:41; Deut 3:14). However, "Jair the judge," a descendant of "Jair, the son of Manasseh," cast out the Gentiles and reclaimed the land about 260 years later and called it Havvoth-jair again.

Those who drive out the unbelieving forces who oppose God from among His people, teach God's Word, transmit faith, and lead people back to the right path will receive blessings throughout their following generations.

3. Jair Was Buried in Kamon

Jair died and was buried in Kamon (Judg 10:5). The word *Kamon* is derived from the word קוּם (*qûm*), which means "to rise." Hence, *Kamon* means "a high place."

Later on, Hezekiah, the king of the southern kingdom of Judah, who enlightened the people through a religious revolution, died, and all Judah and the inhabitants of Jerusalem honored him by burying him "in the upper section of the tombs of the sons of David" (2 Chr 32:33). Just like in the time of Hezekiah, Jair's burial in a high place was an indication of the people's respect for his deeds and their desire to honor him throughout the generations.

When the light of the Word of God works forcefully, unrighteousness, unlawfulness, evil and unbelief will disappear from all aspects of our lives, and righteousness, justice, goodness and faith will grow and become brighter. We must lift up the gospel of the cross of Jesus Christ who came to a world that is totally darkened by sin. We must become enlightened by faith and shine the light of this gospel brightly so as to cast away the forces of darkness (Isa 60:1–3; Ps 119:105; Matt 5:16).

8. Jephthah – יִפְתָּח / Ιεφθαε

He will open it up, God will open it up

Background
Jephthah was the son of a harlot and Gilead was his father. Because of his lowly birth, he did not receive an inheritance in his father's house and was driven out by the sons of Gilead's wife (Judg 11:1–2).

Period of Activity
The Ammonites and the Philistines afflicted the Israelites for 18 years (Judg 10:7–8) and Jephthah reigned as judge for six years (Judg 12:7).

God called Jephthah in order to save the Israelites who were oppressed by the Gentiles for 18 years after the death of Jair. The name *Jephthah* is יִפְתָּח (*yipttâ*) in Hebrew and means "he opens." This word is derived from פָּתַח (*pātaḥ*), which means "to open," "to liberate," "freedom," and "to be released."

1. Jephthah Saved His People from the Oppression of the Ammonites

The Israelites forsook God and served the Baals and the Ashtaroth, the gods of Aram, the gods of Sidon, the gods of Moab, the gods of the sons of Ammon, and the gods of the Philistines (Judg 10:6). As a result, God sold them into the hands of the Philistines and into the hands of the sons of Ammon (Judg 10:7) and made them suffer oppression for 18 years (Judg 10:7–8).

The word *afflicted* in this verse is וַיִּרְצְצוּ (*vayěrōṣěṣû*), in the active emphatic voice of the word רָצַץ (*rāṣaṣ*), meaning "to crush," "to shatter," and "to break." This word vividly describes how the Ammonites and the Philistines brutally and mercilessly oppressed the Israelites as a lion pounces upon its prey and tears it to pieces.

(1) Jephthah's emergence was the result of God's plan to save the Israelites after they had earnestly repented.

The Israelites suffered under the Ammonite oppression and called upon God (Judg 10:10). They put away the foreign gods from among them and began to serve God until He could not bear their misery any longer (Judg 10:16). The Israelites' repentance moved God's heart. The Hebrew word for the phrase, "could bear their misery no longer" is קָצַר (qāṣar) and means "unbearably anxious," "impatient," and "vexed." Like the heart of a parent willing to jump into a ball of fire to save a dying child, God's mercy burned in Him so that He could not help but save Israel (Hos 11:8).

We have to remember that Jephthah saved Israel from the oppression of the Ammonites because of God's burning love and zeal toward His people Israel.

When the inhabitants of Gilead found themselves in an urgent situation because of the attack by the sons of Ammon, they assembled and decided that the one to lead them in fighting against the sons of Ammon would be Jephthah, who had been driven away to the land of Tob. They promised that he would be made head over all the inhabitants of Gilead if he defeated the sons of Ammon (Judg 10:17–18; 11:4–10). The process through which Jephthah emerged appears to be the work of man, but it was actually part of God's sovereign plan to save the Israelites after He saw their repentance and heard their cries.

(2) Jephthah viewed the nation through the eyes of faith.

Jephthah was driven to the land of Tob because he was the son of a harlot, and the worthless fellows of Tob gathered themselves about him and followed him (Judg 11:3). The Hebrew word for *worthless fellows* is רֵיקִים (rēyqîm) in Hebrew and means "men of debauchery," "wandering swindlers with no permanent residence" and "shallow people."

However, Jephthah did not gather with the worthless fellows to do evil. It can be inferred that he guided them in faith and was active to save Israel. Based on the fact that the elders of Gilead asked Jephthah to become their chief for the war against the Ammonites, Jephthah must have been renowned for bravery and possessed strong patriotism based on faith despite his humble birth as the son of a harlot and his ties with the worthless fellows (Judg 11:4–6).

When the elders promised, "...that you may go with us and fight with the sons of Ammon and become head over all the inhabitants of Gilead," Jephthah responded with unwavering faith, saying that he could gain victory if the Lord gives the sons of Ammon up to him (Judg 11:8–9).

In addition, when Jephthah was made head and chief over Gilead, he spoke all his words "before the LORD" at Mizpah (Judg 11:11). The word *before* is פָּנִים (*pānîm*) in Hebrew, and it means "toward the face." Thus, Jephthah presented his whole heart toward the face of God when he spoke his words. With the war against the Ammonites ahead of him, Jephthah reported to God about his current situation and prayed for victory.

(3) Jephthah's perspective on history was firmly founded upon faith. Jephthah sent messengers to the king of Ammon and pointed out the injustice of his attack on Israel (Judg 11:12–13). Jephthah was not looking to go to war at the beginning; he was looking for peace with Ammon if possible.

Afterwards, Jephthah sent a second messenger and cited, reason-by-reason based on history, why it was unjust for Ammon to request the land east of the Jordan River (Judg 11:14–17).

Jephthah was very well-informed about Israel's history with Ammon from the time of the Exodus to the wilderness journey and until the entrance into Canaan. He understood very well that it had all been part of God's plan for salvation.

> **Judges 11:23** Since now the LORD, the God of Israel, drove out the Amorites from before His people Israel, are you then to possess it?

Jephthah tried his best to settle matters peacefully with the Ammonites, but in the end, he prayed, "…May the LORD, the Judge, judge today between the sons of Israel and the sons of Ammon" (Judg 11:27) and displayed great faith through his reliance on God for a solution.

Then the Spirit of the Lord came upon Jephthah (Judg 11:29), and risking his life, he crossed over to where the Ammonites were and attacked them (Judg 12:3). The Lord gave the sons of Ammon into the hands of Jephthah, and he struck them down with a great slaughter from Aroer to the entrance of Minnith, 20 cities, and as far as Abel-keramim until the Ammonites surrendered (Judg 11:32–33).

2. Jephthah Made a Hasty Vow

As Jephthah was going out to war, he vowed that he would offer up as a burnt offering whatever comes out of the doors of his house to meet him when he returns home in peace (Judg 11:31). When he victoriously came back to his house in Mizpah, his daughter—his one and only child—came out to meet him with tambourines and with dancing (Judg 11:34). He

lost strength and felt faint at the miserable thought that he had to offer his only daughter as a burnt offering (Judg 11:35). Amidst great
regret and grief, Jephthah did according to his vow after the two-month
period of comfort that his daughter requested (Judg 11:39).

Jephthah's hasty vow led to the sacrificial death of his one and only child.
The Bible tells us that we must not delay in paying our vows to the Lord
even if it hurts (Deut 23:21–23; Num 30:2; Ps 15:4; Prov 20:25). Thus,
we must not blindly or hastily make a vow to the Lord.

On the other hand, Jephthah's daughter returned after the two months
she requested and allowed herself to be offered as a sacrifice according to
her father's vow. This was truly a noble act of obedience worthy to be com-
memorated (Judg 11:36–40). Even as she faced this unthinkable and guilt-
less death, she confessed that her father's victory against Ammon was totally the result of God's work. She testified that God had done according
to His promise with her father and that he, too, must act according to
his vow to the Lord (Judg 11:36).

Although Jephthah's daughter may have been bitterly grieved for her
premature death, her genuine faith was a consolation to her father, whose
heart was broken in despair. She sublimated her human pain to firm faith.
Here lies the proof that Jephthah had raised his daughter well to become
a woman of faith. The period of the judges had been a spiritually dark
period, but the inclusion of Jephthah's name in Hebrews 11:32 as a person
of faith supports this belief. The faith of Jephthah and his daughter was
exemplary, and it became a custom for the Israelites to commemorate
this event annually by mourning for the daughter of Jephthah for four
days (Judg 11:39–40).

3. Jephthah Triumphed in Battle Against the Tribe of Ephraim

After Jephthah's victory over Ammon, the men of Ephraim became envious and started a quarrel, saying that since they were not called to fight
against the Ammonites they would burn down Jephthah and his house
(Judg 12:1). Actually, Jephthah had asked for help from the sons of
Ephraim but they had refused (Judg 12:2). The sons of Ephraim were selfish and shrewd opportunists who would sit back and not make any effort
until there was victory. Then, they would seize the glory.

Furthermore, the sons of Ephraim spoke against the men of Gilead and slandered their legitimacy by calling them "fugitives of Ephraim" (Judg 12:4). This became the direct cause of a civil war within Israel. Jephthah struck and killed the men of Ephraim and seized those fleeing at the fords of the Jordan so that 42,000 Ephraimites were killed (Judg 12:5–6).

At the fords of the Jordan, Jephthah identified the Ephraimites by their pronunciation. The Ephraimites were not able to pronounce "Shibboleth" (meaning "stream") correctly and thus said, "Sibboleth" (meaning "ear of grain," with the root meaning of "load" or "burden"). Although the Ephraimites spoke the same language, their dialect would pronounce the Hebrew character שׁ (š) as ס (s). Ultimately, the Ephraimites lost 42,000 of their men. Their envy brought about such a great loss that it could have led to their annihilation (Judg 12:6).

As the son of a harlot, Jephthah was despised and forced to endure the hardship of a concubine's child, but God trained him and raised him up as a judge and a great leader over Israel at just the right time. When the Israelites were greatly oppressed at the hands of the Ammonites, God saved them through Jephthah and opened the gates of salvation. In actuality, this was done according to the meaning of Jephthah's name, "God will open it up." Jephthah died six years after becoming a judge and was buried in one of the cities of Gilead (Judg 12:7).

In the New Testament, Peter was able to escape from prison when the church prayed together fervently for him. He passed by the first and second guards, and the iron gate that led to the city opened by itself (Acts 12:5–12). Likewise, God will open the gates of heaven and answer our prayers if we do not cease to pray when we are confronted with a crisis and cannot see the way ahead (1 Sam 12:23; 1 Thes 5:17; Luke 3:21–22).

9. Ibzan – אִבְצָן / Εσεβων
Splendid, brilliant

Background
Ibzan was from Bethlehem (Judg 12:8). However, judging from the fact that the Bethlehem in which Jesus was born is often called "Bethlehem in Judah" (Judg 17:7, 9; Ruth 1:2) or "Bethlehem Ephrathah" (Gen 35:19; 1 Sam 17:12; Micah 5:2), it is presumed that Ibzan's hometown Bethlehem was not the Bethlehem in Judah but the Bethlehem in the land of Zebulun. Elon, the judge who succeeded Ibzan, was a Zebulunite, and this increases the probability that Ibzan's Bethlehem was the Bethlehem in the land of Zebulun (Judg 12:12).

Period of Activity
After Jephthah, Ibzan ruled as Israel's judge for seven years (Judg 12:8–9).

The Israelites were guided by the strong faith of Jephthah, a major judge, during his 6-year reign, and they were able to recover their faith and restore order. Upon this sturdy foundation, three minor judges reigned over Israel after him. Ibzan reigned for seven years, Elon reigned for ten years, and Abdon reigned for eight years (Judg 12:9, 11, 14). Judging from the fact that the Hebrew word אַחַר (*'aḥar*), meaning "after," is used in the phrase, "judged Israel after him" for each of the three minor judges, there was no overlap during the 25 years of their reigns. Information regarding the name, birthplace, burial place and years of reign is recorded for all three judges. However, all that is recorded about Ibzan is the wedding feasts for his 30 sons and 30 daughters. For Abdon, the record only indicates that he had 40 children and 30 grandchildren. Whereas for Elon, there is no record at all of his activity.

Ibzan reigned as Israel's judge for seven years after Jephthah. Ibzan is אִבְצָן (*'ibṣān*) in Hebrew and means "splendid" and "brilliant." It comes from a Chaldean word בּוּעַ (*bûaʿ*), which means "to swell up."

Riches and honor reached their peak during the time of King Solomon, which followed immediately after the time of continuous wars under the reign of David. Likewise, Ibzan succeeded Jephthah when Israel finally regained stability after a time of struggle, and he was able to enjoy a life of splendor and brilliance as the meaning of his name.

1. Ibzan Had 30 Sons and 30 Daughters

> **Judges 12:9** He had thirty sons, and thirty daughters whom he gave in marriage outside the family, and he brought in thirty daughters from outside for his sons. And he judged Israel seven years.

Ibzan had 60 children throughout his life so he probably also had many wives. There is no record of his deeds as the leader of the nation. The only record about him states that he had many wives through whom he had many children and that he gave them away in marriage. Judging from the record, "He had thirty sons, and thirty daughters whom he gave in marriage outside the family, and he brought in thirty daughters from outside for his sons" (Judg 12:9), it can be presumed that during his seven-year reign, his main focus was on marrying his children off.

The Bible states that he reigned as judge over Israel, but there is no record of him fighting to save the nation or serving the people. Rather than being faithful to his duties as judge, Ibzan's heart was more inclined to the benefits that came with his position as judge.[49]

2. Ibzan Lived an Extravagant Life

Since Ibzan had 60 children, celebrating weddings and birthdays all year around for his wives and children would have taken up most of his time. It seems that Ibzan got all of his children married during his reign as judge. Getting 60 children married in seven years of his reign probably averaged about eight to nine weddings per year. Even one wedding is a big event for a family. What a busy work it must have been to have about eight to nine weddings every year for seven years! What is more shocking is that he married all his children off to people outside the family.

> **Judges 12:9** He had thirty sons, and thirty daughters whom he gave in marriage outside the family, and he brought in thirty daughters from outside for his sons....

The Hebrew word for *outside* is חוּץ (*ḥûṣ*) and means "apart from the inside," "outside the camp," and "external." This word חוּץ (*ḥûṣ*) was normally used in the Old Testament to refer to areas "outside of the camp," unclean areas for people who had lost the right to remain inside the holy camp and were cast out (Exod 29:14; 33:7; Lev 4:12).

The Bible emphasizes, by reiterating the fact that Ibzan's children were married to people "outside the family" and "from outside," that these marriages were with unclean Gentiles who had nothing to do with God's covenant. These weddings were probably a great financial burden on the people of Israel since they were not ordinary marriages but marriages to foreigners who lived far away. They also occurred eight to nine times a year.

Ibzan probably focused on marriages with foreigners for his children because the Israelites had suffered greatly in the past due to foreign oppression, and he didn't want that to occur anymore. Thus, he devised this marriage policy in order to develop amicable relationships with the foreign nations and to secure peace for the nation.

According to Judges 10:7–8, the reigns of the minor judges, Ibzan, Elon and Abdon overlapped with the period of Israel's oppression at the hands of the Philistines.[50] Even under the oppression of the Philistines, Ibzan never tried to fight off the Gentiles by trusting and relying upon God and thus free the nation from the gentile oppression. Instead, he used frequent marriage alliances to secure peace, which left the people vulnerable to sinful and idle lives.

Israel's history has shown that marriages with foreigners often have fatal results. King Jehoshaphat of southern Judah was godly, but he allied himself by marriage with King Ahab's family (2 Chr 18:1). There was peace for a short time (1 Kgs 22:44), but later the seed of the royal offspring almost dried up because of King Ahab's daughter, Athaliah (2 Kgs 11:1). In addition, during King Solomon's time, his marriage to gentile women led to the introduction of many idols (1 Kgs 11:1–8).

Thus, there is little doubt that the 30 daughters-in-law that Ibzan brought in from foreign countries also brought with them the detestable idols of the Gentiles. Thus, although it appears as though Ibzan's marriage policy maintained peace, it was only temporary. The nation of Israel intermingled with Gentiles so that they worshipped various idols, and sin disseminated rapidly.

On the outside, Ibzan's life-resumé appears brilliant and splendid. However, with his selfish governance and imprudent alliances with gentile nations, he neglected the people to live idly in sin. He also brought in idols and the people fell into greater sin as a result.

Jesus' life resumé shows no record of a selfish life or a life of splendor for Himself (Matt 20:28). Philippians 2:7 states that He "emptied Himself" and took on the form of a bondservant and became like man. What about our life resumé? Do you have a splendid life resumé like Ibzan's that the world acknowledges? Or do you have a resumé like Jesus' in which you have emptied yourself?

10. Elon – אֵילוֹן / Αιλων
Oak tree

Background
Elon was from the tribe of Zebulun. He was buried in Aijalon in the land of Zebulun after he died (Judg 12:12). There is almost no record of Elon's achievements.

Period of Activity
Elon became a judge of Israel after Ibzan and judged for ten years (Judg 12:11).

Elon became judge of Israel after Ibzan and judged for ten years. The name Elon (אֵילוֹן, *'êlôn*) means "oak tree." The name originates from the word אַיִל (*'ayil*) and this word is used in the Bible with the following four meanings.

First, it means "ram" (Gen 22:13; Isa 1:11).

Second, it refers to "doorpost," "jamb," and "pilaster" (1 Kgs 6:31; Ezek 40:36, 48).

Third, it signifies "man with power," "leading man" and "strong man" (2 Kgs 24:15; Ezek 17:13; 31:11; Exod 15:15).

Fourth, it means "terebinth" or "oak" (Isa 1:29; Hos 4:13).

The four meanings share a common connotation of "strength." The word אַיִל; (*'ayil*) is derived from the word אוּל (*'ûl*), which means "noble," "powerful," and "strong." Considering the meaning of these words, it appears that Elon became judge because he was strong and able.

1. The Record of Elon's Life Was the Shortest

There are no record of Elon's deeds, whether positive or negative, other than the statement, "Then Elon the Zebulunite died and was buried at Aijalon in the land of Zebulun" (Judg 12:12). This shows that Elon lived an ordinary life with no extraordinary event. It is regrettable that Elon did not leave behind any spiritual or aspiring achievement despite being a person of capability and strength.

The ten years of Elon's rule were peaceful ones without any distinct foreign attacks. Thus, had he combined his strength with that of the nation for great achievements, surely there would have been some record regarding his life in the Bible.

When our lives are assessed, instead of being people whose lives contain nothing noteworthy, we should be people who work faithfully with the abilities we are given in order to achieve many things that are delightful in God's eyes (Matt 25:21, 23; 1 Cor 4:1–2).

2. The Land Was Not "Undisturbed" During Elon's Time

The word *peace* is associated with the judges until Gideon. The land was "undisturbed" during the time of the judge Othniel, Ehud, Deborah and Gideon (Judg 3:11, 30; 5:31; 8:28). The word *undisturbed* is שָׁקַט (*šāqaṭ*) and means "to be calm," "to be tranquil," and "to be at peace." This does not refer to a mere state of rest from the Gentiles' oppression, but to the blessing of being liberated from enemies' attacks, oppression and suffering. This blessing was given when the Israelites repented and returned to God. Joshua 11:23 implies that peace is a state of rest from war that the Israelites received as God's blessing; and in Jeremiah 30:10, peace alludes to eternal rest in heaven.

The times of the minor judges, Ibzan, Elon and Abdon were not associated with the expression, "and there was peace." It was because faith that obeys God and totally relies on Him was not established during their combined 25-year rule. During this time, Judges 13:1 states that the Israelites again did evil in the sight of the Lord.

Elon ruled ten years, much longer than the judges preceding and succeeding him. However, there is no indication that during these ten years there was any effort to purge the nation of the idols according to God's will or to fight off foreign attacks. These ten years were quiet and dull, yet there was no true peace given by God.

There is a short account regarding Epaphroditus in the New Testament. Philippians 2:25 introduces him saying, "But I thought it necessary to send to you Epaphroditus, my brother and fellow worker and fellow soldier, who is also your messenger and minister to my need." Philippians 2:30 states, "Because he came close to death for the work of Christ, risking his life to complete what was deficient in your service to me." It is a short but touching and beautiful life resumé. Our life resumés must not be like Elon's, an empty and shameful one because we have done nothing for the church, which is the body of Christ. We must all live valuable lives so that we can possess a meaningful resumé like that of Epaphroditus who labored for God's work.

11. Abdon – עַבְדּוֹן / Αβδων

Slave, servant

Background
It is presumed that Abdon was from the tribe of Ephraim. He was the son of Hillel the Pirathonite (Judg 12:13, 15).

Period of Activity
He became judge after Elon and ruled for eight years (Judg 12:14).

Abdon was the last of the minor judges. He judged Israel for eight years after Elon (Judg 12:15). Abdon's father, Hillel, was a Pirathonite, and Abdon was buried in Pirathon after he died (Judg 12:15). It is specifically recorded that he was "buried at Pirathon in the land of Ephraim, in the hill country of the Amalekites," and this means that the Israelites possessed land in the hill country of the Amalekites. During the time of Gideon, the Amalekites had helped the Midianites attack Israel (Judg 6:3, 33; 7:12). This land now became Ephraim's possession because invasions of Gentile nations, including those of the Amalekites, had ended. This marked a turning point in the history of the judges as the land regained peace. Examination of "The Chronology of the Period of the Judges" on page 307 reveals that there were no foreign attacks or oppression in the second half of Abdon's rule.

The name *Abdon* is עַבְדּוֹן (*'abdôn*) in Hebrew, derived from the word עָבַד (*'ābad*), which means "to serve," "to attend to," and "to become a slave." Thus the name עַבְדּוֹן (*'abdôn*) has a meaning of "slave" or "servant." The name of Abdon's father, Hillel (הִלֵּל) means "he has praised." He did not give his son a name meaning "servant" and "slave" so that his son may become a slave to other men. Here, we see traces of his desire for his son to live as God's faithful servant.

1. Abdon Was a Man of Superior Abilities, but His Only Achievement Was Having Many Wives and Children

About 20 years prior to the time of Abdon, the tribe of Ephraim warred with Jephthah, and 42,000 men were killed at the fords of the Jordan (Judg 12:4–6). The entire tribe of Ephraim was in danger of annihilation.

Then, only about 20 years later, an Ephraimite man, Abdon, became the judge of Israel. This indicates that Abdon must have possessed preeminent abilities. Nonetheless, despite his ability, there is no record of his deeds for the nation. The only record regarding Abdon is that he had many children and many wives.

> **Judges 12:14** And he had forty sons and thirty grandsons who rode on seventy donkeys; and he judged Israel eight years.

Abdon had 40 sons so he must have had many wives as well. Despite his position as judge, a leader of the nation, he spent his time focusing on having many women and siring many children. God called him as a judge, but he accepted the Gentile custom of taking many wives. This shows that Abdon's time appeared to be peaceful outwardly, but there was actually spiritual complacency and corruption through sin.

2. Although Abdon Was a Judge, He Was Preoccupied Only with His Personal Affairs

A few years of Abdon's rule coincided with a part of the 40-year oppression by the Philistines.[51] Abdon's interest was not in saving his people who were crying out under Philistine oppression in one part of the nation, but in marrying off his children. Judges 12:14 states that he had 30 grandchildren. Thus, in a similar way to Ibzan (Judg 12:9), Abdon was absorbed in his sons' marriages during his time as judge.

Abdon's other interest was living a wealthy life. His 40 sons and 30 grandchildren rode on 70 donkeys. Abdon's family must have been extremely wealthy considering that only those of high stature rode on donkeys at the time. The name Abdon means "servant" and "slave." His duty was to live as a servant of God and foresee the coming suffering; he was supposed to awaken the nation from their spiritual numbness (Matt 24:45–46).

Nonetheless, he made no effort to fulfill his calling as "a servant of God" to govern the people and to save the distressed nation. Rather, he worked as "a servant of man," exerting his strength and investing his life only in his private affairs. We, too, have precious callings, but we need to truly examine ourselves to see if we only seek after our own interests and not those of Christ Jesus (Phil 2:21) and if we are absorbed in futile things in order to satisfy our greed (Ps 39:6).

12. Samson – שִׁמְשׁוֹן / Σαμψων

Man of sun, like the sun, sunshine

Background

Samson was the son of Manoah from Zorah of the family of the Danites (Judg 13:2). Zorah was a city located about 24 km (15 mi) west of Jerusalem, across Beth-shemesh where the temple of the sun god was located.

Period of Activity

Samson became a judge in Israel and ruled for 20 years (Judg 15:20; 16:31).

God gave the Israelites into the hands of the Philistines for 40 years because again they did what was evil in God's sight (Judg 13:1). It was while Samson was in Mahaneh-dan, between Zorah and Eshtaol, that the Spirit of the Lord began to stir him (Judg 13:25) and he was called as the savior of Israel from the Philistine oppression (Judg 13:5).

The name *Samson* is שִׁמְשׁוֹן (*šimšôn*) in Hebrew and means "sunlight," "like the sun," and "man of the sun." The name originates from the word שֶׁמֶשׁ (*šemeš*), which means "sun." In actuality, Samson, like the sun, was brilliant; he was a great warrior who fought fearlessly against the Philistines with strength, courage and passion.

1. Samson Was Born After the Angel's Annunciation

Samson was the son of Manoah (מָנוֹחַ: "resting place") from Zorah of the family of the Danites (Judg 13:2). Manoah's wife could not bear children, and the angel of the Lord appeared to her and said, "Behold…you shall conceive and give birth to a son…and he shall begin to deliver Israel from the hands of the Philistines" (Judg 13:2–7). After Manoah's wife heard the angel's annunciation, she conceived and gave birth to a son whom she named Samson. This scene is reminiscent of the angel Gabriel's annunciation to Mary, "And behold, you will conceive in your womb and bear a son, and you shall name Him Jesus" (Luke 1:31).

The child grew and the Lord blessed him and the Spirit of the Lord began to stir him in Mahaneh-dan (Judg 13:24–25). Even before Samson was born, God had a sovereign plan to use him to save Israel.

2. Samson Sought the Opportunity to Attack the Philistines

Samson went down to Timnah, a land about 7 km (4.5 mi) west of his home Zorah, and saw a daughter of a Philistine and planned to take her as his wife. Timnah was the land that Joshua had given to the tribe of Dan after the conquest of Canaan (Josh 19:40–43), but the Amorites later took it over, followed by the Philistines (2 Chr 28:18).

Samson's parents opposed Samson taking a wife from among the uncircumcised Gentiles, but Samson was stubborn to the end (Judg 14:1–3). Samson wanted to use the marriage as an excuse to strike the Philistines. He thought that if he married a Philistine woman, he would have increased contact with the Philistines and then he could find the right opportunity to strike them. For this reason Judges 14:4 states, "However, his father and mother did not know that it was of the Lord, for He was seeking an occasion against the Philistines. Now at that time the Philistines were ruling over Israel." This shows that it was God's will to strike the Philistines through Samson.

3. Samson Proposed a Riddle to the Philistines

Samson and his parents were on their way to Timnah to meet the Philistine woman when they arrived at a vineyard. There, a young lion suddenly attacked them. Samson had nothing in his hands, but the Spirit of the Lord came upon him mightily so that he tore the lion, the king of beasts, at once and killed it (Judg 14:5–6). The phrase, "the Spirit of the LORD came upon him mightily," means that by His sovereignty, God intervened so that this event occurred. This is a presage of how Samson would become as courageous as a lion and perform great work of saving the people against the Philistines.

Some time later, when Samson returned to take the woman, he saw that a swarm of bees and honey were in the body of the lion that he had killed. He ate the honey and also gave some to his parents and they ate it, but he did not tell them where he had gotten the honey (Judg 14:8–9). It is unlawful to touch a corpse even if he were not a Nazirite, but Samson did not abide by the law and touched the animal's carcass (Num 19:11).

Using the experience of the honey and the lion's carcass, Samson presented a riddle to the 30 Philistines during the seven days of the feast. Whoever solved the riddle within the seven days would receive 30 linen wraps and 30 changes of clothes (Judg 14:10–14). The riddle was "out of the eater came something to eat, and out of the strong came something sweet" (Judg 14:14). The wisdom of the Philistines was not enough to solve this riddle because it was based on Samson's personal experience with the honey and the lion's carcass. Through this event Samson wanted to expose the ignorance of the Philistines so that he might use it as an opportunity to gain dominance over them in the war against them.

Even after three days had passed, the Philistines could not solve this riddle. Thus, on the seventh day[52] they threatened Samson's wife saying, "Entice your husband, that he may tell us the riddle, lest we burn you and your father's house with fire" (Judg 14:15). In addition, they intimidated her saying, "Have you invited us to impoverish us? Is this not so?" (Judg 14:15b). The Hebrew word for the phrase, "impoverish us," is יָרַשׁ (yāraš) and it is a military term, referring to the act of conquering land and casting out its inhabitants with the intent to govern. They made an accusation against her, saying that she, a Philistine, had sided with Samson in order to conquer their land when, at that time, the Philistines were ruling over Israel (Judg 14:4; 15:11).

The Philistines' wicked threats and intimidation indicate that Samson's riddle was not a simple riddle presented during a feast to have a good time. Samson used this riddle in order to attempt to dispossess the Philistines of their control and to seek freedom from their oppression. The Philistines, however, appeared to have been aware of Samson's intention to a certain extent. This is why they tried so hard to solve his riddle and even resorted to threatening to burn Samson's wife and her father's house with fire.

Then Samson's wife pleaded with Samson in tears that he might tell her the answer to the riddle. She pressed him so hard that he told her the answer (Judg 14:17a).[53] Samson's wife then told the answer to her people (Judg 14:17b), hence the Philistines were able to answer the riddle easily. Knowing what had happened, Samson said to them, "If you had not plowed with my heifer, you would not have found out my riddle" (Judg 14:18b).

At this time, the Spirit of the Lord came upon Samson mightily so that he went down to Ashkelon in Philistia, killed 30 of them, took their spoil, and gave the clothes to those who had solved the riddle. Greatly angered, he went to his father's house (Judg 14:19). Then the father of Samson's wife gave her to Samson's friend (Judg 14:20).

What can we learn from the riddle that Samson presented?

First, Samson lost the bet with the Philistines because he did not keep the secret. Samson brought disaster upon himself by telling his wife the secret, which he did not even tell his parents, just because she pleaded earnestly (Judg 14:17).

Second, despite the fact that Samson had married a Gentile woman, touched a corpse, and drunk alcohol, thus breaking the rules of a Nazirite, the Spirit of God came down mightily upon him so that he could conquer the Philistines (Judg 14:19). This shows us that God advances the work of salvation to its end despite human weaknesses and shortcomings. The salvation of Israel rested totally upon God's grace, not upon Samson's strength.

Third, the Philistines were initially confident that the wisdom of the 30 Philistines would be great enough to solve the riddle of one man, Samson, but they were not able to solve it at all. There is no way of knowing or to understand the wisdom of heaven with earthly wisdom (1 Cor 1:20–21; 2:6–11). There is no way of knowing God's work without the Holy Spirit of God (1 Cor 2:10). Only those who fear God and have a close relationship with Him can know God's secrets (Job 28:28; Prov 1:7; 9:10; Ps 25:14; John 15:14–15).

4. Samson Triumphed by the Mighty Power of the Lord's Spirit

After a while, in the time of the wheat harvest, Samson decided to forgive his wife, who had disclosed the answer to the riddle, and to seek to reconcile with her. He took a young goat with him and looked for her, but her father had already given her to one of Samson's 30 Philistine companions because he had thought that Samson hated his daughter (Judg 14:11, 20).

Samson was greatly angered, and he caught 300 foxes, placed torches between their tails, lit them and released them in the standing grain of the Philistines. The heat of the fire terrified the foxes and everywhere they ran became a bed of fire, and in the end all the Philistine vineyards and groves were burned up (Judg 15:1–5). Angered by what had happened, the Philistines burned Samson's wife and her father (Judg 15:6) and, in turn, Samson slaughtered many of the Philistines who had killed his wife and father-in-law (Judg 15:7–8a).

After this, Samson went down and lived in the cleft of the rock of Etam where the beasts lived (Judg 15:8b), while the Philistines camped in Judah in order to take revenge upon Samson. When the Philistines attacked, the people of Judah could have joined forces with Samson to win the battle, but astonishingly 3,000 men of Judah gathered in order to hand him over (Judg 15:9–13).

Samson could have broken off the ropes with which the men of Judah bound him, but he allowed them to bind him because he did not want to cause trouble for his people (Judg 15:13). However, the moment the Philistines came to take the captured Samson, the Spirit of the Lord came upon him mightily so that the two new ropes that were binding his arms dropped like flax burned with fire (Judg 15:14).

The foolishness and selfishness of the people of Judah became apparent when 3,000 men attempted to hand Samson over to the Philistines. This incident reminds us of Judas who looked for an opportunity to hand Jesus over after receiving the 30 pieces of silver and finally betrayed him with a tender kiss as a sign to the Roman soldiers, telling them to bind Him well and take Him away (Mark 14:43–46; John 18:3–5). At the time, Jesus could have appealed to His Father so that more than 12 legions of angels would be at His disposal (Matt 26:53), but He did not attempt to avoid the cup of the cross; He laid down His own life as the redemption offering (John 10:17–18). However, Jesus resurrected after three days and broke the bonds of death and destroyed the work of the devil (Heb 2:14; 1 Jn 3:8).

The Spirit of the Lord (God's Holy Spirit) came upon Samson and he was able to take the fresh jawbone of a weak donkey and kill a thousand Philistines until their bodies formed a huge heap. Samson called the place *Ramath-lehi*, meaning "jawbone hill," in remembrance of the place (Judg 15:15–17).

After this intense battle, Samson became very thirsty and exhausted, and he called on the Lord, saying, "You have given this great deliverance by the hand of Your servant, and now shall I die of thirst and fall into the hands of the uncircumcised?" (Judg 15:18). God responded by splitting "the hollow place that is in Lehi so that water came out of it" (Judg 15:19). Samson then drank and his strength returned and he revived. Thus, he named the well *En-hakkore* (עֵין הַקּוֹרֵא), meaning "spring of the one calling," to commemorate the place (Judg 15:18–19).

If God had not performed the miracle at En-hakkore in accordance with Samson's cry to Him, he would have been captured by the Philistines. Although we may be at the point of death, if we totally rely on God and pray earnestly to Him, then He will answer us immediately, give us new strength and restore us so that we may be restored from despair.

The Bible states the following regarding the source behind Samson's ability to obtain victory during the on-going retaliatory battles: "And the Spirit of the LORD came upon him" (Judg 15:14). The Hebrew word for the phrase, "came upon him," is צָלַח (ṣālaḥ) in Hebrew and means "to advance," "to penetrate," and "to rush." Thus, this means that the mighty Spirit of God rushed upon Samson from above in a way similar to a powerful waterfall. When the work of the Lord's Spirit is fully upon us, nothing is going to be impossible. We will be able to fulfill the task God has given us and gain victory in our battles against Satan, our enemy (Eph 5:18).

5. Samson's Ultimate Mistake Was in Disclosing the Secret Behind His Power

After killing a thousand Philistines, Samson again went in to a harlot in Gaza. When the Gazites found out about this, they plotted to kill him, but Samson rose in the night and took hold of the doors of the city gate and the two posts and pulled them up along with the bars. Then, he put them on his shoulders and carried them up to the top of the mountain which is opposite Hebron (Judg 16:1–3).

After this, Samson came to love a woman in the valley of Sorek named Delilah (Judg 16:4). Then the lords of the Philistines came up to her and promised her 1,100 pieces of silver each if she could find out the source of Samson's strength (Judg 16:5). There were five lords of the Philistines, and thus she would receive a total of 5,500 pieces of silver (Josh 13:3; Judg 3:3). Considering that the pieces of silver are shekels of silver, 5,500 shekels of silver was a sum large enough to tempt Delilah's heart.[54] Samson lied to Delilah when she tried to find out the source of his strength. First, he told her that if she bound him with seven fresh cords, he would lose his strength. Then, he told her that if he were bound tightly with new ropes, he would lose his strength. The third time, he told her that if seven locks of his hair were woven into a web and fastened with a pin, he would become weak (Judg 16:6–14).

However, Delilah enticed him and pressed him every day with her words so that his soul was annoyed to death (Judg 16:16). In the end, Samson told her "all that was in his heart" and revealed that he was not to shave his head (Judg 16:17). Delilah saw that he had "told her all that was in his heart" and while he was asleep, she had the seven locks of his hair shaved off (Judg 16:18–19). Thus, Samson broke the vow of the Nazirite not to have a razor come upon his head (Num 6:5).

Samson, not knowing that the Spirit of the Lord had left him because his hair had been shaved off, awoke from his sleep and tried to shake himself free, but he had no strength. He was full of great strength when he had the sense of duty, but now he was helpless. The Philistines seized him and gouged out his eyes. He was bound with bronze chains like an animal and was forced to grind grain in the prison (Judg 16:21).

6. Samson Grabbed the Last Chance to Fulfill His Task and Killed the Largest Number of Philistines in His Life

The stone with which Samson was forced to grind was not the small grinding stone that the women used. It was a heavy millstone that slaves and the animals used(Matt 18:6). The Philistines praised Dagon their god and said, "Our god has given our enemy into our hands, even the destroyer of our country, who has slain many of us" (Judg 16:24). When they were in high spirits, they called for Samson so that he might amuse and entertain them (Judg 16:25). There were about 3,000 men and women who were watching as Samson entertained them (Judg 16:27). At this time, while Samson endured all sorts of indignity and humiliation, he stood between the two pillars that supported the temple and he cried out to God saying, "O Lord God, please remember me and please strengthen me just this time, O God, that I may at once be avenged of the Philistines for my two eyes" (Judg 16:28).

Then, Samson bent with all his might, and the temple fell along with the pillars so that all the lords of the Philistines and the people who were in it were crushed. Thus, the number of Philistines whom he killed at his death was more than all those whom he killed in his life (Judg 16:30). Samson's family took his body and buried him between Zorah and Eshtaol in the tomb of Manoah his father (Judg 16:31).

At one point, Samson shone with great light like the sun in his tremendous strength, but his life ended tragically because he went to Gaza and spent the night with a prostitute (Judg 16:1–3), and he fell in love with a woman in the Valley of Sorek whose name was Delilah (Judg 16:4). He did not keep the purity of his Nazirite vow and became sexually corrupt. As a result, he gave in to Delilah's continuous urging and revealed his secret to her.

Just as Delilah persistently enticed Samson, Satan also looks for opportunities to tempt believers, prowling about like a roaring lion (1 Pet 5:8). The seduction of a woman may be sweet, but it is like a double-edged sharp sword that leads to death (Prov 5:3–5). That's why Micah 7:5 states, "Do not trust in a neighbor; do not have confidence in a friend. From her who lies in your bosom guard your lips."

Samson was like the sun for the Israelites during the 40 years of Philistine oppression. He was supposed to shine the light of great hope for the Israelites as they were living in great misery. However, he could not withstand the pleasures of the flesh and lost the light of godliness and purity of his Nazirite vow. When he lost his two eyes, he became totally trapped in darkness. Those who do not keep the Word of God and are negligent in the duties that God has entrusted to them, ultimately end up in utter darkness (Ps 119:105).

The author of Hebrews records Samson as a man of faith (Heb 11:32). Although Samson lost his two eyes because he gave away his secret, he earnestly repented and cried out to God. Because he seized his final opportunity, God acknowledged his life as a life of faith.

Even today, how many times have we been tempted by this evil world so that we easily forget and discard the duties that have been entrusted to us? We cannot lift our heads before God if we consider all of our great shortcomings. Thus, like Samson, we should never miss the opportunity to repent when it is given (Gen 27:34, 36, 38; Ps 103:8–9; Heb 12:17).

If we have a contrite spirit and repent of our sinful lives with all of our heart, we can accomplish, like Samson, the great work of God, which is greater than any work we have done until now (Ps 34:18; 51:17; Isa 57:15; 66:2). We are forsaken sinners destined to die, but what greater grace could there be than receiving another chance to fulfill our duties?

God is ever patient and, in His patience, He overlooks our sins. He does not remember the sins that we have repented of and does not ask about them again (Ezek 33:14-16). God is like the sun (Ps 84:11). When we truly repent, the dark clouds of sin disappear, and the light of God's love shines again.

מדבר צין הוא קדש

עמלק

ים המלח

מדבר סיני

מדבר פארן

מדבר שור

שבט

שבט

שמעון

ארץ פלשתים

באר שבע

אלכסנדרי

ארץ גשן

פתם

רעמסס

צען

לוח המסעות במדבר
אשר על פי ה'יסעו ועל פי ה'יחנו

א' רעמסס'	טו' רתמה'	רט' הרהגדגד'	
ב' סכת	טז' רמן פרץ	ל' ימבתה	
ג' אתם	יז' לבנה	לא' עברנה	
ד' פיהחירת	יח' רסה	לב' עציונבר	
ה' מרה	יט' קהלתה'	לג' מדברצין	
ו' אילם	ד' הרספר	לד' הרההר	
ז' ים סוף	דא' חרדה	לה' צלמנה	
ח' מדבר סין	דב' מקהלה	לו' פונן	
ט' רפקה	דג' תחת	לז' אבת	
יו' אלוש	דד' תרח	לח' דיבןגד	
יא' רפידם	דה' מתקה	לט' עלמן דבל	
יב' מדברסיני	דו' חשמנה	מ' הרי עברים	
יג' קברתהתאוה	דז' מסרות	מא' ערבה מואב	
יד' חצרות	דח' בני יעקן		

PART FIVE

From Saul to David

David is the focal point and the most important figure in the genealogy of Jesus Christ. Why is David so important?

In Matthew 1:1–17, the name "David" appears five times (Matt 1:1, 6, 17). Of the three periods that make up Jesus' genealogy, David is the last person of the first 14 generations and the first person in the second set of 14 generations. He is the only person whose name appears twice in the genealogy. In addition, David is the only one who is recorded with the title, "king," among all the kings that appear in the genealogy (Matt 1:6). This shows us that the Old Testament prophecy that a king would come from the tribe of Judah was initially fulfilled through King David (Gen 49:10; Micah 5:2). However, the ultimate fulfillment of this prophecy is accomplished by the coming of the Messiah, the King of kings (Matt 1:1, 3, 6, 16).

In order to shed light upon David's life, we must first examine Saul's life. Although Saul became the first king of Israel and the channel for the establishment of true theocracy in Israel, he was abandoned by God after his disobedience and was forced to hand over the throne to David (1 Sam 15:23, 26–28). Saul was used as a stepping stone for the emergence of David's royal lineage, which would open the path for the coming of Jesus Christ.

Let us now turn our attention to the divine administration of redemption in the genealogy of Jesus Christ as revealed through the lives of David and Saul during the time of the unified kingdom.

CHAPTER 25

The History of King Saul

The prophet Samuel judged Israel in the latter years of the period of the judges until Saul became king. However, Samuel became old and he appointed his sons, Joel and Abijah, as judges over Israel, but they did not walk in the ways of their father. Instead, they went after dishonest gain and took bribes and perverted justice (1 Sam 8:1–3). At this time, all the elders of Israel gathered together and came to Samuel saying, "Now appoint a king for us to judge us like all the nations" (1 Sam 8:4–5).

In Hebrew, the name *Saul* (שָׁאוּל) means "desired" and "asked." It originates from the word שָׁאַל (*šāʾal*), meaning "to inquire" or "to request." Saul was the first king that the Israelites received as a result of their entreaty. He came to the throne at the age of 40 and reigned for 40 years (1050–1010 BC) over Israel (1 Sam 13:1; Acts 13:21).

The Israelites requested for a king because their hearts were lured away by the powerful governments headed by kings in the foreign nations. This request signified that they abandoned God and did not acknowledge Him as their true king (1 Sam 8:19–20; 10:19; 12:12–13, 17, 19).

God's ultimate purpose for leading the Israelites out of furnace-like Egypt was to establish His covenant with them, make them His people, and to become their God according to His pledge to their ancestors, Abraham, Isaac and Jacob (Deut 4:20; 29:13; 1 Kgs 8:51; Jer 11:4). For this reason the Bible repeatedly states, "Then I will take you for My people, and I will be your God" (Exod 6:7) and "I will also walk among you and be your God, and you shall be My people" (Lev 26:12; Exod 19:4–6; 2 Kgs 11:17; 2 Chr 23:16; Ezek 37:27; 2 Cor 6:16).

Accordingly, the Israelites were a people who were under the reign of God, but by asking for a visible king, they went against God's covenant. This was the Israelites' sin of forgetting the grace of God, which protected them until this point, and the sin of pride wherein they desired to provide their own salvation and protection. Because of the Israelites' act of betrayal, God lamented, "Listen to the voice of the people in regard to all that they say to you…they have rejected Me from being king over them" (1 Sam 8:7).

Through the prophet Samuel, God warned the people that they would face difficulties and suffer abuses if a king reigned over them (1 Sam 8:10–18). *First*, the young men and women ("your sons" and "daughters") would be recruited by the king (1 Sam 8:11–13). *Second*, he would take the best of their fields and animals (1 Sam 8:14–15, 17). *Third*, he would take their male and female servants, the best young men, and donkeys and would use them for his work (1 Sam 8:16). *Fourth*, he would take a tenth of their flocks (1 Sam 8:17). Thus, the king would make servants out of all the people and oppress them, and God will not answer the people when they cry out because of the king's tyranny (1 Sam 8:18).

However, the Israelites ignored God's warning and Samuel's advice and were persistent in requesting for a king (1 Sam 8:19–20), so that God ultimately allowed it (1 Sam 8:21–22).

Eventually, the Israelites were greatly distressed and suffered immeasurably at the hands of Israel's many evil kings. In reality, Saul recruited the people of the kingdom for his personal purpose (1 Sam 14:52). This was the result of the people's desire to be set free from the reign of God, the true King.

1. The Selection of Saul

(1) Private anointing

Saul met the prophet Samuel as he was out looking for his father's lost donkeys. The day before Saul arrived, God told the prophet Samuel, "…you shall anoint him to be prince over My people Israel" (1 Sam 9:15–16). Samuel ran into Saul about the time the prophet was going up to the high place to offer sacrifices, and God said, "Behold, the man of whom I spoke to you" (1 Sam 9:17). The prophet Samuel implied kingship for Saul when he said, "And for whom is all that is desirable in Israel? Is it not for you and for all your father's household?" (1 Sam 9:20). Startled, Saul said humbly, "Am I not a Benjamite, of the smallest of the tribes of Israel, and my family the least of all the families of the tribe of Benjamin? Why then do you speak to me in this way?" (1 Sam 9:21). Samuel again strongly hinted of Saul's royal destiny by placing him at the head of the table among the feast's 30 attendees. Saul was served the best portions, which were especially prepared for him (1 Sam 9:22–24).

Then Samuel went into the city and went up to the roof with Saul and spoke to him. Upon daybreak the next day, Samuel and Saul walked to the edge of the city and after all the servants had passed them and Saul was left standing alone, Samuel anointed Saul with oil and made him king (1 Sam 9:25–10:1).[55] After Saul was anointed with oil, the Spirit of the Lord came down upon Saul mightily so that he prophesied and was given a new heart. These became signs that God had established him as king (1 Sam 10:6–7, 9–10).

(2) Saul appointed king

Samuel called the people to Mizpah in order to choose a king. The prophet Samuel gave an order for 1,000 people from each tribe to come forth according to God's command, and he made them draw lots. First, the tribe of Benjamin was chosen. Then, the Matrite clan was taken from among the tribe of Benjamin. From among them, Saul, the son of Kish, was chosen (1 Sam 10:17–21). They took Saul who was hiding among the baggage and he was taller than the others from his shoulders upward (1 Sam 10:22–23). All the people were pleased with him and they shouted, "Long live the king" (1 Sam 10:24).

Certain worthless men among the people asked, "How can this one deliver us?" (1 Sam 10:27) and they despised Saul. However, the Spirit of the Lord came down mightily upon Saul so that he obtained a great victory in the battle against Nahash the Ammonite and saved the distressed people of Jabesh-gilead (1 Sam 11:1–11). Then, all the people went to Gilgal and made Saul king and offered sacrifices of peace offerings before the Lord (1 Sam 11:15).

2. Saul's Reign

(1) Battle against the Philistines

Saul became king at the age of 40, and he faced a great battle against the Philistines in the second year of his reign (1 Sam 13:1). The Philistines had 30,000 chariots and 6,000 horsemen. Their people were as many as the sand on the seashore (1 Sam 13:5). The Israelites, who had lost their will to fight against the Philistines, were in hiding, trembling with fear (1 Sam 13:6–7).

The prophet Samuel was to come and give an offering for the people before going out to war. However, he did not arrive even after seven days, which was the appointed time set by Samuel, and the people began to scatter. Then, Saul disobeyed God's Word by offering a burnt offering even though he was not a priest, and the prophet Samuel arrived as soon as Saul was done with the burnt offering (1 Sam 13:8–10). The prophet Samuel announced that God had forsaken Saul as a consequence of this disobedient act and that He would choose another man after His own heart to appoint as the new king (1 Sam 13:13–14).

Saul broke the law which states that only priests can offer sacrifices. He could not wait until the day ended and acted rashly and thoughtlessly, and consequently he received the fearful judgment of losing the throne.

On the contrary, Saul's son Jonathan was victorious in his battle against the Philistines through his strong faith in God (1 Sam 14:6). When Jonathan and his armor-bearer went into the camp of the Philistines and slaughtered some 20 men, God caused a "great trembling" to come upon the camp. Then the Philistines began to strike each other with swords and fell into a state of confusion so that the Israelites were victorious (1 Sam 14:15–22). Their victory on that day was totally the result of God's salvation which He had bestowed upon the Israelites (1 Sam 14:23).

After this victory, he used Saul to fight against "all his enemies on every side, against Moab, the sons of Ammon, Edom, the kings of Zobah, and the Philistines" and He gave them victory. God struck the Amalekites and delivered the Israelites from the hands of those who plundered them (1 Sam 14:47–48). Harsh war against the Philistines did not cease as long as Saul lived (1 Sam 14:52).

(2) War against Amalek

God was determined to completely destroy the Amalekites, the descendants of Esau's grandson Amalek (Gen 36:12, 16; 1 Chr 1:36) who harassed the Israelites continuously since the Exodus (Exod 17:8–16; Num 24:20; Deut 25:17–19; Judg 3:13; 10:12). God remembered how the Amalekites had opposed the Israelites in their wilderness journey, and He commanded King Saul to completely annihilate them (1 Sam 15:2–3). On the other hand, God protected the Kenites who had shown kindness to the Israelites on their journey from Egypt (1 Sam 15:6; Num 10:29–32).

God commanded Saul, "Now go and strike Amalek and utterly destroy all that he has, and do not spare him; but put to death both man and woman, child and infant, ox and sheep, camel and donkey" (1 Sam 15:3). However, Saul disregarded God's Word and spared Agag, the king of

Amalek, and "the best of the sheep, the oxen, the fatlings, the lambs, and all that was good" (1 Sam 15:9). He did not wholly obey God's command.

The prophet Samuel received a revelation regarding Saul's sin and rebuked Saul severely. However, Saul was busy making excuses instead of repenting.

First, Saul lied. He had disobeyed God's command, but he said, "I have carried out the command of the LORD" (1 Sam 15:13). *Next,* he shifted the blame to the people. He said, "They have brought them from the Amalekites, for the people spared the best of the sheep and oxen, to sacrifice to the LORD your God" (1 Sam 15:15, 21). He placed the blame on the people in order to conceal his own sin, showing his cowardice. Then the prophet Samuel made the crucial announcement regarding Saul's dethronement, saying, "Because you have rejected the word of the LORD, He has also rejected you from being king" (1 Sam 15:23, 26). After Samuel made this announcement and turned to go, Saul seized the edge of his robe and it tore (1 Sam 15:27). The tearing of the robe was symbolic of how his throne would be given to someone else (1 Sam 15:28). King Saul was rejected because he did not obey the command that God gave through the prophet Samuel.

> **1 Samuel 15:22** And Samuel said, "Has the LORD as much delight in burnt offerings and sacrifices as in obeying the voice of the LORD? Behold, to obey is better than sacrifice, and to heed than the fat of rams."

Truly, obeying God is better than offering sacrifices. Disobeying God's command is like the sin of divination. The law not only prohibits the practice of divination (sorcery and witchcraft), it states that anyone who practices such things must be stoned to death (Exod 22:18; Lev 19:26; 20:27; Deut 18:10–12).

In addition, being "stubborn" before God is like the sin of bowing to idols (1 Sam 15:23). The word *stubborn* is defined as "unreasonably or perversely unyielding."[56] In Hebrew, it is פָּצַר (*pāṣar*), meaning "to display pushiness" (i.e., arrogance, presumption). It connotes pride and conceit. Whether they relate to big or small things, there are many times when we set God's Word aside and become stubborn and proud in our own thoughts. Additionally, like King Saul, we become shameless and make excuses; by hiding our wrongdoing we try to display our own righteousness, placing the blame on others for our mistakes. If we obey God's Word as He has spoken, then the power of His Word is revealed and

God is glorified. However, when we oppose God's Word and disobey, our sins will cry out from within and will be revealed (Ezek 21:24), just as the sound of bleating of the sheep, and the lowing of the oxen which Saul had hidden reached Samuel's ears (1 Sam 15:14). Thus, the act of boasting of our deeds before God or hiding our sins from God is a vain and shallow tactic.

After this event, the prophet Samuel secretly met with Jesse's son David and anointed him with oil and made him king (1 Sam 16:13). God decided to reject Saul after he repeatedly disobeyed God's commands.

God holds firmly onto the people who hold onto God's Word. However, God has no choice but to reject those who disobey the Word and those who do not repent even to the end. God cannot use such people.

3. Relationship Between Saul and David

God chose David as king in the place of Saul and anointed him with oil at a time when there seemed to be no need for a new king.

(1) The emergence of David

The prophet Samuel cried out all night to God in distress on the day he heard that God regretted making Saul king because of his sin of disobedience (1 Sam 15:11). The prophet Samuel's heart was probably heavy-laden with bitter sadness since he had to relay the message that, although God had anointed Saul with great expectation (1 Sam 10:1), He now regretted that He had made Saul king. Samuel never went to see Saul again until the day he died because he grieved so much over Saul (1 Sam 15:35).

God spoke to the grief-stricken Samuel and asked, "How long will you grieve over Saul…?" and He commanded him, "Fill your horn with oil, and go; I will send you to Jesse the Bethlehemite" (1 Sam 16:1). God had commanded Samuel to take a heifer and go to Bethlehem as though he was coming to give a sacrifice offering, and then to invite Jesse to the sacrifice. Samuel, who was old and gray (1 Sam 12:2), obeyed God even though he could have been killed by Saul (1 Sam 16:2-4).

At first, the prophet Samuel saw the outer appearance of Jesse's oldest son Eliab and wanted to anoint him with oil and make him king. However, God told him that Eliab would not be king and that God had already rejected him. God said, "…for man looks at the outward appearance, but the LORD looks at the heart" (1 Sam 16:7). Thus, Jesse brought out his second son Abinadab, then his third son Shammah, until he made all his seven sons pass before Samuel, but there was no one among them whom the Lord has chosen to become king. Samuel said that he would not sit down to eat until the youngest son arrived. So Jesse sent and brought his youngest son David in. Now he was ruddy, with beautiful eyes and a handsome appearance. Thus, God said, "Arise, anoint him; for it is he" (1 Sam 16:12). Judging from the fact that David was tending the sheep alone when he was anointed with oil, he must have been about 15 years old.[57]

David was a mere shepherd boy who was not even called when the family offered sacrifices, but God anointed David and made him the sovereign king of Israel (1 Chr 17:7; Ps 78:70–71). Because God looks at the heart of man, if the heart is pleasing to God, then even the lowly and outcast can become great people who fulfill God's will (Acts 13:22).

Samuel anointed David with oil and from that day forward, the Spirit of the Lord came down mightily upon David (1 Sam 16:13). On the other hand, the Spirit of the Lord departed from Saul, and an evil spirit terrorized him (1 Sam 16:14). This is quite a contrast. Saul summoned David so that he might be freed from his agony. When David, whom the Lord was with, played the harp, Saul would be refreshed and be well, and the evil spirit would depart from him (1 Sam 16:23).

Sometime later, the Philistine army attacked Israel. The Philistines had a hero named Goliath whom no one could defeat. He was a giant whose height was six cubits and a span (approx. 9.5 feet, or 2.9 m). He wore a bronze helmet on his head and was clothed with scale-armor that weighed 5,000 shekels of bronze (approx. 126 pounds, or 57 kg). He also had bronze armor on his legs and a bronze javelin slung between his shoulders. The shaft of his spear was like a weaver's beam and the head of his spear weighed 600 shekels of iron (about 15 pounds, or 6.8 kg; 1 Sam 17:5–7). Goliath was fully armed and unbeatable. He also had a shield-carrier who walked before him (1 Sam 17:7, 41).

Goliath appeared before Israel's army morning and evening for 40 days and taunted the Israelites to start a fight, but Saul and all of Israel lost their motivation to fight at the sight of such an intimidating figure. They were greatly disturbed and trembled with fear (1 Sam 17:11). 1 Samuel 17:11 states, "When Saul and all Israel heard these words of the Philistine, they were dismayed and greatly afraid."

At this time, Jesse sent his youngest son David to the battlefield in order that he may bring back news about his sons (1 Sam 17:18). This was part of God's plan to use David to save Israel from her dangerous predicament. David went to the front line to meet his brothers and heard Goliath's insults against God (1 Sam 17:22–23). While all the people were greatly afraid and were fleeing from Goliath (1 Sam 17:24), David was not intimidated by Goliath's daunting physique. He said boldly, "For who is this uncircumcised Philistine, that he should taunt the armies of the living God?" (1 Sam 17:26). David's oldest brother Eliab rebuked him, but he was not at all deterred. He went to King Saul and encouraged him, saying he should not despair because of Goliath and volunteered to fight Goliath (1 Sam 17:28–32).

When David tended his father's sheep, he was able to chase a lion or a bear that took a lamb from the flock by the help of the Lord; he rescued it by striking the beast to death. Based on these experiences, he was certain that this uncircumcised Philistine who insulted God's army would become like those beasts and that God would save him (1 Sam 17:33–37).

After hearing David's words, Saul clothed David with his garments, put a bronze helmet on his head and armed him with his armor. Since David had not tested the armor and the weapons, he went out to fight in his ordinary shepherd's clothes (1 Sam 17:39, 50). He took his stick in his hand and chose for himself five smooth stones from the brook. He put the stones in the shepherd's bag which he had; and with a sling in his hand, he approached Goliath (1 Sam 17:40). Disdained, Goliath asked, "Am I a dog, that you come to me with sticks?" and cursed David by his gods. The Philistine threatened to make David's flesh food for the birds of the sky and the beasts of the field (1 Sam 17:43–44).

Yet, with even more courage, David proclaimed to Goliath, "You come to me with a sword, a spear, and a javelin, but I come to you in the name of the LORD of hosts, the God of the armies of Israel, whom you have taunted" (1 Sam 17:45, 47). Goliath rose and drew near. David ran quickly toward him. He put his hands into his bag, took a stone, and slung it. This stone struck Goliath on his forehead, and he fell facedown to the ground. David defeated and killed the Philistine using a sling and a stone. Then, David drew Goliath's sword from its sheath and cut off his head with it (1 Sam 17:49–51). When the Philistines saw that their champion was dead, they fled. The Israelites were greatly victorious (1 Sam 17:51b–54).

(2) Saul was displeased with David

When David returned victorious from the battle against the Philistines, the women sang "Saul has slain his thousands, and David his ten thousands" (1 Sam 18:7). As David's fame rose, Saul could no longer contain his anger at the thought that he would lose the throne to David.

> **1 Samuel 18:8** Then Saul became very angry, for this saying displeased him; and he said, "They have ascribed to David ten thousands, but to me they have ascribed thousands. Now what more can he have but the kingdom?"

The word *displeased* is רָעַע (*rāʿaʿ*) in Hebrew and means "to break," "to shatter," "to crack," and "to harm." This means that Saul's heart was scarred and irreversibly broken into pieces. The word *angry* is חָרָה (*ḥārâ*) in Hebrew and means "to burn," "to be kindled," and "to feel wrathful." This shows that Saul's anger burned to the highest degree.

Saul was greatly distressed and his emotions ultimately worked themselves up into a furor. As a result, an evil spirit came down mightily upon Saul and "he raved in the midst of the house" (1 Sam 18:10). The word *rave* is נָבָא (*nābāʾ*) in Hebrew and means "to prophesy," but is also used in a negative sense, as "to prophesy falsely." It signifies that Saul cried out like a crazy man. According to the *New Oxford American Dictionary*, the word *rave* means "to talk wildly or incoherently, as if one were delirious or insane."[58] Saul, possessed by an evil spirit, tried to kill David twice by throwing a spear at him (1 Sam 18:10–11).

When Saul's displeasure peaked, it turned into anger. Because of this anger, the evil spirit came down mightily, and this in turn led to the attempts on David's life. This shows us the fearful result of the feeling of displeasure. Thus, Ephesians 4:26–27 states, "Be angry, and yet do not sin; do not let the sun go down on your anger, and do not give the devil an opportunity." If there is anger in your heart, you are giving the devil an opportunity (cf. Gen 4:4–7).

After this, Saul gave his daughter Michal to David and made him his son-in-law, but he tried to kill David once again by throwing a spear (1 Sam 19:9–10). Saul also sent messengers to David's house to kill him, but Michal secretly let David out through a window so that he could escape (1 Sam 19:11–12).

For about 10 years thereafter (1020–1010 BC), Saul attempted to kill David and David was relegated to the life of a fugitive.[59]

The image of a frantic Saul who wanted to kill David out of envy calls to mind the image of the religious leaders who frantically tried to kill Jesus because of envy (Matt 26:2–5; Mark 14:1; Luke 6:11; 22:2; John 5:18; 7:1, 25, 30; 8:57–59; 10:31–33, 39; 11:53). However, just as David overcame evil with good and became king, Jesus Christ died on the cross and resurrected on the third day defeating the power of death, and He will come again in the end time to receive glory as the King of kings and the Lord of lords (1 Cor 15:25–26; Rev 17:14).

4. The Wretched Fall of Saul and His Entire Family

King Saul's disbelief had reached its peak. He committed a grave sin by sending his sycophantic servant Doeg the Edomite to massacre 85 priests (1 Sam 22:6–22, especially verse 18).

Then, King Saul was killed, along with his three sons, in the battle against the Philistines on Mount Gilboa. Saul was wounded in battle, so he fell upon his own sword and met a tragic end to his life (1 Sam 31:1–13).

The Philistines cut off his head, and fastened his headless body on the wall of Beth-shan (1 Sam 31:1–10; 1 Chr 10:1–6). When the inhabitants of Jabesh-gilead heard what had been done, they took the headless body down from the wall and burned it; they took the bones and buried them under the tamarisk tree at Jabesh and fasted for seven days (1 Sam 31:11–13; 1 Chr 10:11–12).

King Saul's remaining son, Ish-bosheth, came to the throne at the age of 40 and opposed David for two years, but eventually failed (2 Sam 2:8–10). He also met a tragic end when his two servants, Rechab and Baanah, struck him in the belly and killed him (2 Sam 4:1–8).

Saul's younger daughter, Michal, was David's wife, but she was cursed so that she had no child to the day of her death (2 Sam 6:23) because she had condemned David for dancing unclothed when the Ark of the Covenant was being brought back to Jerusalem.

We must not forget that another reason for the downfall of Saul's royal lineage was Saul's massacre of the Gibeonites. During the conquest of Canaan, Joshua had entered into a peace treaty with the Gibeonites in the name of the LORD. God did not allow him to kill the Gibeonites. From that time on, Joshua made them hewers of wood and drawers of water for the congregation and for the altar of the Lord (Josh 9:21–27).

However, King Saul committed a great sin before God by breaking this treaty, and as a result there was a three-year famine in the latter years of King David's reign (2 Sam 21:1–2). Because the covenant with the Gibeonites had been made so long ago, the people did not realize that the cause of the famine was related to the Gibeonites. However, God did not overlook the sin of breaking a covenant made in God's name. He made Saul's royal family face the consequences of their sin and punished them for killing the Gibeonites.

When the remaining seven descendants from Saul's royal family were handed over to the Gibeonites and hanged, prayer for the land moved God's heart (2 Sam 21:3–14). The seven men were the two sons of Saul's concubine Rizpah, Armoni and Mephibosheth, and the five sons of Saul's daughter Merab (2 Sam 21:8). Saul's concubine Rizpah truly showed a mother's love when she guarded the bodies of her two sons day and night from the birds of the sky and the beasts of the field. David was moved by this sad and pitiful woman's devotion, so he took their bones and buried them along with the bones of Saul and Jonathan (2 Sam 21:10–14). This was truly an hapless ending of Saul's family.

The devastating collapse of Saul's royal family line was caused by the sins that King Saul committed. *First*, King Saul despised the Word of God by not keeping it (1 Sam 13:8–14; 15:9, 22–23).

Second, instead of asking the Lord, he inquired of a female medium (1 Chr 10:13–14). When the Philistines attacked, King Saul disguised himself and went to see a medium at En-dor (1 Sam 28:3–19).

Third, he broke a covenant made in the name of God (2 Sam 21:1–14).

In actuality, the collapse of Saul's family was the result of God's extensive penal measures (Exod 20:5; 34:7; Num 14:18). Saul's death is a clear example of the final end of a person who repeatedly disobeys God's Word and who does not repent.

Israel found itself in the midst of a great crisis because of the disobedience of its first king Saul, but God chose David as the new king. Through David, God established a theocratic kingdom and began to work out His administration of the redemptive history by preparing for the coming of Jesus Christ.

CHAPTER 26

The History of King David

The prophet Samuel anointed David, Jesse's eighth son, as king when he was around the age of 15 (1 Sam 16:13). Then he entered the king's palace and played the harp to treat King Saul who had been tormented by an evil spirit that fell upon him (1 Sam 16:21–23). After David killed Goliath with a sling during the battle against the Philistines, the women responded with song as they played, "Saul has slain his thousands, and David his ten thousands" (1 Sam 18:7). As a result of this incident, Saul became indignant with David and began to pursue him.

However, God was with David so that the people praised him and his fame rose continuously (1 Sam 18:16, 30). Even King Saul realized that God was with David (1 Sam 18:28). Thus, Saul was envious of David and tried to kill him by throwing spears at him while he played the harp (1 Sam 18:11; 19:9–10). Saul also commanded messengers to go to David's house to kill him (1 Sam 19:11).

David found himself in a predicament and, realizing that the only One who could save him was God, he earnestly called out to Him for his life. Psalm 59 is the poem that David wrote at this time. The heading of Psalm 59 states, "When Saul had sent men to watch David's house in order to kill him." Saul's messengers had come to David's house and were lying in ambush in order to kill him the next morning (1 Sam 19:11). In Psalm 59, David refers to Saul's messengers as men who have "set an ambush for my life," "fierce men," men who have launched "an attack against me" (Ps 59:3), men who "howl like a dog and go around the city" (Ps 59:6, 14), "men of bloodshed" (Ps 59:2), men who "belch forth with their mouth" and men who have "swords in their lips" (Ps 59:7).

David was in a life-threatening situation where the sovereign king who had the entire kingdom in his hand was pursuing him relentlessly to destroy him. This is why David appealed to God to deliver him from his enemies and to raise him securely to a high place where they could not reach him (Ps 59:1–2). David boldly confessed his innocence and pleaded with God to rise, see his situation, and help him (Ps 59:3–4). He asked his righteous God to destroy the proud and evil men (Ps 59:11–13).

David had conviction that God was his refuge during his days of tribulation; he believed that God's strength was his strength and that God was his stronghold. He confessed that he would sing of God's strength and lovingkindness in the morning (Ps 59:9–10, 16–17). David faced the injustice of having his enemies trying to harm him with lies and deceit. Fierce enemies gathered their strength and prowled about looking to take his life. Yet, he stood firm with his faith in God and sang with conviction that the dawn of salvation would come. He sought and waited for God's mercy until the end.

God heard David's prayers and, using Michal who lowered David down from the window, He opened the path of escape (1 Sam 19:11–17). This was the beginning of David's long, long life of refuge.

1. David's Life of Refuge

The Bible records very detailed accounts of David's life of refuge (1 Sam 19–31). His flight began about 1020 BC, not too long after killing Goliath. His fugitive life lasted for about 10 years from this time until 1010 BC when David became king in Hebron. During his years of refuge, David faced many uncertainties and endured many hardships. Such experiences helped him to understand the hardships of others and to become a true leader who could overcome all kinds of adversities.

David's life of refuge can be divided into three stages.

Stage 1	The journey from Ramah to the forest of Hereth (About 1020–1018 BC, 1 Sam 19:18–22:23)
Stage 2	The journey from Keilah to the Wilderness of Ziph (About 1017–1015 BC, 1 Sam 23:1–26:25)
Stage 3	The journey from Gath, "the land of the Philistines," to Ziklag (About 1014–1010 BC, 1 Sam 27:1–2 Sam 1:27)

David took refuge in 16 locations. David's places of refuge seem to point to Jesus, the refuge for believers. Only God is our true refuge (2 Sam 22:3; Ps 14:6; 46:7, 11; 91:2, 9; 142:5; 144:2; Jer 16:19; Joel 3:16).

1 Ramah → 2 Gibeah (where Jonathan was) → 3 Nob → 4 Gath →
5 Cave of Adullam → 6 Mizpeh of Moab → 7 Forest of Hereth

The first stage of David's flight covered Naioth at Ramah to the forest of Hereth. During this stage, Saul's pursuit was so ferocious that David was completely absorbed in his search for places of refuge. This is evident from the reference map "David's Flight from Saul" (see endpapers), which shows that David had taken refuge in gentile lands like Philistia and Moab and that his first stage of flight was longer than the second and third. This was the period in which the 85 priests of Nob were massacred, and people began to gather around David. In the cave of Adullam, about 400 men (1 Sam 22:2) gathered and created a large community. Henceforth, David was not alone but was joined by a large group of people (1 Sam 22:6; 23:5, 8, 24, 26; 24:2–4, 22; 25:13, 20; 27:2–3, 8; 29:2, 11; 30:1, 3, 9, 30–31). This group of people was with David until he went up to Hebron after his life of refuge had ended (2 Sam 2:1–3).

2 Samuel 23:8–39 and 1 Chronicles 11:10–47 mention David's three mighty men and thirty chief men. These men gathered during the time of David's refuge. They stayed around, remaining faithful to David even after many people had left him during times of trial and adversities. We can gather from this that David's time of refuge was part of God's special plan. It was a period of blessing prepared by God for the final victory.

1 Ramah / רָמָה / 1 Sam 19:18–24

Ramah, meaning "high place," is located approximately 8 km (5 mi) north of Jerusalem. In later years, it became the border region between the northern kingdom of Israel and the southern kingdom of Judah. God who resides in the highest place is our place of refuge (Job 25:2).

With the help of Michal, David barely escaped Saul's attempt to kill him. Then, he fled first to Ramah because the prophet Samuel was there.

David reported to Samuel all that Saul had done to him. Together, they went and stayed in Naioth (1 Sam 19:18, Naioth was a "prophet school" during Samuel's time).

Saul heard that David was in Naioth and sent messengers to kill him (1 Sam 19:19–20). Three times he sent messengers to bring or to kill David, but they all came back prophesying instead (1 Sam 19:21). Then, Saul personally set out for Naioth, and he also prophesied until he reached Naioth. When he came before Samuel, he stripped off his clothes and prophesied, and he lay naked all that day and all that night (1 Sam 19:23–24). David was able to use this opportunity to escape.

Here, Saul's act of stripping off his clothes seems to show how he would later be stripped of his throne. Saul should have realized that he cannot stop God's work and that it is not God's will for him to kill David. However, Saul did not give up his plan to kill David.

2 To Jonathan at Gibeah / אֶל־יְהוֹנָתָן הַגִּבְעָתָה / 1 Sam 20:1–42

Gibeah was a city that belonged to the tribe of Benjamin (Judg 19:14; 20:10) as well as being Saul's hometown (1 Sam 10:26; 11:4). After Saul became king and defeated the Philistines, he named this place "Gibeah of Saul" and made it the capital city (1 Sam 15:34; cf. 1 Sam 23:19). *Gibeah* means "hill" or "small mountain," and the name *Jonathan* (יְהוֹנָתָן) means "the LORD has given."

David left Samuel and fled from Naioth in Ramah and went to seek Jonathan in Gibeah (1 Sam 20:1). Jonathan loved David as he loved his own life and had entered into a covenant with him in the past. At the time, Jonathan stripped off his robe and gave it to David, along with his armor, including his sword, bow and belt (1 Sam 18:3–4).

David survived Saul's numerous attempts to kill him (1 Sam 18:11, 17, 21, 25; 19:1), and his life was always in danger as if he were at the threshold of death. David came to Jonathan and confessed, "There is hardly a step between me and death" (1 Sam 20:3). These words expressed David's weakened and worried state of mind as he found himself suffering unjustly and pushed into problematic situations.

Before continuing his flight from Saul, David wanted to confirm Saul's intentions for a final time. This was because if David were fleeing when Saul had no intention of killing him, he would be eternally denounced as

Tel Zafit, Gath

Tel Maon, the Wilderness of Maon

A flock of sheep in Adullam

▲ A cave in Adullam | Scenery in Adullam ▶

Wadi Paran

▲ Tel Adullam | Jordan, near Madaba ▶

◀ A view toward Ramah | Pine trees on Mount Hereth ▲

Wadi Rum in southern Jordan

▲ A view from Tel Ziph | Ziklag, a view from Tel esh-Sharia ▶

Keilah

Ada Canyon in Wadi Paran

A flock of sheep in the vicinity of Carmel

Cattle at the foothill of Tel esh-Sharia

Wadi Arugot by the Dead Sea

▲ Nubian ibexes in En-gedi | David waterfall in En-gedi ▶

Acacia tree in Wadi Paran

The Judean desert from Mount Scopus

an unfaithful servant. It was Saul's own son, Jonathan, who gave David great help during this critical time.

It was when David fled from Naioth in Ramah to Jonathan that the two men made an agreement to protect one another. Jonathan promised to protect David as he requested (1 Sam 20:12–13) and asked David to protect him and his descendants in the future (1 Sam 20:14–16).

The New Moon festival came and Saul sat down to eat, but when he noticed that David's seat had been empty for two days, he commanded that David be brought to him and be killed (1 Sam 20:31). Jonathan defended and spoke out for David; enraged, Saul hurled his spear at him to strike him down (1 Sam 20:33). Jonathan realized that his father was determined to kill David. So he met with David using the sign with the arrows they had agreed upon.

As a sign of gratitude to Jonathan for saving his life, David fell to the ground and bowed three times to Jonathan, and they kissed each other and wept together, but David wept more (1 Sam 20:41). Jonathan had treasured David's life as his own and did everything in his power to help him. He consoled David as he suppressed his sorrow and encouraged David saying, "Go in safety, inasmuch as we have sworn to each other in the name of the LORD, saying, 'The LORD will be between me and you, and between my descendants and your descendants forever'" (1 Sam 20:42). After this, David and Jonathan had their last meeting in a forest in the Wilderness of Ziph (1 Sam 23:15–18).

Jonathan must have provided immeasurable strength and comfort for David during these critical times when his life was in danger. The name *Jonathan* means "the LORD had given." And indeed, Jonathan was a great and special gift from God to David—someone as precious as his own life.

Jonathan was Saul's son. If David were to die, Jonathan was the next in line to be king. Nevertheless, he saved David from trouble and acknowledged that it was God's will that David, not he, become king. His father Saul opposed God's sovereignty and was desperate to kill David, but Jonathan trusted wholly in God's sovereignty and only thought of David's safety.

Jonathan's brotherly love for David was "more wonderful than the love of women" (2 Sam 1:26). It overlooked all conditions and circumstances; it was unchanging from beginning to end, and it was without deceit. This kind of love would have been impossible without faith. Therefore,

Jonathan's love serves as a testimony to the greatness of his faith (1 Sam 14:6). Later, when Jonathan died along with his father Saul at the battle of Gilboa, David lamented for Jonathan by singing the "song of the bow" (2 Sam 1:18–27). David repaid Jonathan for his kindness and kept his promise by sparing the life of Jonathan's son, Mephibosheth (2 Sam 9; 21:7).

3 Nob / נֹב / 1 Sam 21:1–9

Nob was a city located about 1 km (0.62 mi) northeast of Jerusalem in a location where one could look down toward Jerusalem. It was also called "the city of priests" (1 Sam 22:19). The name *Nob* means "high place" and "high or lofty place of worship."

Jesus Christ died on the cross and resurrected on the third day. Then He was lifted high in glory to the right hand of God's throne (1 Tim 3:16; Heb 1:3; 7:26). Jesus, who resides in a place higher than the heavens, is our true refuge.

After confirming Saul's intention to kill him during his stay with Jonathan, David departed from Jonathan and began to live as a fugitive. The first place that David chose when he found himself in this difficult situation was Nob. Nob was the site of the tabernacle where sacrifices were offered to God, so David went to inquire of God regarding the future (1 Sam 22:10, 15).

Ahimelech the priest trembled in fear as he greeted David (1 Sam 21:1). Ahimelech was the king's son-in-law, and he was shocked to see that David, Israel's hero, had come alone without an entourage. He trembled from fear that something was wrong. That's why Ahimelech asked, "Why are you alone and no one with you?" (1 Sam 21:1).

David hid the fact that he was fleeing and answered that he had come alone because the king had commissioned him with a secret matter (1 Sam 21:2). David lied out of selfishness. He thought that if Ahimelech knew that he was fleeing from Saul, Ahimelech would not help him for fear of Saul's revenge. Thus, not knowing that David was fleeing, Ahimelech gave David bread and the sword of Goliath as David requested (1 Sam 21:8–9).

Doeg, the chief of Saul's shepherds (1 Sam 21:7), happened to be there at the time. Later when David was hiding in the forest of Hereth, Doeg reported to Saul that David had come to Nob (1 Sam 22:9, 22). As a result, Ahimelech and all the priests of his father's household were wrongly accused of treason, and the city of Nob was put to the sword. Men, women, children, infants, oxen, donkeys and sheep were all brutally killed (1 Sam 22:18–19). Saul's servants did not want to kill the priests, so Saul commanded Doeg to kill the 85 priests (1 Sam 22:17–18). Thus, David's lie became the cause of a calamity, a bloodshed of many innocent people.

4   Gath / גַּת / 1 Sam 21:10–15

Gath was located about 37 km (23 mi) southwest of Nob and about 42 km (26 mi) northeast of Gaza. It was one of the five cities of the Philistines. This city was located inland, to the south of Ekron. Since it was the easternmost city of the five cities of Philistia, Gath was the closest to Judah. The champion, Goliath the Philistine, was also from Gath (1 Sam 17:4).

Gath means "winepress." A winepress is a device where grapes are trampled and crushed to extract the juice (Lam 1:15; Isa 16:10). Just as people trample upon the grapes, the winepress imagery is also used to describe God's judgment (Rev 14:19).

David was afraid of Saul, so he rose up from Nob and went to Achish king of Gath in Philistia (1 Sam 21:10). David fled to Gath because it was close by and because he thought that Saul would not pursue him all the way into the territory of his own enemy. However, Achish's servants recognized David as the man who had killed Goliath the Philistine and reported it to King Achish (1 Sam 21:11). David greatly feared Achish, and he disguised his sanity before them. He barely saved his life by acting insane, scribbling on the doors of the gate and letting his saliva run down into his beard (1 Sam 21:13–15).

David wrote Psalm 56 when the Philistines seized him in Gath."The heading of Psalm 56 in the King James Version states "To the chief Musician upon Jonathelemrechokim." "Jonathelemrechokim" is a title of a poem which means "the silent dove of far-off places." This was a song lamenting his misery at being in a foreign land, far away from his home where God's tabernacle was located.

David could not settle anywhere safely because of the many people who secretly reported to Saul about his whereabouts (1 Sam 23:22–23, Ps 56:6; cf. 1 Sam 19:19; 23:7, 13, 19; 24:1; 26:1). It was truly a life-threatening run of a fugitive because he had to furtively move from one place to another, constantly seeking safety day and night. This was why

David entered the Gentile land of the Philistines in order to escape Saul's sword. However, David probably found himself drowning in sorrow as he realized he could not live safely even as an exile from his own country.

David did not know when his dangerous and nerve-wracking life of refuge would end. So in Psalm 56:8a, he states, "Thou hast taken account of my wanderings." This was a confession of his conviction that God had taken account of the days of his wretched wanderings due to his enemy's pursuit. At the same time, it is an earnest entreaty to God to remember the suffering and pain he sustained during his wanderings.

David felt such bitter sorrow during his refuge in Philistia that he prayed to God to put his tears in "Your bottle" (signifying a leather bag or pouch; Ps 56:8). How much did he cry that he could put his tears in a bottle?

Surrounded by enemies who sought to kill him, David suffered tremendously from the fear of being killed. Yet he realized that even this suffering was God's grace given to him according to His providence and thus confessed that he would trust in God to the end (Ps 56:3–4). Furthermore, he vowed to "praise his word" (Ps 56:4, 10; KJV). Though the present may have been an unbearable trial for him, David was determined to hold onto the immutable promises of God. His great confession of faith was that he will hope only in the LORD who fulfills His promises.

David saw that his enemies finally turned back when he trusted and prayed to God (Ps 56:9); and those who had pursued him left him unharmed (Ps 56:4, 11). God helps those who remember His Word and trust that He will keep His promises so that the evil one may not touch them (1 Jn 5:18). Although we find ourselves in the midst of tribulation too great to escape from, if we call out to God in tears, He will put our tears into His bottle and comfort us. He will keep an account of all our sufferings and repay our enemies.

David wrote Psalm 34 as he reminisced about his dramatic escape from King Achish of Gath.[60] The heading for Psalm 34 states, "A Psalm of David when he feigned madness before Abimelech, who drove him away and he departed." When it was known that he was the one who had killed Goliath, David found himself in a terribly volatile situation. In that life-threatening moment, it was through God's answer to his prayers that he was able to feign insanity and to escape alive. In Psalm 34:4 David confessed, "I sought the LORD, and He answered me, and delivered me from all my fears," and in Psalm 34:6 he confessed, "This poor man cried and the LORD heard him, and saved him out of all his troubles" (Ps 34:17–18). David received concrete and immediate answers as he found himself facing death, so he proclaimed in Psalm 34:5, "They looked to Him and were radiant, and their faces shall never be ashamed."

David lifted up to God his confession of hope through praises even when he was at the brink of death, and he was saved. God promises us that we surely will not be ashamed if we trust in the Lord and do not lose hope even in distressed circumstances when there seems to be no way out. (Ps 22:5; 25:3).

5   The Cave of Adullam / מְעָרַת עֲדֻלָּם / 1 Sam 22:1–2

Adullam was located about 16 km (10 mi) east-southeast of Gath and about 17 km (10.5 mi) northwest of Hebron. The name *Adullam* means "refuge," "hiding place" and "segregated place." Psalm 119:114 states, "You are my hiding place and my shield; I wait for Your word." Only God is our true refuge and hiding place (Ps 32:7).

David barely escaped to the cave of Adullam after his brush with death at Gath. Adullam was the city given to the tribe of Judah after the conquest of Canaan (Josh 12:15; 15:35).

David's brothers and his father's entire household went down to the cave of Adullam when they heard that he was there (1 Sam 22:1). It was a common practice at the time to kill the whole family because of one person (1 Sam 22:18–19), so David's family had come to be with David in the cave to seek refuge from King Saul. At this time, about 400 men—all those who were suffering trials, in debt and embittered—gathered around David (1 Sam 22:2). The young David gained understanding, patience, humility and broad-mindedness as he ruled over these people and began to acquire the qualities he needed to become the king of Israel.

While David was in the cave of Adullam, the Philistine army was camped close by in the valley of Rephaim. There, David had a craving for cool water from the well in his hometown and said, "Oh that someone would give me water to drink from the well of Bethlehem which is by the gate!" (2 Sam 23:15; 1 Chr 11:17). Immediately, the three mighty men broke through the camp of the Philistines and drew water from the well of Bethlehem that was by the gate. When David received the water for which the men risked their lives to fetch, he did not drink it, but poured it out to the Lord and said that it was "the blood of the men" (2 Sam 23:16–17; 1 Chr 11:18–19).

Psalm 142 is David's song about his loneliness and adversity while he was in the cave. The heading for Psalm 142 states, "Maskil of David, when he was in the cave. A prayer." Here, David describes his painful hardships and experiences as "my complaint" (Ps 142:2), "my trouble" (Ps 142:2), "when my spirit was overwhelmed within me ... for I am brought very low" (Ps 142:3–6). However, even in the midst of this tearful situation, David was full of hope and made this confession of faith, "You are my refuge, my portion in the land of the living" (Ps 142:5).

6 Mizpeh (Mizpah) of Moab / מִצְפֵּה מוֹאָב / 1 Sam 22:3–4

Moab, the son of Lot's older daughter, was the ancestor of the Moabites (Gen 19:37). The name *Mizpeh* means "watchtower." Mizpeh in Moab was a region located east of the Dead Sea, so David had fled very far. The name of the Lord is a strong tower (Prov 18:10), and only the Lord is a tower of strength against the enemy (Ps 61:3).

David fled from the cave of Adullam to Mizpeh in Moab. David's ancestor, Ruth (great grandmother), was a Moabitess and Saul was at war against Moab at the time (1 Sam 14:47) so he was able to entrust his parents to the king of Moab for a while (1 Sam 22:3).

As he entrusted his parents to the king of Moab, David said, "Please let my father and my mother come and stay with you until I know what God will do for me" (1 Sam 22:3). Although he faced uncertainty as he fled from Saul, he had conviction that God had planned and was guiding his every move as part of His providence. That's why even as he was entrusting his parents to the Gentile king, he did not succumb to human worries, but trusted only in God's sovereignty.

Although he was being pursued by the king of his nation and could barely take care of himself, David did not neglect his parents. He was especially concerned for their welfare and safety and took care of them. David possessed the true faith to fear the God above while respecting his parents on earth.

After David had left his parents with the king of Moab (1 Sam 22:4), he stayed in the stronghold (מְצוּדָה, *mĕṣûdâ*). Some believe that this "stronghold" refers to one of the strongholds in Moab, and others believe that this is Masada. The name *Masada* means "stronghold in the mountain," and it is a stronghold made of impregnable rocks located about 16 km (10 mi) south of Engedi, on the west coast of the Dead Sea.

⑦ The Forest of Hereth (Hareth) / יַעַר חָרֶת / 1 Sam 22:5–23

The forest of Hereth is located somewhere between Keilah and Adullam and is thought to be nearer to Keilah, but the exact location is unknown. The name *Hereth* means "a dense forest." Jesus Christ is also described as the "green tree" (Luke 23:31) and the "large tree" (Matt 13:31–32). Jesus Christ is the large and dense forest of life that can embrace the entire people of God.

Through the prophet Gad, David received the command to go into the land of Judah and went into the forest of Hereth (1 Sam 22:5).

Meanwhile, Saul heard from his servant Doeg that the priest Ahimelech "inquired of the LORD for him [David], gave him provisions, and gave him the sword of Goliath the Philistine" (1 Sam 22:9–10). Then Saul commanded Doeg to kill Ahimelech and the 85 priests in Nob and brutally massacred the men, women, infants, children and even the animals of Nob the city of priests (1 Sam 22:18–19).

Only one of Ahimelech's sons, named Abiathar, escaped with his life and fled to David to tell him what had occurred. David confessed that the cause of these deaths lay with him and told Abiathar to stay with him (1 Sam 22:20–23).

David's heart probably felt like it would collapse in misery as he thought about how Ahimelech and all the innocent priests were killed because of him. David was overcome with righteous indignation as he thought about Doeg and the bloody massacre he had committed.

David wrote Psalm 52 in the midst of great anguish and frustration. He called Doeg a "mighty man" (Ps 52:1) and pointed out that the terrible massacre in Nob was the result of Doeg's deceitful tongue. He also called him a "sharp razor, O worker of deceit" (Ps 52:2–3). If we use our tongues wisely, we can be like good medicine that heals and saves lives (Prov 12:18; 16:24), and we can refresh and delight those who listen (Prov 15:23; 23:16; 27:9), but tongues like Doeg's which plot against others are like a sharp sword that strikes and kills (Ps 57:4).

Those who do not rely on God but on their own strength and wealth like Doeg may appear to prosper for the moment, but they will be snatched up from their tents forever. They will be uprooted from the land of the living and be totally destroyed (Ps 52:5, 7). However, those who firmly trust in God even in times of despair will be as secure as the evergreen olive tree (Ps 52:8).

Stage 2 – The Journey from Keilah to the Wilderness of Ziph

1017–1015 BC, about three years, 1 Sam 23:1–26:25
(Route marked in red on see endpapers, "David's Flight from Saul")

---

[8] Keilah → [9] Wilderness of Ziph → [10] Wilderness of Maon → [11] Wilderness of Engedi → [12] Wilderness of Paran → [13] Carmel → [14] Wilderness of Ziph

---

About 400 people came and gathered around David at the cave of Adullam, which was the fifth place of refuge (1 Sam 22:2). At Keilah, which begins the second stage of David's life of refuge, this number increased to 600 (1 Sam 23:13; 27:2).

All of the places in which David took refuge during this second stage were in the wilderness except for Keilah, the first place of refuge. David received the bitter answer from God that the people of Keilah would give him up into the hand of Saul (1 Sam 23:12). As a result, he was forced to escape from Saul's grasp and roam about in the wilderness. He spent the next three years fearfully wandering in uninhabited places, teeming with beasts. He went from the Wilderness of Ziph (1 Sam 23:15) to the Wilderness of Maon (1 Sam 23:24) to the Wilderness of Engedi (1 Sam 24:1) and to the hill of Hachilah in the Wilderness of Ziph (1 Sam 26:1–3). When David heard that Samuel had died, he took refuge in a distant land, in the Wilderness of Paran (1 Sam 25:1).

After David was anointed as king of Israel, he first had to endure the extreme suffering and countless bouts of despair in the terrifying and desolate wilderness before he could enjoy the comfort and power that comes with being the most powerful person in the kingdom. Furthermore, he was tried through excruciating pains of solitude, which resulted from the backstabbing and betrayal by even his own people whom he saved.

8 · Keilah / קְעִילָה / 1 Sam 23:1–13

Keilah was an important city located in Judah almost 14 km (about 9 mi) northwest of Hebron. The name *Keilah* means "fortress" and "strategic place." A fortress is a large fortified place and a defense facility. God is our true fortress (2 Sam 22:2, 33; Ps 18:2; 91:2; 144:2).

David faced another unexpected problem at the same time as he received the sad news about the massacre of the priest Ahimelech and many others. While David was residing in the forest of Hereth, the Philistines attacked Keilah and plundered the threshing floors (1 Sam 23:1). The Philistines had come all the way into Keilah, Israel's strategic fortress, in order to plunder food.

At this time, David did not act of his own accord. Instead he asked God, "Shall I go and attack these Philistines?" As a result of his life in refuge, David had obtained the faith to inquire of God first before doing anything. So God answered David, "Go and attack the Philistines, and deliver Keilah" (1 Sam 23:2). However, the people around him tried to dissuade him, saying that the situation was not in their favor and that it was not the right time for them to strike the Philistines. Then, David inquired of God again, and God confirmed, "Arise, go down to Keilah, for I will give the Philistines into your hand" (1 Sam 23:4).

Even in the worst predicaments, David trusted and obeyed the Word of God only. Consequently, he gained a great victory in his battle against the Philistines. At the same time, he obtained livestock as booty and saved the people of Keilah (1 Sam 23:5). With the victory at Keilah, people probably no longer viewed David as a fugitive, but began to recognize him as the savior and leader of Israel.

David obeyed God and saved Keilah by driving out the Philistines, but someone reported to Saul that David was in Keilah (1 Sam 23:7), and David's whereabouts were exposed. Saul rejoiced saying, "God has delivered him into my hand, for he shut himself in by entering a city with double gates and bars," and he summoned all the people to war (1 Sam 23:7–8). Even though it was only right that the people of Keilah should stand on the side of David their savior, they turned on him as soon as Saul uttered his threats against them. David must have felt an immense sense of disappointment and betrayal.

David had to quickly flee from Keilah following God's Word given to him through the Urim and Thummim (1 Sam 23:9–12). The Bible describes David's flight from Saul as "they went wherever they could go" (1 Sam 23:13). This means that whenever David was pursued by Saul, he went wherever he could go to avoid danger, wherever was best in the given situation, without having a fixed course or destination. Regarding David's life of refuge, the Bible comments, "And David stayed in the wilderness in the strongholds, and remained in the hill country in the Wilderness of Ziph. And Saul sought him every day…" (1 Sam 23:14).

David escaped death many times, drank the bitter cup of betrayal and rebellion, and lived a wandering life of a fugitive. However, David never placed his hope in man, so he never blamed anyone. Instead, he learned to have faith that drew close only to God and to only seek after His consolation.

9   The Wilderness of Ziph / מִדְבַּר זִיף / 1 Sam 23:14–23

The Wilderness of Ziph was located about 6 km (4 mi) southeast of Hebron. It was a secure city in Judah located among the mountains in Maon (Josh 15:24, 55) and a village located in the southern part of the central mountainous regions in Judah (Josh 15:24). Ziph is זִיף (*zîp*) in Hebrew and means "to dissolve." Ziph originates from the Hebrew word זֶפֶת (*zepet*) which means "to melt." Through trials, God melts away all the impurities in our lives so that we may possess faith as pure as refined gold (Job 23:10; Ps 12:6; 26:2; 66:10; 105:19).

David left Keilah and stayed in the wilderness in the strongholds, and remained in the hill country in the Wilderness of Ziph located in the central mountainous regions in Judah about 20 km (12 mi) southeast of Keilah (1 Sam 23:14a). Saul looked for David every day in order to kill him, but God did not deliver him into his hand (1 Sam 23:14). This means that nothing can be achieved without God's consent no matter how much one may try (Matt 10:29).

David met Jonathan for the last time in the woods of the Wilderness of Ziph. Jonathan helped David to rely wholly on God when David was most weakened by despair. Furthermore, Jonathan imbued David with hope by telling him that he would surely become king (1 Sam 23:15–18). He gave David confirmation that his father Saul's hands would not touch him, and told him that even Saul knew that David would become king of Israel (1 Sam 23:17). Even in this overwhelming situation, all of

Jonathan's words of faith reached David like the voice of God and probably gave him more strength than thousands of troops and horses.

However, David had to flee to the Wilderness of Maon in the Arabah to the south of the Judean Wilderness (יְשִׁימוֹן, yĕšîmôn; "desert" or "wasteland"), because the people of Ziph had reported David's whereabouts to Saul (1 Sam 23:24).

David stayed in the land of Ziph twice during his life of refuge, and twice the people of Ziph exposed David's location to Saul (1 Sam 23:19; 26:1). The city of Ziph was over 40 km (25 mi) from Gibeah, and yet the people traveled all the way to the capital city of Gibeah in order to expose David to Saul (1 Sam 23:19; 26:1). The people of Ziph were diligent in searching out David's whereabouts and reporting it to Saul (Ps 54:1), as if it was their duty to place David into Saul's hands (1 Sam 23:20). As a result, David found himself in a desperate situation where he was surrounded by Saul and his men while he was hiding in the woods of the Wilderness of Ziph (1 Sam 23:26).

David wrote Psalm 54 when he was cornered in a situation that was humanly impossible to solve. The heading of Psalm 54 states, "When the Ziphites had gone to Saul and said, 'Is not David hiding among us?'"

While his enemies were seeking his life (Ps 54:3), the first thing David did was call out to God, "Save me, O God, by Your name" (Ps 54:1). During his times of tribulation, he relied on the name of God who is faithful to His covenants, and at the same time David experienced His help. This enabled him to give thanks before the name of God (Ps 54:6). All the feelings of anger and betrayal toward the people of Ziph disappeared, and David thanked God for His help in times of trouble and praised His name (Ps 54:4, 7).

Whenever we face an imminent crisis during our lifetime on earth, we should not resort to blame and resentment or give in to complaints regarding our situation. What we need to do instead is to rely on God's name in times of trouble and seek His help until the end (Ps 143:11).

10 The Wilderness of Maon / מִדְבַּר מָעוֹן / 1 Sam 23:24–29

David moved to the Wilderness of Maon, which is located about 8 km (5 mi) south of the Wilderness of Ziph. Maon was a city belonging to the tribe of Judah, located in the central mountainous regions in Palestine

(Josh 15:55). It was a rugged mountainous region located about 13 km (8 mi) south of Hebron. The name *Maon* means "residing" and "habitation." The word "residing" refers to the act of settling down in a specific place. The Almighty God is a secret shelter in which all believers must reside forever (Ps 27:5; 31:20; 91:1–2).

Saul found out that David was in the Wilderness of Maon and went there to kill him. Saul was on one side of the mountain and David was on the other. David, who had escaped numerous life-threatening situations thus far, was in a desperate predicament, about to be captured and killed by Saul (1 Sam 23:26). 1 Samuel 23:26 describes this situation as, "Saul and his men were surrounding David and his men to seize them."

Right about that time, Saul received an urgent report that the Philistines had attacked, and he had no choice but to abandon the pursuit of David in order to go and fight the Philistines. David and Saul were separated in this place so they called it the "Rock of Escape" (סֶלַע הַמַּחְלְקוֹת, *sela'hammaḥēlēqôt*) (1 Sam 23:28). God protected David so that Saul could not cross over to him, and He took Saul away from him.

This miraculous event shows us that God governs all history and even controlled the timing of the Philistines' attack in order to fulfill His plan of salvation.

[11] The Wilderness of Engedi / מִדְבַּר עֵין גֶּדִי / 1 Sam 23:29–24:22

Engedi was the name of the spring and stream located to the east of Hebron, as well as the name of the Judean wilderness just to the west of the Dead Sea (Josh 15:62). The name *Engedi* means "spring of the young goat." Coming to a spring in the barren and scorched wilderness is an encounter with a precious life-giving place of refuge. Jesus Christ provides living waters to thirsting human beings so that they may never thirst again (John 4:10, 14; Rev 21:6). He guides us to the springs of the water of life (Rev 7:17).

David stayed in a cave near the Wilderness of Engedi, as he was hiding from Saul (1 Sam 23:29; 24:3). Later, when Saul returned from his battle against the Philistines, he heard that David was in the Wilderness of Engedi (1 Sam 24:1). Then, he took 3,000 chosen men from all throughout Israel and went to the Wilderness of Engedi to find David. There, Saul had to go into a cave to relieve himself (1 Sam 24:2–3).[61]

At that time, David happened to be hiding deep inside the same cave. The opportunity had come for David to take revenge on Saul. Yet David did not take advantage of the opportunity; he merely cut off the edge of Saul's robe in silence (1 Sam 24:3–4). In addition, he did not allow his men to harm Saul (1 Sam 24:7). David acted in this manner because Saul was the Lord's anointed, and David believed that God would directly intervene in regard to this matter (1 Sam 24:12). David cut off a piece of Saul's robe in order to prove his innocence and faithfulness (1 Sam 24:10–11), but even this act bothered his conscience (1 Sam 24:5). In truth, David's conscience of faith was pure (Acts 23:1; 24:16).

Although David had the perfect opportunity to take revenge on Saul, he abstained from killing him. Moreover, David assumed a humble attitude and exalted his enemy as "king," while referring to himself as "a dead dog, a single flea" (1 Sam 24:14). David humbly said to Saul, "my hand shall not be against you" (1 Sam 24:13). This instantly melted Saul's wicked and obstinate heart and he acknowledged David's royal authority. Saul then made David swear by the name of God that he would not destroy Saul's descendants (1 Sam 24:20–22).

Then Saul lifted up his voice and wept, "You are more righteous than I; for you have dealt well with me, while I have dealt wickedly with you" (1 Sam 24:17). Saul repented, even if it was just for that moment, and he then went home (1 Sam 24:22).

The image of David entrusting judgment to God and desiring to overcome evil with good calls to mind Jesus who entrusted everything to God and walked the way of the cross silently through all the jeering and mockery.

David wrote Psalm 57 based on his experience in the cave. The heading for Psalm 57 states, "When he had fled from Saul into the cave." David described his painful experience with the words, "My soul is among lions; I must lie among those who breathe forth fire, even the sons of men, whose teeth are spears and arrows, and their tongue a sharp sword" (Ps 57:4).

During times of despair, David trusted completely in God and cried out to him, "To God who accomplishes all things for me" (Ps 57:2). He also made a resolution to awake the dawn and to give thanks and praise to God (Ps 57:8–9). In Psalm 141, which he wrote as he reflected upon his time in Engedi, he prayed, "Keep me from the jaws of the trap which they have set for me, and from the snares of those who do iniquity" (Ps 141:9).

Even as he experienced intense suffering, he felt secure and did not give way to anxiety nor did he complain. Instead, he woke up at dawn and cried out to God and did not cease singing praises and giving thanks.

After David parted with Saul, he and his men went up to the stronghold (מְצוּדָה, mĕṣûdâ; 1 Sam 24:22). The stronghold mentioned here is believed to be the impregnable fortress of Masada (Μεσσαρα, LXX) located about 16 km (10 mi) south of Engedi. It is believed that David passed through this place during his life of refuge.

⟦12⟧ The Wilderness of Paran / מִדְבַּר פָּארָן / 1 Sam 25:1

The Wilderness of Paran was a desert located northeast of the Sinai Peninsula. Kadesh-barnea, from which Moses sent the 12 spies, was also part of the Wilderness of Paran (Num 13:3, 26). Hagar and Ishmael also took refuge in the Wilderness of Paran after Abraham cast them out (Gen 21:21). The name *Paran* means "land with many caves," so it is presumed that it was a place where people could easily take refuge in times of danger. God is like a cave where we can take refuge from all the unjust threats of this world (Ps 32:7; 119:114).

David was shocked to hear that the prophet Samuel had died, so he went down to the Wilderness of Paran with a troubled heart. David fled very far away from his stronghold, to the Wilderness of Paran, which was the southernmost point David had reached during his flight. With the death of the only spiritual leader who could curb King Saul, it was likely that Saul would threaten David's life with more vigor. Therefore, it was probably David's best choice to flee to a very distant place.

Samuel was the nation's lamp who had provided light in the spiritually darkened era of the judges. He was the nation's father and a great prophet. When David first fled from Saul after Samuel anointed him, the first place he fled to was Naioth in Ramah where Samuel was. The prophet Samuel was like a great pillar in David's heart. David was shaken up by the news of the death of Samuel, the spiritual father and great prophet. He probably felt an anticipation of dread in his already burdened heart. This must have drained all the strength from him.

Carmel was located about 11 km (7 mi) south-southeast of Hebron, and the name means "vineyard" and "orchard." Isaiah 27:3 states, "I, the LORD, am its keeper" (keeper of the vineyard). The vineyard that the almighty God keeps is the refuge for all believers (Isa 5:7).

David entered Carmel in Maon from the Wilderness of Paran (1 Sam 25:2), in a truly difficult predicament again. Not only was the king of the nation pursuing him with his army by day and night so that he had to flee to the wilderness, but the multitude who followed him had grown to 600 people so he had to bear the burden of feeding them as well.

David sought help from a rich man named Nabal living in Maon in order to obtain food for his people. He sent ten young men to Nabal as he was shearing his sheep (1 Sam 25:5–8) in Carmel which was about 2 km (1.2 mi) from Maon. Nabal was very rich and had 3,000 sheep and 1,000 goats (1 Sam 25:2). However, David's young men returned with nothing but insults from Nabal (1 Sam 25:9–11).

Not only did David save Israel numerous times and protect people's lives and possessions, he also acted as a protective barrier for Nabal's shepherds and flock when he was living as a refugee in the wilderness (1 Sam 25:15–16). Nonetheless, Nabal treated David like an evil servant who had fled from his master Saul and turned him down without a second thought, saying, "Who is David? And who is the son of Jesse? There are many servants today who are each breaking away from his master" (1 Sam 25:10).

Nabal's refusal of David's request was a ruthless act of returning a good favor with evil. The name *Nabal* means "flat" and "tasteless" and is used to refer to a foolish person. In accordance with his name, Nabal was harsh and evil in his dealings (1 Sam 25:3). Even his servant said of him, "he is such a worthless man that no one can speak to him" (1 Sam 25:17).

Infuriated, David took 400 soldiers and advanced toward Carmel where Nabal was shearing his sheep, intending to kill him. However, one of his servants told Nabal's wife Abigail about this urgent situation and spoke well of David (1 Sam 25:14–17). Abigail wasted no time and went to meet David with all the best provisions she had hurriedly prepared (1 Sam 25:18–20). When she saw David, she fell down at his feet with her face to the ground (1 Sam 25:23–24a). She called her husband's act of ingratitude "evil" and pleaded for the blame to fall upon her as she humbly requested, "And please let your maidservant speak to you, and listen to the words of your maidservant" (1 Sam 25:24b). Abigail's gentle and wise words appeased David's anger and prevented him from taking revenge on his enemy by shedding blood with his own hands (1 Sam 25:25–28). It was just as it is written, "And a soft tongue breaks the bone" (Prov 25:15).

Abigail also gave David conviction regarding God's protection.

> **1 Samuel 25:29** And should anyone rise up to pursue you and to seek your life, then the life of my lord shall be bound in the bundle of the living with the LORD your God; but the lives of your enemies He will sling out as from the hollow of a sling.

The "bundle of the living" that Abigail referred to came from the ancient Near Eastern practice of wrapping up treasures or precious articles for safe keeping. The word *bundle* from "bundle of the living" is צְרוֹר (*sĕrôr*), meaning "bundle," "parcel," and "pouch." It is derived from צָרַר (*sārar*), meaning "to bind" and "to wrap." This means that God had especially wrapped up David's life like His precious treasure so that he would be safe and unharmed.

The phrase, "shall be bound," is the participle form in the passive voice of the Hebrew word צָרַר (*sārar*), and it shows that David was continuously receiving God's protection. The phrase, "shall be bound in the bundle of the living," is the repetition of the same Hebrew word and shows that God had safely wrapped up David's life like a very precious and special treasure in the "bundle of the living," so that his life would not be harmed no matter how hard the enemy tried. More importantly, David was not wrapped up alone in the bundle of the living; he was wrapped up "with the Lord."

This statement about the Lord who is sovereign over life being "wrapped up" in the bundle of the living with David must have been an unforgettable encouragement and comfort to David every time danger approached during his life of refuge.

Abigail was a woman who possessed historical insight, and she knew that David would become king. She had conviction that God would appoint David as "ruler over Israel" and told him that he should not stain himself by killing Nabal with his own hands (1 Sam 25:30–31). Here, the word *ruler* used in this passage is נָגִיד (*nāgîd*) in Hebrew meaning "leader," "ruler," and "captain." It is another way of referring to the king. Abigail was convinced that David would become a great king in the future.

Abigail's words were a great comfort at a time when David was especially lonely and exhausted after Samuel's death. Her words were as strong as the words of a prophet that rekindled the spiritual wick of his stagnant faith and brightened his soul. Just as the name *Abigail* means "joy of my father," she was a joy to her father because she was intelligent and beautiful with a compassionate heart, poised and wise in all her dealings. Her wise teachings became the "fountain of life" that turned aside snares of death from her household (Prov 13:14). In truth, each and every word spoken by faith is full of the flavor and charm of godliness, "like apples of gold in settings of silver" (Prov 25:11).

When Abigail returned home after meeting with David, she found a drunk and merry Nabal holding a feast fit for a king in his house. She did not tell him anything until the morning dawned (1 Sam 25:36). After Nabal awoke from his wine, Abigail told him all the things that David had planned and had done. As soon as Nabal heard this, his heart died within him so that he became as a stone. About ten days later, the Lord struck him, and he died suddenly (1 Sam 25:37–38). David witnessed how God Himself had avenged those who insulted him so that he did not have to use the sword himself (Deut 32:35, 41, 43; Isa 35:4; Rom 12:19; 1 Thes 4:6; Heb 10:30).

As soon as Nabal died, Abigail became David's wife in accordance with his proposal (1 Sam 25:39–42), and Abigail accompanied David through the remainder of his life of refuge (1 Sam 27:3; 30:5, 18).

Nabal received the grace of life from a man of God, David, but he scorned his words and received just retribution. The final state of the ungrateful, foolish man who repaid grace with evil was truly wretched. Ultimately, he was struck down and killed by the hand of God, not by the hand of David. Let us also examine ourselves today. Have we not forgotten the grace that we've received from God? Have we not ignored His requests for us in our lives?

[14] The Wilderness of Ziph / מִדְבַּר זִיף / 1 Sam 26:1–15

As we have already seen, the Wilderness of Ziph was David's ninth place of refuge. It was located about 6 km (4 mi) south-southeast of Hebron.

Ziph was a secure city in Judah in the mountainous regions of Maon (Josh 15:24, 55) and a village in the southern part of the central mountainous region in Judah (Josh 15:24).

David hid in the hill of Hachilah in the Wilderness of Ziph (1 Sam 26:1–3). When Saul heard a report about this, he took 3,000 of his men with him to pursue David. That night Saul fell into a deep sleep (1 Sam 26:2, 5) that God had caused upon him (1 Sam 26:12). In the past, David had faced danger from the people of Ziph (1 Sam 23:19). This time, he sent spies (1 Sam 26:4) and confirmed that Saul's army was coming. David, accompanied only by Abishai, went into the heart of the encampment of Saul and his army. When Abishai said that he would strike Saul down with one stroke of the spear (1 Sam 26:8), David told him not to kill Saul. Instead, David quietly took the spear and the water jug near Saul's head. Just as David had only cut off a piece of Saul's robe in Engedi and did not kill him (1 Sam 24:4–11), he left Saul untouched again (1 Sam 26:9–11).

From a distance, David rebuked Abner the general for not doing a good job of guarding Saul and said that he must "surely die." Then he pleaded with Saul to stop pursuing him (1 Sam 26:15–20). Just as he had humbly lowered himself at Engedi by calling himself "a dead dog, a single flea" (1 Sam 24:14), again he humbled himself before Saul by referring to himself as "a single flea" (1 Sam 26:20).

Although David had had two opportunities to kill Saul and usurp the throne, he waited until the appointed time when God Himself would crown him. David truly lived a God-centered life.

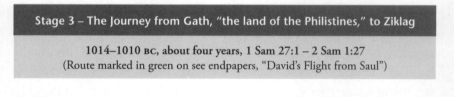

Stage 3 – The Journey from Gath, "the land of the Philistines," to Ziklag

1014–1010 BC, about four years, 1 Sam 27:1 – 2 Sam 1:27
(Route marked in green on see endpapers, "David's Flight from Saul")

15 Gath → 16 Ziklag

The third stage of David's life of refuge, from the Philistine land of Gath until the conclusion of his flight at Hebron, started about six years since the beginning of his flight. When he found himself in extreme danger once again, he was forced to take asylum in Philistia (Gath and Ziklag).

When King Saul found out that David had fled to Gath in the land of the Philistines, he no longer searched for him (1 Sam 27:4).

While David was hiding from Saul in Ziklag, many men from the tribes of Gad, Benjamin, Judah, and Manasseh came to the rugged wilderness where David resided, and enlisted as soldiers (1 Chr 12:1–22). In fact, men came to David every day until a "great army" had been formed. 1 Chronicles 12:22 states, "there was a great army like the army of God."

In 1010 BC, the Philistines defeated Saul in the battle at Mount Gilboa and he and his three sons (Jonathan, Abinadab and Malchi-shua) died in the battle (1 Sam 31:1–6). With his death, Saul's endless pursuit came to a close along with David's life of refuge. David was now able to return to Hebron (2 Sam 2:1–3).

15   Gath / נַת / 1 Sam 27:1–4

As we have already seen, Gath was the fourth stop on David's fugitive journey. It was also one of the five cities of the Philistines, and it means "winepress."

After David had parted with Saul at the hill of Hachilah, he thought that fleeing to Philistia was his best choice, and so he returned to King Achish of Gath for the second time.

There were 600 warriors with David at this time (1 Sam 27:2) and each man had his own household (1 Sam 27:3), so it is estimated that the total number of people who journeyed with David was over 2,000. David also had his two wives, Ahinoam and Abigail, with him (1 Sam 27:3).

Saul heard that David was in Gath and stopped pursuing him. 1 Samuel 27:4 states, "Now it was told Saul that David had fled to Gath, so he no longer searched for him."

16   Ziklag / צִקְלַג / 1 Sam 27:5 – 2 Sam 1:27

Ziklag was located in the southern end of Judah (Josh 15:31), and the name means "winding." David resided there until he heard that Saul had died (2 Sam 1:1). David's journey until he arrived at his final place of refuge in Ziklag was truly full of winding turns. God had led him to Ziklag so that he could safely conclude his journey.

While King Saul pursued him, David left the land of Israel, the land of the covenant, and took refuge in Gath, one of the cities of the Philistines. When David went to King Achish of Gath, he allowed David to stay in Ziklag and he remained there in Philistia for a year and four months (1 Sam 27:6–7).

It was wrong of David to enter the land of the Philistines without first inquiring of God (1 Sam 27:1). Coincidentally, a war broke out between the Philistines and the Israelites, and David had to take part in the war on the side of the Philistines. However, the Philistine commanders were against David's participation in the war and said, "in the battle he may become an adversary to us" (1 Sam 29:4). This is why David had to return to Ziklag without having to fight against his own people even though he had advanced up to the Philistine camp at Aphek (1 Sam 29:1a).

By God's providential work, David was able to avoid the tragedy of warring against his own people. Yet, another trying and desperate situation awaited him. He left the Philistine camp of Aphek and returned to Ziklag on the third day, only to find Ziklag ablazed by the Amalekites and the Israelites' wives and children taken away (1 Sam 30:1–2). David and all the people were so distressed and grieved that they lifted their voices and wept until there was no strength in them to weep (1 Sam 30:4). It was truly a moment of despair and bitterness.

Thinking that all their families had been killed, David's warriors were momentarily so enraged that they wished to stone David. 1 Samuel 30:6 describes the situation, "Moreover David was greatly distressed because the people spoke of stoning him, for all the people were embittered, each one because of his sons and his daughters. But David strengthened himself in the Lord his God." The word *distressed* is יָצַר (*yāṣar*) in Hebrew and means, "to bind," "to tie up," "to be restricted," and "to be cramped." Thus, he found himself in a difficult and grievous position, but he immediately realized his wrongdoing and gathered himself together by relying on God.

David repented and inquired of God, and God told him to pursue the Amalekites and he will surely overtake them and rescue all that they had taken (1 Sam 30:7–8). Thus, he took his 600 men with him to pursue the Amalekites. However, some of the men lagged behind due to exhaustion from the three-day trip from Aphek to Ziklag (1 Sam 30:1). David left behind 200 men at the Brook Besor, and he continued to pursue Amalek with 400 men (1 Sam 30:9–10). David slaughtered the Amalekites from twilight until the evening of the next day and recovered all that they had taken. He rescued his two wives (Abigail and Ahinoam) and took many sheep and cattle as spoil (1 Sam 30:17–20).

David distributed the spoils evenly amongst the people, including the 200 men who had stayed back at the Brook Besor, and this became the ordinance regarding the spoils of war for Israel to this day (1 Sam 30:24–25). David even sent some of the spoil to the elders of Judah, and to his friends (1 Sam 30:26–30). This shows us that David secretly helped the people of Judah even while he was residing in the land of the Philistines, and that he stayed in contact with the elders of Judah and maintained amicable relationships with them.

Even in situations where we find ourselves in serious trouble by making a wrong decision, God will surely restore us by giving us new strength and courage as long as we realize our faults, repent, turn back to God, rely on Him and inquire of Him.

Until now we have examined the route David took as he spent nearly ten years escaping from the hands of Saul. A large number of David's most beautiful poems (psalms) was written during this time. Thus they are full of David's cries and laments that stem from despair and bitter pain, the desperate longings for God, and the joy of experiencing God's great work of salvation from severe tribulations, and finally, thanksgiving to God.

Psalm 31 is known as the poem that David wrote while Saul was pursuing him. David sought God's help while he was being pursued and demoralized by the enemy; still he thanked and praised God for His salvation from all the pain, anxiety, sorrow, grief and suffering caused by his enemy.

David described the painful situations he faced due to Saul's pursuit in various ways.

First, "My eye is wasted away from grief, my soul and my body also" (Ps 31:9).

Second, "For my life is spent with sorrow, and my years with sighing; my strength has failed because of my iniquity, and my body has wasted away" (Ps 31:10).

Third, "Because of all my adversaries, I have become a reproach, especially to my neighbors, and an object of dread to my acquaintances; those who see me in the street flee from me" (Ps 31:11).

Fourth, "I am forgotten as a dead man, out of mind, I am like a broken vessel" (Ps 31:12).

Fifth, "For I have heard the slander of many, terror is on every side; while they took counsel together against me, they schemed to take away my life" (Ps 31:13).

Most people in situations like these fall into despair and give up on life. However, David cast away the forces of despair at once. He confessed, "But as for me, I trust in You, O Lord, I say, 'You are my God'" (Ps 31:14). This confession reveals David's firm and unwavering faith; he trusted in God even when all situations around him seemed hopeless.

Furthermore, David cried out, "My times are in Your hand; deliver me from the hand of my enemies, and from those who persecute me" (Ps 31:15). "My times" refer to all his times, the past, the present and the future. Thus, "my times are in your hand" is a great confession of faith that his whole life was in the sovereign hands of God, not just a specific period of time.

As he lived through the times of trial, he was able to see through faith that the enemy would be put to shame and that the wicked who persecuted him would be silent in Sheol (Ps 31:17–18). Then, David praised God saying, "How great is Your goodness" (Ps 31:19). There were two reasons that David was so moved to praise God.

First, it was because of the grace that God had stored up for David (Ps 31:19a). Even when David faced trials, he realized that God had stored up His grace for him from long ago. The expression *stored up* is צָפַן (*sāpan*) in Hebrew and means "to hide" and "to treasure up." This indicates that God had especially prepared good things, from long ago, to bestow upon David. While David was in trouble, many people did not expect him to be blessed with enormous glory and great fame as a king established by God. However, even in the worst of situations, God knew his blessed path and prepared good things to give to him. Through his prayers, David realized God's benevolent providence and, unable to contain his astonishment, he praised God greatly.

Second, God hid David in the "secret place" (Ps 31:20).

The term, "secret place," is סֵתֶר (*sēter*) in Hebrew and is derived from סָתַר (*sātar*), meaning "to cover" and "to hide." Saul continuously pursued David with an unwavering intent to kill him. David experienced the grace of God for God covered David in places where his enemies could not find him. God kept him in a secret shelter of His presence, a covering that protected him from the "conspiracies of man" and the "strife of tongues." He was so moved by this grace that he could not help but praise God.

There were times when David's troubles grew more and more severe each day and he was seized with terror that he momentarily doubted that God was protecting him and said, "I am cut off from before Your eyes" (Ps 31:22). However, David was inspired by the love of God, who answered his prayers immediately when he cried out in times of crisis, and praised Him again. He confidently beseeches those who trust in the Lord and seek Him,, "Be strong, and let your heart take courage" (Ps 31:24). Even in the midst of trials, David persevered, pushing on with courage because he had come to understand God's plan to make him king over Israel and give him victory and glory.

After all, it was God's complete protection that guarded David from numerous near-death situations. At a quick glance, David's life of escape could seem like a waste of time. However, God was training David to have faith like pure gold (Job 23:10) prior to establishing him as king just as He trained Moses in the wilderness for 40 years and prepared him prior to the Israelites' exodus (Acts 7:29–30).

Through the ten years of life as a fugitive, David attained and learned the faith and obedience necessary to become the king of a newly established nation. He had the ability to build up military and political power and the wisdom needed to rule over the people. As a fugitive, he experienced the difficulties of a life so low, which taught him to understand the hearts of the people and allowed him to mature to a person who possessed a generous heart. God was molding David into a leader of faith who could fulfill His administration in the history of redemption.

2. David's Accession to the Throne

(1) David becomes king of Judah in Hebron.

David heard from a young Amalekite boy that Saul and Jonathan died in battle, and he mourned, wept and fasted until the evening (2 Sam 1:11–12). He also lamented over them with a song of lamentation (2 Sam 1:17–27).

After this, David inquired of God if he should go up to one of the cities in Judah, and God commanded him to go to Hebron (2 Sam 2:1). When David went to Hebron, the men of Judah came and anointed David king of Judah (2 Sam 2:4, 11). David thus became king 15 years after the prophet Samuel first anointed him (1 Sam 16:13) at the age of about 15 (1025 BC).[62]

Pursued by Saul, David began his life of escape for about ten years from the age of 20, five years after he was anointed at the age of about 15. The precious prime of his youth from the age of 20 until the age of 30 was spent in the wilderness, in caves, in mountains, and in foreign countries, living in fear. Therefore, he must have felt a great emotional uplift when he became king. David was able to advance from being a shepherd boy to the chief leader of Israel as the result of the sovereign providence of God, the ruler of all history (1 Chr 17:7; Ps 78:70–71).

David sang the words of Psalm 18 when he ascended the throne. The heading for Psalm 18 states, "A Psalm of David the servant of the Lord, who spoke to the Lord the words of this song in the day that the Lord delivered him from the hand of all his enemies and from the hand of Saul." Deeply moved when he finally became king, David confessed that it was God who delivered him from his powerful enemies and from those who hated him (Ps 18:17). David also realized that God lit his lamp and helped him overcome all obstacles in the past and confessed, "For You light my lamp; the Lord my God illumines my darkness. For by You I can run upon a troop; and by my God I can leap over a wall" (Ps 18:28–29).

The ten years of suffering while he was fleeing from Saul until he became king, David described as "darkness." The word *darkness* is חֹשֶׁךְ (*hōšek*) in Hebrew and refers to a state of pitch darkness with no light. David literally lived in darkness, devoid of sunlight; he hid in the cave of Adullam and the cave of Engedi during his flight from Saul. Furthermore, he went through suffering, despair and life-threatening danger without a single ray of light or hope on numerous occasions. Later, he was able to confess that it was God who had freed him from the darkness of his suffering and made him king.

In addition, the word *wall* is שׁוּר (*šûr*) in Hebrew and refers to a wall. David describes in Psalm 18:29 and 2 Samuel 22:30 that he could leap over the wall only by God's help. He overcame the biggest obstacle, that is Saul and his enemies, by trusting and relying only on God. At last, he was enthroned as king in the city of Hebron.

At the same time, however, Abner, who was Saul's servant, made Saul's son Ish-bosheth king of Israel when he was forty years old (2 Sam 2:10).

① **Battle at the pool of Gibeon**

As soon as he became king, David first blessed and praised the people of Jabesh-gilead for giving a burial for Saul (2 Sam 2:4–7). Then, David had his first war since becoming king. At the pool of Gibeon, he fought against Israel who enthroned Saul's son, Ish-bosheth (2 Sam 2:8–17). David was victorious in this battle, but 20 men, including Asahel (Joab's brother), died and 360 men from Israel's army were killed (2 Sam 2:30–31). This was the start of David's rise to become king over the whole nation.

② Abner's death

Since Abner had made himself strong in the house of Saul, he was accused of having relations with Rizpah, Saul's concubine. When Ish-bosheth spoke strongly to Abner regarding the matter, Abner became very angry over Ish-bosheth's words and said to him, "Am I a dog's head that belongs to Judah?" The word *head* is רֹאשׁ (r'ōš), which can also mean "chief" in Hebrew. Hence, Abner's argument can be understood as "Am I only like a dog's head that takes sides with David?" (2 Sam 3:6–11).

Because of this incident, Abner betrayed Ish-bosheth and met with David, promising him that he would help David establish a unified kingdom (2 Sam 3:20–21).

Then, Joab, commander of David's army, heard about this on his way back from the battle. So he had Abner, who was on his way back after meeting with David, brought back to Hebron and killed him by striking him in the belly. This was in retaliation against Abner for killing his younger brother Asahel, but he probably also felt threatened that Abner might take his place (2 Sam 3:23–30).

Now, David did not know that Joab had sent messengers to call Abner back to Hebron (2 Sam 3:26b). When he heard that Joab had killed Abner, David cursed him saying, "I and my kingdom are innocent before the Lord forever of the blood of Abner the son of Ner. May it fall on the head of Joab and on all his father's house; and may there not fail from the house of Joab one who has a discharge, or who is a leper, or who takes hold of a distaff, or who falls by the sword, or who lacks bread" (2 Sam 3:28–29).

David commanded Joab and all the people who were with him, "Tear your clothes and gird on sackcloth and lament before Abner," while David himself lifted up his voice and wept at the grave of Abner. All the people came to persuade David to eat bread while it was still day, but David vowed that he would not taste bread or anything else before the sun went down (2 Sam 3:35). The people who saw this scene put aside their suspicion that David had commanded Joab to kill Abner and began to have more confidence in him (2 Sam 3:37).

③ Ish-bosheth's death

Ish-bosheth had two groups of followers, whose leaders were named Rechab
and Baanah. They went to the house of Ish-bosheth as he was taking his
mid-day rest and struck him in the belly. Then, they beheaded him and
brought his head to David. They expected to be rewarded by David, but
instead David had the two men killed on the spot for the sin of betraying
their own king (2 Sam 4:5–12).

David had previously vowed to Saul and to Jonathan that he would
not cut off the descendants of the house of Saul (1 Sam 20:15; 24:21–
22), and he kept this vow until the end. When David trusted in God
and did not avenge himself on his own enemies, God made Saul's house
to crumble by itself. David possessed a totally God-centered faith; he
waited for God to work in His time instead of taking revenge into his
own hands.

(2) David becomes king over all of Israel.

When Ish-bosheth died, all the elders of Israel came to David in Hebron.
They said to David, "Previously, when Saul was king over us, you were
the one who led Israel out and in. And the LORD said to you, 'You will
shepherd My people Israel, and you will be a ruler over Israel'" (2 Sam
5:2). This reveals that David had been the true leader even during the
period in which Saul ruled over Israel, and that David had become king
in accordance with the Word of God.

Thus, the elders of Israel made a covenant with David before the
Lord and poured oil over David and anointed him king over all of Israel
(2 Sam 5:3; cf. 1 Chr 11:1–3). This was the third time that David had
been anointed. David was first anointed at about the age of 15 (1 Sam
16:13) and was anointed a second time in Hebron as the king of Judah
(2 Sam 2:3–4, 11).

David became king at the age of 30 and ruled for 40 years until he
was 70 years old. He reigned seven years and six months in Hebron and
33 years in Jerusalem (2 Sam 5:4–5; 1 Kgs 2:11; 1 Chr 3:4; 29:27).

① David captures the stronghold of Zion.

As soon as David became king over all of Israel, he recovered the city of
Jerusalem first. It was occupied by the Jebusites, and David established
it as the nation's new capital (2 Sam 5:6–9; 1 Chr 11:4–8). David became
greater and greater since the Lord, the God of hosts, was with him (2

Sam 5:10). Those whom God is with grow steadily stronger, while those whom God is not with, and those whom He has cast away, grow continually weaker (2 Sam 3:1).

② **Victory from a continuous war against the Philistines**
The Philistines came to attack David when they heard that he had become king (2 Sam 5:17–18; 1 Chr 14:8–9). David inquired of God, and He said, "Go up, for I will certainly give the Philistines into your hand" (2 Sam 5:19; 1 Chr 14:10). David was greatly victorious at Baal-perazim which means "the LORD who breaks out." This name was given to signify that God had scattered the Philistines (2 Sam 5:20–21; 1 Chr 14:11–12).

The defeated Philistines once again attacked Israel and camped in the valley of Rephaim (2 Sam 5:22; 1 Chr 14:13). Again, David obeyed God's command to make a surprise attack from behind and was greatly victorious (2 Sam 5:23–25; 1 Chr 14:14–16).

③ **Failure of the first attempt to bring the Ark of the Covenant to the city of David**
After the war with the Philistines, David attempted to relocate the Ark of the Covenant to the city of David. Why?

First, he wanted to unify the public sentiment which had been divided between the north and the south.

Second, he wanted to establish the Word of God as the governing ideology for the new unified kingdom. The Ark, containing the two tablets upon which the Ten Commandments were written, represented the presence of the Word.

According to 2 Samuel 6 and 1 Chronicles 13, after David had established Jerusalem as the nation's capital, he wanted to relocate the Ark of God from Baalah of Judah (Kiriath-jearim) where it had been for quite a long time. David consulted with the captains of the thousands and the hundreds, even with every leader, and after gaining the consent of all the assembly of Israel (1 Chr 13:1–2), he carefully selected 30,000 men (made up of soldiers and civilians) and went down with them (2 Sam 6:1). They carried the Ark of God on a new cart, and Uzzah (Uzza) and Ahio, sons (actually considered to be grandsons) of Abinadab,[63] drove the cart toward Jerusalem (1 Chr 13:7). When the cart came to the threshing floor of Nacon (Chidon), the oxen stumbled and the Ark almost fell to the ground (1 Chr 13:9). Uzzah reached out toward the Ark of God and took hold of it and died instantly (2 Sam 6:6–7; 1 Chr 13:9–10). David became angry because of the Lord's outburst against Uzzah and he called the place "Perez-uzzah," which means "to burst out against Uzzah" (2 Sam 6:8; 1 Chr 13:11). Uzzah took hold of the Ark out of a desire to save it, but God struck him and killed him. This was because God had said that only the consecrated sons of Kohath were to carry the Ark on their shoulders and that those who touched the Ark would die (Num 4:15; 3:30–31; 7:9; 10:21; 1 Chr 15:2). Thus, it was a sin for it was against the Law to carry the Ark in a new cart instead of carrying it on their shoulders; having Uzzah and Ahio, the sons (grandsons) of Abinadab, carry the Ark instead of the sons of Kohath; and touching the Ark, which would kill even the sons of Kohath. No matter how good the intent was, there is a retribution when it is done against God's Word.

④ **The Ark of the Covenant is transported to the city of David at the second attempt.**

David feared transporting the Ark of God after Uzzah's death, and the Ark was moved to the house of Obed-Edom where it stayed for three months (2 Sam 6:10–11; 1 Chr 13:12–14). During those three months, Obed-Edom's whole household was greatly blessed on account of the Ark of God.

David heard this news, and he had the Ark carried upon the shoulders to bring to the city this time. As the Ark was entering the city of David, he was so overjoyed that he took off his clothes and, wearing just a linen ephod, he leaped and danced joyously like a child. His wife Michal, the daughter of king Saul, was watching from her window, unmoved and joyless when she saw David dancing, as the Ark of God was entering the city of David, and she despised him in her heart (2 Sam 6:16). Then, she rebuked the king for not upholding the dignity of a king (2 Sam 6:20), and as a result God made her childless to the day of her death (2 Sam 6:23).

The word *dancing* in 2 Samuel 6:14 is כָּרַר (*kārar*) in Hebrew and is written in the participle mood of the pilpel stem, which means that David was whirling and dancing continuously and with passion. 2 Samuel 6:14 states that David was dancing "with all his might" and 2 Samuel 6:16 states that David was "leaping and dancing." He could not contain himself for he was overjoyed and thankful for the grace of God, who allowed him to finally restore the Ark. It was also an act of confession that the true king of Israel is not he, but God.

3. The Davidic Covenant and Victories in Battles

(1) The Davidic Covenant

After uniting the national sentiment and establishing a theocratic government founded upon the Word of God, David consulted with the prophet Nathan about building a temple for God (2 Sam 7:1–2). Most people, once they have gained power and are settled, usually become idle and proud, looking after their own welfare and glory. However, when David resided in his palace in peace, he planned to build a temple for God. David thought of God first; his faith was truly a God-centered faith. Although God said to him, "You have shed much blood, and have waged great wars; you shall not build a house to My name," God soon entered into a covenant with David and promised him that He would construct the temple through David's son.

① **The content of the covenant**

God regarded David's desire to build His temple as praiseworthy and entered into a covenant with him. God's unilateral covenant with David contains the following three elements.

First, a promise regarding David himself

God promised that He would make David a great name (2 Sam 7:8-9; 1 Chr 17:8). He also promised that David's house and his kingdom would endure forever and that his throne would be established forever (2 Sam 7:11, 16). In addition, God promised that David would lie down with his fathers when his days were complete (2 Sam 7:12).

Second, a promise regarding the nation of Israel

God promised that Israel would be firmly planted, that it would not have to be moved again, that the wicked would not afflict them, and that they would have rest from their enemies (2 Sam 7:10–11; 1 Chr 17:9–10).

Third, a promise regarding David's descendants

In 2 Samuel 7:12–13 God promised, "…I will raise up your descendant after you, who will come forth from you, and I will establish his kingdom. He shall build a house for My name, and I will establish the throne of his kingdom forever" (1 Chr 17:11–12). Here, the word *descendant* (זֶרַע, *zeraʿ*) is written in the singular form, and it primarily refers to King Solomon and the promise that he would build the temple. However, a nation's throne cannot be established forever by Solomon, a fallible human being. Thus, from a redemptive perspective, the word *descendant* refers to Jesus Christ who would come in the future.

② The fulfiller of the Davidic Covenant

The Bible introduces Jesus Christ who is to come as the fulfiller of the Davidic Covenant.

First, the Bible testifies that Jesus Christ is a descendant of David (Acts 2:30; 13:23; 2 Tim 2:8; Rev 22:16). John 7:42 states, "Christ comes from the descendants of David, and from Bethlehem, the village where David was" and Romans 1:3 states that Jesus Christ was "born of a descendant of David according to the flesh."

Next, the Bible testifies that Jesus Christ possesses the eternal throne. In Psalm 89:4, He promised, "I will establish your seed forever, and build up your throne to all generations"; and in Psalm 89:36, He promised, "His descendants shall endure forever, and his throne as the sun before Me" (Ps 89:29). In Isaiah 9:7, He also promised, "There will be no end to the increase of His government or of peace, on the throne of David and over his kingdom, to establish it and to uphold it with justice and righteousness." Jesus Christ fulfilled all these promises and established the eternal throne. This is why the angel Gabriel proclaimed regarding Jesus Christ, "He will reign over the house of Jacob forever; and His kingdom will have no end" (Luke 1:33).

③ David's prayer of thanksgiving (1 Chr 17:16–27)

David thanked God deeply for His covenant and earnestly hoped for its fulfillment. In 2 Samuel 7:25–26, David prayed, "Now therefore, O LORD God, the word that You have spoken concerning Your servant and his house, confirm it forever, and do as You have spoken, that Your name may be magnified forever, by saying, 'The LORD of hosts is God over Israel'; and may the house of Your servant David be established before You."

David did not grumble although his desire to build the temple was not accepted. Instead, he gave earnest thanksgiving to God for His willingness to have it built through his son, and by doing so, he demonstrated the faith of total obedience. Total obedience is laying down our own will to hold on to God's will and obeying with overflowing joy and thanksgiving just as David did.

(2) David is victorious at war (1 Chr 18:1–17).

David defeated the Philistines (2 Sam 8:1), Moab (2 Sam 8:2), Zobah and Aram (2 Sam 8:3–8), and Edom (2 Sam 8:13–14) in battles. Then, Hamath (2 Sam 8:9–10) sent him tribute. This is the fulfillment of the promise "I will give you rest from all your enemies" that God made through the Davidic Covenant (2 Sam 7:11). David was victorious in all his battles because wherever he went, God Himself gave him victory (2 Sam 8:6, 14). In addition, David administered justice and righteousness for all his people, and the nation became more stable (2 Sam 8:15).

David was also victorious in war against Ammon. When Nahash, the king of the Ammonites died, David remembered the kindness that Nahash had previously showed him and sent some of his servants with his condolences. However, Nahash's son, Hanun misunderstood David's intention and thought he had sent spies. Therefore, he took David's servants and shaved off half of their beards and cut off their garments in the middle as far as their hips and sent them away (2 Sam 10:1–4).

In light of the culture of those times, this kind of action represented the highest degree of insult and it led to a war between David and Ammon. Ammon united with the people of Aram, but the Israelites were victorious. Thus, the forces of evil may insult the people of God without good reason, but God's people ultimately will gain victory.

4. David's Transgression

(1) Adultery with Bathsheba

After the war with Ammon, in the springtime when the rainy season had passed and the dry and warm season had come, Israel's army destroyed the Ammonites and was besieging Rabbah (2 Sam 11:1). At this time, David was in Jerusalem and committed the great sin of adultery with Uriah's wife Bathsheba (2 Sam 11:2–5). David saw Bathsheba, the wife of his loyal servant, bathing and he lay with her.

Why did David commit such a sin?
First, he had become spiritually idle.

> **2 Samuel 11:2a** Now when evening came David arose from his bed and walked around on the roof of the king's house….

David did not go to war with his soldiers (2 Sam 11:1). The nation was in the middle of a head-on battle against Ammon, so David should have been in the battlefield with his men. Even if he had not participated in the war, if he had been a king who was truly awake, he should have been living a godly life and praying for his men who were at war. Nonetheless, as an indication of his spiritual idleness, David arose from his bed in the evening, not even in the morning, and leisurely walked around the roof of his house (2 Sam 11:2). Thus, spiritual idleness and laziness become the path for sin (Prov 19:15).

Second, he could not overcome the lust of the eyes.

> **2 Samuel 11:2b** …and from the roof he saw a woman bathing; and the woman was very beautiful in appearance.

David was walking around his roof and "from the roof he saw" a woman bathing, and noticed she was very beautiful. If David had immediately moved away from that place when he saw the woman bathing, he may not have ended up committing the grave sin. However, he probably continued to watch Bathsheba and became captivated by her beauty. Ultimately, David was not able to overcome the lust of his eyes and lost the ability to overcome the temptation (1 Jn 2:16).

All the desires of mankind begin from "seeing." For this reason Job said, "I have made a covenant with my eyes; how then could I gaze at a virgin?" (Job 31:1). The more you look at something that tempts your desire, the stronger the greed becomes. Thus, people who continue to look with interest at something that they know is wrong are already in sin. And when sin is full-grown, it gives birth to death (Jas 1:15).

Third, he lost a proper sense of judgment.

David told his servants to enquire about the woman, and one said, "Is this not Bathsheba, the daughter of Eliam, the wife of Uriah the Hittite?" (2 Sam 11:3). Eliam was the son of Ahithophel, David's advisor, and Bathsheba was Ahithophel's granddaughter (2 Sam 23:34). Uriah was one of the 37 mighty men (2 Sam 23:39; ref 1 Chr 11:41), and he was risking his life in fighting against the Ammonites at that time.

David should have immediately cast away the thought of sin as soon as he found out that Bathsheba was the wife of his faithful servant Uriah. The sin that began with "seeing" had already seduced his heart, and he lost all proper sense of judgment so that he ultimately committed the sin of adultery.

(2) David killed Uriah, Bathsheba's husband.

David heard that Bathsheba had conceived as a result of their adultery, so in order to cover up his sin, he sent word to Joab and called Uriah from the battlefield. Thus, Uriah stood before King David without knowing why, and David calmly asked him about the welfare of Joab and the people and the state of the war. Then, David told Uriah to go and sleep in his own house, and he sent a king's feast from the palace as a present (2 Sam 11:6–8). David wanted Uriah to sleep with his wife so that he could say that the child that Bathsheba would give birth to was Uriah's, and not his. However, Uriah, the loyal servant, felt that he would not be comfortable sleeping in his home while his superiors and subordinates were risking their lives and fighting in a war. Instead of going home, Uriah slept at the door of the king's house with all the servants (2 Sam 11:9, 13).

Thus, David wrote a letter to Joab and sent it by the hand of Uriah. In the letter, David commanded Joab to place Uriah in the front line of the fiercest battle so that he would be struck down and killed (2 Sam 11:14–15). Joab did according to David's command and placed Uriah where the enemy's mighty men were so that he was killed. Some of David's innocent servants were also killed as the plan to have Uriah killed was being carried out (2 Sam 11:17–24). What David had done was evil in the sight of the Lord (2 Sam 11:27).

(3) The prophet Nathan's rebuke

About ten months had passed since David sinned, and Bathsheba gave birth to David's son (2 Sam 11:27). David felt a sense of relief, believing that he had committed the perfect crime, and he covered his sin and went on without repenting.

God had been waiting for David's repentance and sent the prophet Nathan to rebuke him. The prophet Nathan told David the story about the rich man who took away the poor man's ewe lamb and then said, "You are the man!" (2 Sam 12:7), as he rebuked David for killing Uriah and for taking his wife Bathsheba.

The prophet Nathan pointed out that David had committed such an act because he despised the Word of God and furthermore, God Himself (2 Sam 12:9–10). The meaning of the name *Nathan* is "conscience" and "he gives." Like the meaning of his name the prophet Nathan was conscientious in delivering God's message to King David without adding or subtracting from His command.

Furthermore, the prophet Nathan warned David that a punishment would fall upon him. *First*, the sword would never depart from his house (2 Sam 12:10). *Second*, evil would be raised up against him from his own household (2 Sam 12:11). *Third*, David's wives would lie with others out in public (2 Sam 12:11-12). *Fourth*, the child that would be born to him would surely die (2 Sam 12:14).

Initially, David's conscience was numb, and he had thought the evil man that the prophet Nathan spoke of was someone else, but after he heard Nathan's rebuke, he confessed, "I have sinned against the Lord," and he truly repented (2 Sam 12:13a). Then God forgave David's sin and said that he would not die (2 Sam 12:13b). According to God's Word, the son that Bathsheba bore died seven days after he was born. (2 Sam 12:18).

(4) David's repentance

David repented earnestly after he heard the prophet Nathan's rebuke. In Psalm 32:3–4, David made a confession regarding the state of his heart while he was trying to cover up his sin: "When I kept silent about my sin, my body wasted away through my groaning all day long. For day and night Your hand was heavy upon me; my vitality was drained away as with the fever heat of summer. Selah."

Although David felt fear and had a guilty conscience in the beginning, he carried on without honestly confessing and repenting of his sin before God. As a result, he felt his body wasting away. He was groaning all day, and he wilted like a plant withering in the heat of summer. No matter how hard he tried to ignore his sin, the sin was always lurking before him so that there was no way to avoid it. At last, he confessed his sin before God.

When David confessed his sin, God poured down the grace of forgiveness. In Psalm 32:5, David said, "I acknowledged my sin to You, and my iniquity I did not hide; I said, 'I will confess my transgressions to the Lord'; and You forgave the guilt of my sin. Selah."

What were the details of David's repentance?

In Psalm 6:6 David confessed, "I am weary with my sighing; every night I make my bed swim, I dissolve my couch with my tears." David drenched his bed with tears every night and drowned his couch until he was weary from shedding tears of repentance. The word *weary* (יָגַע, *yāga'*) refers to the state in which a person is drained of strength and worn out, or out of breath and gasping for air. A true repentance involves a laborious effort of seeking restoration and sincere prayers of tears (Ps 51:1–2).

> **Psalm 51:9–12** Hide Your face from my sins, And blot out all my iniquities. [10]Create in me a clean heart, O God, And renew a steadfast spirit within me. [11]Do not cast me away from Your presence, And do not take Your Holy Spirit from me. [12]Restore to me the joy of Your salvation, And sustain me with a willing spirit.

After his heart-wrenching repentance, David confessed, "How blessed is he whose transgression is forgiven, whose sin is covered! How blessed is the man to whom the Lord does not impute iniquity, and in whose spirit there is no deceit!" (Ps 32:1–2; Rom 4:6–8). We need to receive the grace of forgiveness in order to enjoy true happiness on this earth.

David was a sinner just like us, but the one reason that God loved him was that he humbly confessed his sins before God and earnestly repented.

It is easy for anyone to commit a sin, but one cannot truly repent without the heart-piercing and bone-grinding pain that David went through. Without fervent repentance you are deceiving God and deceiving yourself. Proper repentance is not easy to achieve. True repentance involves acknowledging sin, confessing your sin with a broken heart, cutting it off with great resolution, and bearing fruit through a change in your will.

David's repentance was so heart-wrenching that 1 Kings 15:5 states, "because David did what was right in the sight of the Lord, and had not turned aside from anything that He commanded him all the days of his life, except in the case of Uriah the Hittite." David bore the fruits worthy of repentance (Matt 3:8; Luke 3:8).

Thus, God preserved the covenant He made with David even after he sinned so that the lamp would not burn out from his household (1 Kgs 11:36; 15:4; 2 Kgs 8:19; 2 Chr 21:7; 2 Sam 21:17; 22:29).

5. Absalom's Rebellion

(1) Amnon's sin and Absalom's revenge

Of the many sons of David that appear in the Bible, the most important ones include the first son, Amnon; the third son, Absalom; and Bathsheba's son, Solomon. There was no one in Israel as handsome as Absalom, and there was no defect in him from the sole of his foot to the crown of his head (2 Sam 14:25). He had a younger sister named Tamar, and she was a distinctively beautiful woman (2 Sam 13:1).

David's firstborn, Amnon, was in love with Tamar to the point that he became ill because of his passion for her (2 Sam 13:2). He pretended to be ill and made Tamar bake some cakes for him. He lured her to his bedroom and violated her (2 Sam 13:7–14). After he lay with her, however, he suddenly hated her with a very great hatred and sent her away. David was greatly angered when he heard of all these matters, and Absalom, Tamar's biological brother, did not say anything either good or bad, but he prepared his sword of revenge (2 Sam 13:21–22).

Two years after this incident, on the day that the sheep were sheared, Absalom invited all the king's sons for a feast (2 Sam 13:23). In those days, sheep-shearing day was the most joyous time for shepherds, and it was customary for them to throw a generous feast and to invite neighbors. Absalom killed Amnon during this feast and fled to Talmai, the king of Geshur (2 Sam 13:37). This happened as the fulfillment of God's Word, "the sword shall never depart from your house" (2 Sam 12:10). David mourned for his son every day from the time Absalom fled (2 Sam 13:37). Three years since Absalom had left, David's heart longed to go out to him (2 Sam 13:39).

Joab perceived the king's heart and brought a wise woman from Tekoa and had her pretend to be a mourner. She put on mourning garments without anointing herself with oil and acted like a woman who has been mourning for the dead many days when she met with David (2 Sam 14:1–2). The woman spoke to David according to Joab's instructions. She told David that her two sons had fought and one had killed the other, and now other people wanted to kill the son that was remaining (2 Sam 14:3–7). The remaining son represented Absalom. Although David saw that this woman was instructed by Joab, David allowed Absalom to be brought back to Jerusalem through this incident (2 Sam 14:18–21).

However, David did not see Absalom's face for two years after he returned home (2 Sam 14:24, 28). Then, Absalom set fire to Joab's field and, when Joab came to confront him on the matter, Absalom asked Joab to help arrange a meeting with David and at last he met with David (2 Sam 14:33).

(2) Absalom's rebellion

① David flees

After three years of staying in Geshur (2 Sam 13:38) and two more years since he returned to Jerusalem (2 Sam 14:28), Absalom finally met his father David after a total of five years. Nonetheless, Absalom held an evil grudge against David because David did not meet with him after he returned home to Jerusalem. This ultimately led to Absalom's revolt against David. This revolt had been precisely planned in advance so that Absalom had already provided himself with a chariot and horses. Furthermore, he took over David's seat as judge and ruled over the cases that the people brought, and thus he stole the hearts of the people (2 Sam 15:1–6). Absalom's trials were illegal and gave deceitful and crooked verdicts designed to win people's hearts over. He also falsely denounced his father in order to become king (2 Sam 15:3).

When Absalom became king in Hebron, the hearts of the Israelites were with him (2 Sam 15:13). Instead of fighting against the rebellious Absalom, David chose to leave Jerusalem (2 Sam 15:14). All of David's servants who had pledged loyalty to him passed over the Brook Kidron, weeping in a loud voice, and David followed behind them (2 Sam 15:19–23).[64] Among them was Ittai who had said, "As the Lord lives, and as my lord the king lives, surely wherever my lord the king may be, whether for death or for life, there also your servant will be" (2 Sam 15:21). At this time, the priest Zadok followed David, carrying the Ark of the Covenant because he wished to be with God and with David (2 Sam 15:24). However, David feared that damage might come upon God's glory and sent Zadok and Abiathar back to Jerusalem (2 Sam 15:25–29).

As David went up the ascent of the Mount of Olives, he wept as he went with his head covered and his feet bare. The people with him also did the same (2 Sam 15:30). This is an expression of extreme sadness, disgrace and pain (Esth 6:12; Jer 14:3; Ezek 24:17).

When David heard that Ahithophel, his counselor, was among the conspirators with Absalom, he prayed, "O Lord, I pray, make the counsel of Ahithophel foolishness" (2 Sam 15:31). Later, David came to Bahurim, and a man named Shimei came out cursing David continually and throwing stones at David (2 Sam 16:5–8). Shimei's mocking was severe enough to rip out and tear at David's heart. Abishai was about to kill him, but

David stopped him saying, "Perhaps the Lord will look on my affliction and return good to me instead of his cursing this day" (2 Sam 16:12). As David was being mocked by Shimei, David realized that Absalom's revolt was God's punishment for his sin and he repented thoroughly and sought God's mercy again.

It was about 979 BC, in the latter part of David's reign, when he fled from Absalom.[65] Years had already passed since David was called by God when he was a shepherd at the age of 15; and at this time, he was 61 years old.

David had spent a substantial part of his life escaping, but his most wretched moment was when he was fleeing from his own son. David probably felt devastated that he became a disgraced fugitive, running from his most beloved son Absalom and his men in his old age. On top of that, the mocking of Shimei and other people was probably unbearably painful (Ps 3:2).

David sang the words of Psalm 63 when he was in the Wilderness of Judah fleeing from Absalom. David described his dreadful and despondent state as "a dry and weary land where there is no water" (Ps 63:1). David was thrown from a life of splendor and power in his palace to desolate wilderness, so to the human eye the situation seemed irreversible. Nonetheless, David sought and longed for God each day in order to see God's power and glory even at this point in time. As a result, he confessed that his soul was satisfied as with marrow and fatness (Ps 63:2–5). He confessed that he was so overjoyed that he praised God on his bed and woke up in the night to praise God as if he were singing and laughing joyfully at a banquet table (Ps 63:5–7). This was because God was holding his right hand every step along the way of his tribulation (Ps 63:8).

David also wrote Psalm 3 while he was fleeing from Absalom. Even in the worst situation, David was not afraid. He believed that God would lift his head up again (Ps 3:3). He confessed and cried to the Lord toward His holy mountain even from afar (Ps 3:4). He said he lay down to sleep and did not awake in terror or twist and turn in anxiety all night; rather, he fell into sweet sleep without worries and awoke peacefully to greet the new morning even in the midst of extreme dangers and tribulation when ten thousands of people were set against him all round (Ps 3:5–6). He believed that God had already smitten all his enemies on the cheek and shattered the teeth of the wicked; he had conviction in God's comfort and salvation (Ps 3:7–8).

David lifted his eyes and looked toward heaven during times of adversity. He longed after God's temple and woke up early in the morning to pray. There, he discovered the God of comfort, rest and salvation.

How many times do we wake up early in the morning to enter God's presence to pray during times of tribulation? If we do not lose hope when tribulations and sufferings come our way, but go to the temple and cry out to God, then we will be able to meet the God of salvation. We have to see God's face in order to come alive, and we need to hear God's Word in order to protect our faith and keep our souls alive during times of tribulation.

② **Absalom's failure**

After Absalom became king, he had relations with David's concubines in public in accordance with Ahithophel's conspiracy. As revenge against his father, Absalom gathered the concubines left in the palace (2 Sam 15:16) onto the roof and had relations with them, thus, committing a grave sin that would enrage anyone (2 Sam 16:22). In reality, this was David's punishment for taking Uriah's wife (2 Sam 12:11–12).

Then, Ahithophel advised Absalom to attack David immediately (2 Sam 17:1–4), but Absalom did not give heed to his strategy. Instead, he listened to the counsel of Hushai, David's friend, who advised him to attack David when all of Israel's army had gathered together (2 Sam 17:5–14). This was done because God had planned to bring calamity on Absalom (2 Sam 17:14b), and it earned David enough time to cross the Jordan River.

When Ahithophel saw that his counsel was not followed, he went back to his hometown and hanged himself (2 Sam 17:23). This was the answer to David's prayer that God would make Ahithophel's counsel foolishness (2 Sam 15:31b).

Absalom's army camped in the land of Gilead and was preparing to attack David's army while they were at Mahanaim (2 Sam 17:24, 26). Though the danger of an attack by Absalom was imminent, David's army was so exhausted from the long period of fleeing that they were about to collapse.

It was at this time that three men—Shobi, Machir, and Barzillai—served David and his men (2 Sam 17:27). They brought beds, basins, pottery, wheat, barley, flour, parched grain, beans, lentils, parched seeds, honey, curds, sheep, and cheese of the herd. They provided all these 14 items plentifully, setting them hospitably and abundantly before David and his men. They prepared all this saying, "The people are hungry and weary and thirsty in the wilderness" (2 Sam 17:27–29). The people who had fled from Absalom had lived in regions that lacked good resting places. How precious were the hearts of these men who were sympathetic to their plight? They had no desire to receive a reward or compensation. They served the king and his men out of sincere concern and fear that they might faint and die on the road due to exhaustion.

At the time, David was caught in a situation where no amount of human effort could break him free from the plight. This terrible predicament had driven him to the point of despair and depression that had sapped all life out of him. This was exactly when Barzillai had treated him with warmth and hospitality. Barzillai's heartfelt kindness must have remained deeply memorable in David's heart. With the battle against Absalom looming close, David was greatly comforted and strengthened by Shobi, Machir, and Barzillai.

Shortly after, Absalom's army and David's army came to a head-on confrontation. David's servants defeated Absalom's army in the forest of Ephraim, and there were 20,000 men killed on that day (2 Sam 18:6–8). Then, Absalom happened to meet David's servants and, as he was riding away on his mule, his hair caught fast in an oak (terebinth) tree so that he was left hanging in the air. Here, Joab ignored David's earnest plea not to harm Absalom, but he struck Absalom's heart with three spears (2 Sam 18:9–14).

The most tragic thing about Absalom's death was that he had no son to preserve his name (2 Sam 18:18a). In actuality, he had three sons and one daughter (2 Sam 14:27), but all three sons died early. Absalom lamented this and set up for himself a pillar in his own name (2 Sam 18:18b).

③ **David returns to Jerusalem**

When the battle against Absalom began, David charged his three commanders, Joab, Abishai and Ittai, not to kill Absalom but to deal gently with him for his sake, and all the people who were there heard it because he made this request publicly (2 Sam 18:5, 12). However, Joab went against David's plea and struck Absalom's heart with three spears while he was still alive, suspended in the oak tree. At the same time, ten young men gathered around and brutally killed him (2 Sam 18:14–15). Then, they cast the body into a deep pit in the forest and erected over him a very great heap of stones (2 Sam 18:17).

When David heard that Absalom had died, David was heartbroken and wept greatly, refusing to eat or drink. As soon as he heard the news, he went up to the chamber over the gate and, unable to hold back the flooding tears, he wept saying, "O my son Absalom, my son, my son Absalom! Would I had died instead of you, O Absalom, my son, my son!" repeating the words, "O my son" (2 Sam 18:33). There was no end to David's tears and lament. With no regard to the news of a victorious battle brought by the servant, he cried out loud, "O my son Absalom!"

> **2 Samuel 19:4** And the king covered his face and cried out with a loud voice, "O my son Absalom, O Absalom, my son, my son!"

David wept so much that the day's victory became sorrow for all the people (2 Sam 19:1–2), and the people went by stealth into the city as people who are humiliated steal away when they flee in battle (2 Sam 19:3).

Absalom was a son who killed his oldest brother Amnon, stole his father's throne, and went into his father's concubines in broad daylight! Furthermore, he gathered his troops in order to attack and kill his father. There could be no worse son than him under the heavens; he was struck by heaven and killed, and yet David wept in great sorrow for this son! He said, "Would I had died instead of you, O Absalom, my son, my son!" (2 Sam 18:33b); he would have given his own life to save his son.

Through David's lament for his son, we can see a parent's unconditional love for his child. Absalom had deceived his father from beginning to end and was a heartless son who committed many sins against his father. Yet David forgave him because of his endless love. This scene reminds us of how Jesus continuously prayed on the cross for those who hurled insults and mockery at Him even as blood ran down His body (Luke 23:34). Furthermore, through this, we are able to see how Jesus continuously prays for us in tears at the right hand of God's throne, for Absalom is like us (Rom 8:34). The name *Absalom* is אֲבִישָׁלוֹם ('ăbîšālôm) in Hebrew and means "father of peace." In truth, David was the unchanging father of peace to Absalom.

④ **The people who welcomed David (Shimei, Mephibosheth and Barzillai)**

After the death of Absalom, David did away with "Sheba's rebellion," which had incited Israel, and he returned to Jerusalem and became king (2 Sam

20:1–2, 21–22). Many people came out to greet David when he returned to Jerusalem.

When David became king again, Shimei, the man who had cursed and stoned David, came to David and begged for his life. Shimei was an opportunist who took advantage of the changing times (2 Sam 19:16–23). Unable to contain his rage at Shimei's deceitfulness, Abishai wanted to kill him, but David rebuked Abishai and pardoned Shimei with a generous heart and even vowed that he would not kill Shimei (2 Sam 19:21–23). David was genuinely an understanding person.

Mephibosheth neither cared for his feet, nor trimmed his mustache, nor washed his clothes, from the day David departed until the day he came home, because he was concerned about him (2 Sam 19:24). He did this out of a faithful heart, in order to take part in David's suffering. He was King Saul's grandson and Jonathan's son, and the sole survivor from Saul's household (2 Sam 4:1–4). David remembered his vow to Jonathan (2 Sam 9:1, 7; 21:7) and extended great favor to Mephibosheth by allowing him to eat at the king's table as if he were one of the princes (2 Sam 9:7, 11, 13). Mephibosheth, in turn, did not forget the grace that had been bestowed upon him and was faithful to David in all sincerity.

Even at the old age of 80, Barzillai came down from Rogelim in order to escort David over the Jordan (2 Sam 19:31). He had provided David and his men with a variety of food at Mahanaim when David was fleeing from Absalom (2 Sam 17:27–29). David could not forget this favor and wanted to repay him; he proposed, "I will sustain you in Jerusalem with me" (2 Sam 19:33). However, Barzillai humbly refused the proposal saying, "How long have I yet to live, that I should go up with the king to Jerusalem? I am now eighty years old. Can I distinguish between good and bad? Or can your servant taste what I eat or what I drink? Or can I hear any more the voice of singing men and women? Why then should your servant be an added burden to my lord the king?" (2 Sam 34–35). He said he wanted to die in his own city near the graves of his father and mother (2 Sam 19:37). Barzillai made an honest confession about his old age and sent his son Chimham with David in his stead (2 Sam 19:37; 1 Kgs 2:7).

Barzillai was a rich man with no need of envy for anyone on this earth. However, it is not easy to generously serve others just because one has great wealth. It is impossible unless it is motivated by the benevolence that comes from faith.

The name *Barzillai* בַּרְזִלַּי (*barzillay*) means "man of iron" and "strong iron." The words of iron that the 80-year old man Barzillai spoke out from experience of life and faith still ring in our ears today. This is because: *First*, he feared God. *Second*, he had love in his heart for the servant established by God. *Third*, never expecting any compensation, he only wanted to help the servant of God and did not want to burden him. *Fourth*, although he was very wealthy, he possessed faith with integrity so that he did not live for the pleasures of the flesh.

It is truly people like Barzillai, a modest and faithful servant, that fulfill God's will.

6. David's Latter Years

(1) David's preparation for the construction of the temple

After David suppressed Absalom and Sheba's rebellion, he spent his latter years pouring his heart and soul into preparing for the construction work for the temple (1 Chr 22:1–19).

First, David prepared every detail, from big to small, that would be needed (1 Chr 22:3). David prepared large quantities of iron to make the nails for the doors and for clamps. He also prepared the bronze needed to make the two pillars (Jachin and Boaz). The nails held the doors of the gates and the clamps were used to fasten objects made of wood or stone.

David was able to prepare even for these small things because God had made him understand in writing by His hand upon him, all the details of the pattern (1 Chr 28:12, 19), and David prepared with faith and with the desire to do exactly according to God's command.

Second, David prepared in "great quantity" (1 Chr 22:14–15) and "with all his ability" (1 Chr 29:2). David prepared large quantities of iron (1 Chr 22:3), more bronze than could be weighed (1 Chr 22:3), timbers of cedar logs beyond number (1 Chr 22:4), 100,000 talents of gold and 1 million talents of silver (1 Chr 22:14).[66]

Third, David gave generously from his personal wealth also (1 Chr 29:3). David took charge of the construction of the temple and asked, "Who then is willing to consecrate himself this day to the LORD?" (1 Chr 29:5), and the rulers of the fathers' households, the princes of the tribes of Israel and the commanders of thousands and of hundreds, with the overseers over the king's work, offered willingly (1 Chr 29:6). They brought so much (1 Chr 29:7–8)[67] that it was put in the care of Jehiel the Gershonite

(1 Chr 29:8). The people made their offerings "with a whole heart," and they rejoiced because they had offered so "willingly"; even King David was overcome with joy (1 Chr 29:9).

David confessed that he had prepared for the house of the Lord with "great pains" (1 Chr 22:14). The word *pains* is עָנִי ('ŏnî) in Hebrew and refers to "affliction as a result of war." David had gathered spoils from wars, in which he risked his life, so that they may be used as resources for the construction of the temple (1 Chr 18:8; 20:2).

David praised God with all the assembly on the dedication day for the construction of the temple even before the temple was built (1 Chr 29:10–20) and offered sacrifices to God of 1,000 bulls, 1,000 rams and 1,000 lambs, with drink offerings and sacrifices in abundance (1 Chr 29:21). The king and the people became as one in great gladness, and they experienced God's presence as they ate and drank that day "before the LORD" (1 Chr 29:22).

(2) David's census

David also conducted a census in the latter years of his life. This became the cause of pestilence that came upon Israel for three days. It killed 70,000 people from among the people (2 Sam 24:15).

Why did David conduct a census?

First, there was sin in the nation.

2 Samuel 24:1 states, "Now again the anger of the LORD burned against Israel, and it incited David against them to say, 'Go, number Israel and Judah.'" Because there was sin in the land of Israel, God used the census to judge the nation. What was this sin? God had established David as king by His sovereignty, but the Israelites challenged His sovereignty when they rebelled and followed Absalom and Sheba instead.

Second, David was proud.

1 Chronicles 21:1 (KJV) states, "And Satan stood up against Israel, and provoked David to number Israel." It was Satan who provoked David. The New International Version (NIV) of this verse reads, "Satan rose up against Israel and incited David to take a census of Israel." David had the desire to show off his powers through the census of the people; and Satan provoked David's heart and incited him to take his desire into action. Joab actively tried to stop David (2 Sam 24:3), but David did not take his servant's advice.

It was only after the plague of pestilence that David built an altar at the threshing floor of Araunah and repented earnestly. He bought the threshing floor and the oxen with 50 shekels of silver, and there he offered burnt offerings and peace offerings. God was moved by his entreaty for the land, and the plague was held back from Israel (2 Sam 24:23–25).

The threshing floor of Araunah was the site where Abraham had offered Isaac as a sacrifice (Gen 22:1–19), which later became the site for the temple of Solomon (2 Chr 3:1). This incident with the threshing floor of Araunah seems to be symbolic of the redemptive work of Jesus on the cross. Jesus paid the price with His own blood in the place of sinners and became the peace offering on the cross, so that we could be freed from the curse of death (Rom 3:25; Eph 1:7; Heb 9:11–12).

(3) Adonijah's insurrection and David in his old age

David was old and advanced in age; he could not be kept warm even when he was covered with clothes (1 Kgs 1:1). In other words, he had become so weak that he could not maintain his body temperature. 1 Kings 1:15 states, "Now the king was very old." Thus, his servants brought a beautiful girl, Abishag the Shunammite, to nurse and serve David (1 Kgs 1:3–4a).

However, the Bible states that David did not cohabit with her (1 Kgs 1:4b). After David sinned with regard to Uriah's wife Bathsheba, he wholly repented and, for the rest of his life, he maintained "godliness" and did not sin again. Thus, 1 Kings 15:5 states, "David did what was right in the sight of the LORD, and had not turned aside from anything that He commanded him all the days of his life, except in the case of Uriah the Hittite."

When David became old and could no longer oversee the affairs of the nation, his fourth son Adonijah conferred with Abiathar the priest and Joab the commander of the army. As a result, he exalted himself high and declared himself king (1 Kgs 1:5–7).

Adonijah was a very handsome man and was in great favor with David so that his father had never spoken anything against him at any time (1 Kgs 1:6). However, he later changed and became an atrocious and rebellious son, who gave a fatal shock to his father in his old age.

Shocked by Adonijah's revolt, the prophet Nathan hurriedly met with Bathsheba so that she could inform David of what had happened. She went and inquired of David as to who should become the next king, and Nathan, too, made an effort to ensure that Solomon would become king according to God's will as had already been determined (1 Kgs 1:11–27). God had already vowed that Solomon would succeed David on the throne (1 Chr 22:9–10). Realizing the urgency of the situation, David vowed that Solomon would be king after him, and that he would sit on the throne in his place (1 Kgs 1:30).

All the people rejoiced in Solomon becoming king, and Adonijah's revolt was easily quashed. Realizing that his revolt had failed, Adonijah went and took hold of the horns of the altar to preserve his life (1 Kgs 1:50–53). However, he was later put to death by Solomon after David's death when he asked for Abishag to be given to him as his wife (1 Kgs 2:19–25).

(4) The wretched end of the lives of Abiathar the priest and Joab the commander of the army

Abiathar and Joab had worked with David for a long time and were faithful men who were with him through thick and thin. However, toward the end of David's life, they helped Adonijah become king instead of Solomon whom God had chosen (1 Kgs 1:7). Physically, Adonijah was more striking than Solomon; thus, they reverted to personal choice and reasoning, and elected Adonijah, disregarding God's plan again.

① The end of Abiathar's life

Abiathar was a descendant of Eli and the son of Ahimelech (1 Sam 22:20). His father Ahimelech was a priest, who had bestowed a good favor upon David during his flight from Saul. As a result, Saul killed the whole household of priests in Nob, all 85 of them, and Abiathar was the sole survivor (1 Sam 22:18–23).

During David's reign as king, Abiathar served both God and David faithfully. However, it was toward the end of David's life that he did not follow God's will but decided to go his own way by helping Adonijah. Abiathar deserved to die considering what he had done, but Solomon did not have him killed because he had suffered alongside with David during his difficult times; Solomon only stripped him of his priestly duties (1 Kgs 2:26–27). This was in fulfillment of the prophecy of the man of God (1 Sam 2:27) regarding the house of Eli, that the house of Eli would not minister as priests but that He would raise up a new priest (1 Sam 2:34–36). From this time on, the household of Zadok, a descendant of Eleazar, ministered as priests (1 Kgs 2:35; 1 Chr 6:1–8; 24:1–3).

② The end of Joab's life

Joab was not only David's cousin, but he was also David's comrade who went through life-threatening times during David's flight from Saul's oppression. He had accomplished honorable achievements for the house of David and had become second in power to David (1 Chr 11:6). Nevertheless, the pain he caused David was too great. The Bible records of three killings committed by Joab. All these killings were committed against David's will.

First, David entered into a peace treaty with Abner, the commander of Ish-bosheth's army as part of his effort to unite the nation. Joab killed Abner out of personal vengeance and caused all the people of Israel to think that David had instigated the action (2 Sam 3:12–39). Then David fiercely cursed his loyal servant (2 Sam 3:28–29). Crying out to God that it was too difficult for him to control Joab, David prayed that God would deal with Joab according to his evil (2 Sam 3:39).

Second, Joab brutally killed Absalom during his revolt and brought extreme sorrow to David (2 Sam 18:14–15; 19:1–8).

Third, Joab harbored a jealous and discontented heart, when David appointed Amasa as commander of the army in his place (2 Sam 19:13), and he killed the innocent Amasa with the sword (2 Sam 20:4–10).

For a long time, Joab was a loyal servant and companion who served David well. However, Joab turned into a dangerous man just as David warned Solomon before he died (1 Kgs 2:5–6). Regarding the matter, Solomon also preeminently pointed out that Joab had taken the lives of two innocent men—Abner and Amasa—and said that their blood would return on the head of Joab (1 Kgs 2:31–33).

In the end, Joab, along with the high priest Abiathar, betrayed David by enthroning Adonijah (1 Kgs 1:7) and was killed by Benaiah the commander of the army whom Solomon sent (1 Kgs 2:28–34). He had fled to the tent of the Lord, but Benaiah beheaded him there as he held onto the horns of the altar. What a pitiful end for someone who had been a man of merit!

Both Joab and Abiathar had been loyal servants who had performed distinguished services for the nation and for King David, but they did not properly consider God's will. Instead, they lived according to their own thoughts, and their end was tragic rather than honorable.

(5) David's prophetic song of praise

2 Samuel chapters 22 and 23 contain David's songs of praise. The heading for 2 Samuel 22 opens with, "And David spoke the words of this song to the LORD in the day that the LORD delivered him from the hand of all his enemies and from the hand of Saul." 2 Samuel 22 is a song of praise sung by David when God had given him victory in the wars against the Philistines, Aram, Amalek, Zobah, Edom and others in the early years of his reign after Saul had died (2 Sam 8:1–14; cf. Ps 18). The content of the song in 2 Samuel 22 begins (2 Sam 22:2–3), progresses (2 Sam 22:17–18) and ends with the theme of salvation (2 Sam 22:49–50).

2 Samuel 23:1–7, which continues from 2 Samuel 22, is recorded by David as his last words and life's testament in the twilight years of his 70-year life (2 Sam 23:1a). As he looks back to the eventful life he lived, he gives thanks for God's providence and guidance. He praises God with a hope for the completion of the Messianic kingdom and emphasizes that the "Spirit of the LORD spoke" by him (2 Sam 23:2a).

As God evaluated David's kingdom, He described it first as the light of the morning when the sun rises; second, as a morning without clouds; and third, as when the tender grass springs out of the earth through sunshine after rain (2 Sam 23:4).

First, God described it as "the light of the morning when the sun rises" because the kingdom of God that the Messiah will reign will be like the light bursting out from the morning sun and breaking the darkness of the world, so that all nations will be filled with the light of God's grace (Judg 5:31; Prov 4:18; Matt 13:43).

Second, God described it as "the morning without clouds," because the kingdom of God will be like a refreshing morning with not a speck of cloud. It is like a clear sky where all the clouds of worries and anxieties have been lifted (Ps 58:8). When the Messianic kingdom is established, all sin, death, corruption and all pitch-dark nights will be cast away and a brilliant morning full of prosperity, joy, and happiness will rise up.

Third, God described it as "when the tender grass springs out of the earth, through sunshine after rain." Just as new life sprouts from the ground as the sun shines through after the rain, the grace that shines down from the kingdom of Jesus' righteous reign will give countless number of lives to those who will rise from the place of death. God's kingdom is described as new shoots because, just as new shoots grow and bear fruit, the Messianic kingdom will be increasingly established through the work of salvation (Matt 13:31–32).

However, the wicked who cannot enter the Messianic kingdom will receive judgment. All of them "will be thrust away like thorns" into the lake that burns with fire and brimstone (2 Sam 23:6–7; Rev 20:15; 21:8).

(6) David's final words

Forty years of David's reign flew by after he was anointed as king, and he was now at the advanced age of 70. He reminisced of the joy of striking down Goliath with a sling and a stone, the ten years of escaping from Saul not knowing when his life would come to an end, the aspiring event of being enthroned in Hebron, the joy of unobstructed victories in every battle after he became king of Israel, the shame of committing the sin of adultery with Uriah's wife and his tear-filled repentance, and the trauma of being driven out by Absalom, a heartbreaking and unexpected blow from his beloved son that caused him to flee barefooted into the wilderness again. All these passed by and remain as mere memories.

Before God called David home, David summoned his son, Solomon, and gave his final words (1 Kgs 2:1–9). His words also contained the intimacy of a father's true affection. David did not boast of his own achievements, but gave firm instructions to Solomon to keep the principles and ethics of a king according to the Word of God.

David's final words are divided into two parts: how Solomon should act with regard to God (verses 1–4), and how he should act with regard to the people (verses 5–9). David's instructions regarding what Solomon must do for the people included the honorable treatment of those who had been loyal and had risked their lives for the establishment of God's new kingdom. On the other hand, Solomon was also instructed to bring justice upon those who had challenged or revolted against him. David's instructions regarding what he must do in his relationship with God go beyond their times; they are instructions that every believer today must take to heart.

First, David instructed, "Be strong, therefore, and show yourself a man."

> **1 Kings 2:2** I am going the way of all the earth. Be strong, therefore, and show yourself a man.

The words *be strong* are חֲזַק (*ḥāzaq*) in Hebrew and mean "to be strong," "to be courageous," and "to bind on." The word *man* is אִישׁ (*ʾîš*) in Hebrew, and this word is different from אָדָם (*ʾādām*), which also means "man" or "mankind." The treatment of the word here refers to a strong and coura-geous man. David instructed Solomon to have courage and to become a strong man of vigor.

Both times, during his fight against Goliath and his flight from Saul, David was victorious only through strong faith and courage. Strong faith and courage were the spiritual teachings that David learned throughout his whole life. When Joshua was about to inherit the great task of con-quering the land of Canaan, Moses also instructed Joshua to "be strong and courageous" (Josh 1:6). We can fulfill our duties when we believe that God is with us and when we drive forward toward the work with courage.

Second, David instructed Solomon to keep the Word of God.

> **1 Kings 2:3** And keep the charge of the LORD your God, to walk in His ways, to keep His statutes, His commandments, His ordinances, and His testimo-nies, according to what is written in the law of Moses, that you may succeed in all that you do and wherever you turn,

Here, David charged Solomon to keep two things.

First, he commanded Solomon to keep the charge of the Lord. The word *charge* is מִשְׁמֶרֶת (*mišmeret*) in Hebrew and means "obligation," "service," "charge," and "duty." David was instructing Solomon to fulfill all the obligations and duties that God had entrusted to him.

Second, David charged Solomon to keep God's statutes, command-ments, ordinances and testimonies. The word *statutes* is חֻקָּה (*ḥuqqâ*) in Hebrew and refers to the detailed provisions of the law. The word *com-mandments* is מִצְוָה (*miṣvâ*) in Hebrew and refers to God's commands. The word *ordinances* is מִשְׁפָּט (*mišĕppāṭ*) in Hebrew and refers to judg-ment, and *testimonies* is עֵדוּת (*ʿēdût*) in Hebrew and refers to the recorded Word of God. David charged Solomon to completely abide by all the Word of God.

In the past, as David was fleeing barefoot from his beloved Absalom with his face covered, he probably reflected upon his sin of adultery with Uriah's wife Bathsheba and killing Uriah, and he painfully repented again. Through experience, David learned the importance of keeping God's Word deep in his heart. The blessing for those who keep the Word of God is "prosperity" in whatever they do and wherever they go (Josh 1:7–8; Ps 1:2–3). If Solomon had deeply engraved his father's final words into his heart and had not accepted the idols of the Gentile women, then he would not have caused the nation to experience the tragedy of being divided into two.

Third, David instructed Solomon to walk before God in truth.

> **1 Kings 2:4** so that the LORD may carry out His promise which He spoke concerning me, saying, "If your sons are careful of their way, to walk before Me in truth with all their heart and with all their soul, you shall not lack a man on the throne of Israel."

David instructed Solomon to walk before God in truth. In this verse, the word *truth* is אֱמֶת (*'emet*) in Hebrew and means "truth" and "faithfulness." It refers to keeping an unchanging stable attitude in all circumstances. How can we walk before God in truth? We need to walk before God with all our hearts and with all our souls. The word *heart* is לֵבָב (*lēbāb*) in Hebrew, meaning "inner man" and "will," and *soul* is נֶפֶשׁ (*nepeš*), meaning "soul" and "life." "Heart and soul" is a reiterative expression referring to the whole person. The word *all* is כֹל (*kōl*) in Hebrew and means "the whole." Thus, the command "with all their heart and with all their soul" means to walk before God with your whole heart and your whole soul. No matter what we do, we can be truthful before God if we remain faithful with our heart and soul.

David's final words were a summary of the arduous journey of his life and the understanding he attained through the wind and frost of the 70 years of life. When we engrave these words deep in our hearts and obey them, the light of prosperity will shine brightly before us.

Hitherto, we have examined the life of David, a central figure in the genealogy of Jesus Christ. David's life was full of vicissitudes. When he was young, he was just a normal shepherd boy who tended sheep by green pastures and streams, but he was anointed king at the young age of about 15. He became famous after striking Goliath down with a sling and a stone, after which he became well-known and was invited to enter the palace. When the women sang, "Saul has slain his thousands, and David his ten thousands," David was put into a situation where he had to live a life of a fugitive, running from Saul, for ten golden years of his youth. During this time, David faced hardship each time he acted without inquiring of God first.

At last, at the age of 30, David became king of Judah in the city of Hebron; and at the age of 37, he became king of all of Israel, of both Israel and Judah. Nonetheless, at the apex of his life, he committed adultery with Uriah's wife Bathsheba, and later faced the tragedy of betrayal by his son, Absalom, which caused him to flee barefoot from his palace. After he had barely recovered his throne, he had a holy longing to build the temple and he prepared the resources. In the latter part of his reign he conducted a census and brought upon the land a plague of pestilence that killed 70,000 people.

Thus, David experienced much tumult in his life and had many shortcomings. Yet God evaluated David's life in the following manner after his death.

First, after Solomon offered a thousand burnt offerings on the altar, God appeared to him in a dream and said, "And if you walk in My ways, keeping My statutes and commandments, as your father David walked, then I will prolong your days" (1 Kgs 3:14). Here, God proclaimed that David had walked in God's ways and had kept his statues and commandments.

Second, after both the temple and the palace constructions were completed, God spoke to Solomon in 1 Kings 9:4 and said, "And as for you, if you will walk before Me as your father David walked, in integrity of heart and uprightness, doing according to all that I have commanded you and will keep My statutes and My ordinances." Here, God acknowledged David as having walked before God in integrity of heart and in uprightness.

Third, in 1 Kings 15:5, after Abijah (Abijam) succeeded Rehoboam as king, God stated, "David did what was right in the sight of the LORD, and had not turned aside from anything that He commanded him all the days of his life, except in the case of Uriah the Hittite." God said that David had done what was right in God's eyes all his life except for the incident with Uriah.

Fourth, in Acts 13:22, Paul in a sermon states, "And after He had removed him, He raised up David to be their king, concerning whom He also testified and said, 'I have found David the son of Jesse, a man after My heart, who will do all My will.'" Here, God proclaimed that David was a man after His own heart.

We can learn many important things through God's evaluation of David. Although David had many faults, God embraced David with His abounding love, forgave all his faults and did not remember them. God only remembered how David had kept His statues and commands all his life.

Thus, David is deemed as a good example of an upright person. When God evaluated an upright king, He said, "And Asa did what was right in the sight of the Lord, like David his father" (1 Kgs 15:11). When He evaluated kings who were not wholly devoted to Him, He said, "And he walked in all the sins of his father which he had committed before him; and his heart was not wholly devoted to the Lord his God, like the heart of his father David" (1 Kgs 15:3).

Thus, a "person after God's own heart" does not refer to a perfect person. A person after God's own heart is a person who may have many faults, but repents thoroughly and resolves to live according to God's Word. Such a person keeps the Word of God and obeys it in uprightness. No matter who we may be, there is bound to be shame and many shortcomings if all aspects of our life are scrutinized and revealed. However, the good news is that God will not question our sins and will cover them with the precious blood of Jesus Christ as long as we repent with all our hearts and "bring forth fruit in keeping with repentance" (Matt 3:8; Luke 3:8). We are blessed if we confess our transgressions, receive forgiveness and have our sins covered (Ps 32:1). Yet, those who conceal their transgressions will not prosper all their lives (Prov 28:13), and the burden will weigh down on them so heavily that there is not a moment of peace (Ps 38:4; Isa 48:22; 57:21). The Lord will not listen to the prayers of those whose hearts are wicked (Ps 66:18).

How God evaluates us in the last moment of our lives when we will be judged, is extremely important for it will decide where we will be for eternity. The issue will be whether we repented or not. The sins of which we have repented will be forgotten (Heb 10:17), but evil will cause us to remember the sins of which we have not repented (Ezek 21:24); and each one of us must give account of our own sins to God (Rom 14:12; 1 Pet 4:5).

Before we "fail the test" on that last day, we must reflect upon our past days and examine our faith and confirm it (2 Cor 13:5). Then, we can keep the Word of God for the rest of our days, so that like David we can become people after God's own heart and leave behind a blessed legacy of faith.

עמלק

מדבר צין הוא קדש

ים המלח

עתר

מוקדה

עיר כרמל

שבט

יהו

מדבר סיני

מדבר פארן

מדבר שור

ארץ פלשתים

אלהלד

באר שבע

שמעון

שבט

גת

אשקלון

ארק גשן

פתם

שרה

צען

אלכסנדרי

לוח המסעות במדבר
אשר על פי ה' יסעו ועל פי ה' יחנו

לט' הרהגדגד	טו' רתמה	א' רעמסס
ל' ייטבתה	טז' רמן פרץ	ב' סכת
לא' עברנה	יז' לבנה	ג' אתם
לב' עציןגבר	יח' רסה	ד' פיהחירת
לג' מדבר צין	יט' קהלתה	ה' מרה
לד' הרההר	ך' הרספר	ו' אילם
לה' צלמנה	כא' חרדה	ז' ים סוף
לו' פונן	כב' מקהלה	ח' מדבר סין
לז' אבת	כג' תחת	ט' רפקה
לח' דיבןגר	כד' תרח	יו' אלוש
לט' עלמןדבל	כה' מתקה	יא' רפידים
מ' הרי עברים	כו' חשמנה	יב' מדבר סיני
מא' ערבת מואב	כז' מסרות	יג' קברת התאוה
	כח' בני יעקן	יד' חצרות

CONCLUSION

The Unquenchable Lamp
of the Covenant

God is greater than all (John 10:29) and sovereign over heaven and earth (Acts 4:24; Rev 6:10). It is because God "so loved" the world that He, who is truly immeasurably great (1 Chr 16:25), sent His only begotten Son Jesus Christ to save the sinners (John 3:16). This great love of God is condensed into the genealogy of Jesus Christ and sealed into each of the names (Matt 1). This genealogy is divided into three time periods. The first period is a record from Abraham until David, 14 generations. The second period is a record from David until the migration into Babylon, 14 generations. The third period is a record from the time after the migration into Babylon until Jesus Christ, 14 generations.

The first period, from Abraham until David, deals with the history of Israel, from its birth until the establishment of the united Israel. There was a long period of time, 1,163 years, that extended between the birth of Abraham (2166 BC) to when David ascended the throne in Jerusalem (1003 BC). This long history is compressed into five verses in the genealogy of Jesus Christ in Matthew 1:2–6.

Now, I would like to conclude this book with an examination of God's administration in the history of redemption and the unquenchable lamp of the covenant revealed in the genealogy of Jesus Christ.

1. The Genealogy of Jesus Christ and God's Administration in the History of Redemption

The genealogy of Jesus Christ is a synopsis of God's redemptive work fulfilled through the covenant. Thus, God's amazing administration in the history of redemption is revealed through each person in this genealogy. The following is a synopsis of God's administration in the history of redemption revealed through the first period of the genealogy.

First, the genealogy of Jesus Christ emphasizes God's sovereign choice. Isaac, Jacob, Judah, Perez and Ram were not the firstborn but they appear in the genealogy of Jesus Christ as the firstborn. This is the work of God's sovereign election.

Isaac was Abraham's second son and he had an older brother, Ishmael, but God acknowledged Isaac as the firstborn and placed him in the genealogy of Jesus Christ (Matt 1:2). This was because Isaac was the child of the promise (Gen 21:1–5; Rom 9:7–8).

Jacob was also Isaac's second son. He had an older twin brother, Esau, but God acknowledged Jacob as the firstborn and placed him in the genealogy of Jesus Christ (Matt 1:2). Jacob was able to obtain the birthright and the blessing of the firstborn by the sovereign work of God (Gen 25:23; 27; Rom 9:10–13, 16; Heb 11:20).

Judah was the fourth son among Jacob's 12 sons. However, before Jacob died, he blessed Judah saying, "Judah, your brothers shall praise you; your hand shall be on the neck of your enemies; your father's sons shall bow down to you" (Gen 49:8). This was the prophecy that Judah would become the firstborn.

Perez was one of the twins that Tamar gave birth to through Judah. At first, the other twin, Zerah, stuck his hand out, so the midwife placed a scarlet thread on his hand. Then, the hand withdrew into the womb and Perez came out of the womb first (Gen 38:27–30).

Ram was the second of three sons born to Hezron through his first wife (1 Chr 2:9). However, God placed the second son Ram in the genealogy of Jesus Christ in the place of Jerahmeel, the first son (Matt 1:3).

By observing the lives of each person in the genealogy of Jesus Christ, we are able to confirm over and over again that everything was fulfilled according to God's sovereign choice. God's administration in the history of redemption is based on the foundation of His sovereignty. Our salvation is not achieved through our accomplishments, wealth, power, honor, scholarship or ability, but solely by God's sovereign grace (Eph 2:8–9; Titus 3:5).

Second, the genealogy of Jesus Christ proclaims that He is the savior of the entire universe and the chosen people. God broke the traditional structure of genealogies by including the names of women in the genealogy (Matt 1:3, 5). Furthermore, all the women who appear in the genealogy were Gentiles whom the Jews looked upon with contempt. Tamar and Rahab were Canaanite women and Ruth was a Moabite.

The inclusion of Gentile women, who were generally treated as unworthy, in the genealogy of Jesus Christ teaches us that there is no discrimination based on descent and that anyone can become righteous through faith in Jesus Christ (Rom 3:22; 10:11–13). Ultimately, Jesus Christ is not the savior of just the chosen nation of Israel, but the savior of all believers who receive Jesus Christ by the faith that is bestowed through the grace of God.

Although some people may be outside of Christ or strangers when it comes to the covenants of the promise, all who have become close in Jesus Christ through His blood are part of the same household which possesses the inheritance of heaven (Eph 2:12–13, 19).

Third, the genealogy of Jesus Christ testifies that living faith is the most important platform that fulfills the administration of the history of salvation (Heb 11:6). The three women who appear in the first period of the genealogy of Jesus Christ were great people of faith who advanced the path of Jesus Christ by the sovereign providence of God during times when the generations of the chosen Israel were on the verge of being disrupted.

Judah was the successor of God's covenant which had been passed down from Abraham, Isaac and Jacob, but while Judah had turned his back on this covenant, Tamar, with holy faith and righteous deed (Gen 38:26), risked her life and had relations with Judah, her father-in-law. She possessed a deep spiritual insight that realized that lineage of faith cannot come to a halt, and she wanted to establish Judah's wavering lineage. Thus, through Judah, Tamar gave birth to Perez and Zerah and advanced the genealogy of Jesus Christ (Gen 38:27–30; Matt 1:3).

Rahab was a lowly harlot who made her living by selling her body in the city of Jericho (Josh 2:1). However, she risked her life to hide the two spies whom Joshua had sent, and she protected them until the end (Josh 2:1–6). She possessed great faith which was expressed by her confession, "the LORD your God, He is God in heaven above and on earth beneath" (Josh 2:11), and she did not forget the promise made by the two spies to tie a "cord of scarlet thread in the window," and accordingly she did it (Josh 2:18; Jas 2:25). Realizing that her nation, the city of Jericho, would soon be destroyed, she did not fear the king, but welcomed the two spies in peace and acted in "faith" (Jas 2:25–26; Heb 11:31). Thus, she became the wife of Salmon and a great person of faith who maintained the genealogy of Jesus Christ (Matt 1:5).

Ruth, a Moabitess, was a widow and a Gentile (Ruth 1:4), but she, too, continued the genealogy of Jesus Christ during the spiritually dark times of the judges (Ruth 4:12, 18–22; Matt 1:5). The Moabites were a nation that originally began with the son born of the union between Abraham's nephew, Lot, and his older daughter (Gen 19:30). They were a gentile nation that was banned forever from entering the assembly of the Lord (Deut 23:3).

Though her mother-in-law, Naomi, told her to go back to her country when her husband died, Ruth confessed that Naomi's God would be her God (Ruth 1:16) and sought refuge under God's wings (Ruth 2:12). Much like Abraham who left Ur of the Chaldeans, Ruth left her family and country, and she followed Naomi in faith. As a result, she was guided under God's wings and met Boaz, who took her as wife (Ruth 2:12; 4:13). As a result, she was able to continue the genealogy of Jesus Christ by giving birth to Obed (Ruth 4:17; Matt 1:5).

No matter how complicated a person's past may be and no matter how many problems there were, God regards the living faith of today as more precious than the past. These three women gave their lives for their choice in life without any hesitation because they were convicted that it was the right decision. Consequently, these three women became the crucial links that helped the lamp of the covenant to continue burning in the divine history of salvation. No obstacle on this earth could stand in the way of their living faith for which they risked their lives.

Fourth, the genealogy of Jesus Christ proclaims that Jesus Christ is the fulfiller of the covenants with Abraham and David. The Old Testament opens with the universal proclamation in Genesis 1:1, "In the beginning God created the heavens and the earth," and the New Testament opens with the Messianic proclamation in Matthew 1:1, "The book of the genealogy of Jesus Christ, the son of David, the son of Abraham." The proclamation that the covenants of Abraham and David are fulfilled through Jesus Christ was the same as proclaiming that Jesus Christ is the Messiah.

The core of the covenant with Abraham was the promise regarding the Messiah. The phrases, "in you" (Gen 12:3) and "in him" (Gen 18:18), which appear in the covenant with Abraham mean that the Messiah will come in Abraham and as a descendant of Abraham. In addition, "your offspring" (Gen 15:5 - NIV) and "your seed" (Gen 22:17–18) are singular nouns and ultimately refer to Jesus Christ who will come as a descendant of Abraham (Gal 3:16).

Matthew 1:1 proclaims that Jesus Christ is the "son of Abraham" and testifies that the Messiah promised in the covenant with Abraham is Jesus Christ. The core of the covenant with David is also Jesus Christ. God promised that He would raise up a descendant from David's body and would establish the throne of his kingdom forever (2 Sam 7:12–16). This covenant has never actually been wholly fulfilled within the history of Israel. This is because there was no king who could reign over Israel forever.

Thus, the expression, "Jesus Christ, son of David," is a proclamation that only Jesus Christ is the one "offspring" who can establish the throne of the kingdom forever as God had promised David in the covenant (Luke 1:32–33; Heb 1:8).

Ultimately, after the fall of mankind, God promised that the Messiah would come as the seed of a woman (Gen 3:15), and this promise was reconfirmed and proclaimed again through the covenant with Abraham and the covenant with David.

2. The Unquenchable Lamp of the Covenant

The first period in the genealogy of Jesus Christ begins with Abraham and ends with David. Since God established His covenant with both Abraham and David, this period of the genealogy can be characterized as the time that begins and ends with God's covenant.

The covenant was the lamp of God in every period of history. 2 Chronicles 21:7 states, "Yet the LORD was not willing to destroy the house of David because of the covenant which He had made with David, and since He had promised to give a lamp to him and his sons forever." Here, God's establishment of a covenant is equated with Him giving a lamp. God's covenant established with His Word was God's lamp for that era (1 Chr 16:15; 2 Chr 21:7; Ps 105:8; 119:105; Prov 6:23).

The lamp of the covenant that God establishes never dies out. It is the unquenchable lamp of the covenant that burns eternally until its fulfillment. This is because God entered the covenant with an oath. An oath is a pledge stating that a person's words and deeds are sincere and that what has been promised will be done. In Israel, people often took an oath on the name of the powerful and holy Jehovah, who is One higher than they, in order to prove that their promise was sincere (Gen 21:23; Jer 5:2; Heb 6:16). This is because God does not change the things He has promised, but fulfills them (Ps 132:11). Psalm 110:4 states, "The LORD has sworn and will not change His mind" and Hebrew 6:17 states, "In the same way God, desiring even more to show to the heirs of the promise the unchangeableness of His purpose, interposed with an oath" (Heb 7:21). A covenant established through God's oath is "confirmed" (Ps 89:28) and will not be violated (Ps 89:34). Furthermore, it is an "eternal covenant" (Gen 9:12, 16; 17:7, 13, 19; Exod 31:16; Lev 24:8; 2 Sam 23:5; 1 Chr 16:17; Ps 105:8–10; 111:5, 9; Isa 55:3; Jer 32:40; Ezek 16:60; 37:26; Heb 13:20).

When God entered into a covenant with Abraham, Isaac and Jacob, He also established it with an oath (Gen 22:16–18; 24:7; 26:3; 50:24; Exod 6:8; 32:13; Deut 13:17; 29:12–13). God also entered into a covenant with Moses on the plains of Moab through an oath (Deut 29:12).

God also entered into a covenant with David with an oath (Ps 89:49; 132:11). Psalm 89 states, "Once I have sworn by My holiness" (Ps 89:35) and again, "O LORD, Which You swore to David in Your faithfulness" (Ps 89:49).

Covenants that God establishes with an oath are covenants that are fulfilled, and there is no power on this earth that can stand in the way. No matter how fierce the power of darkness tries to hinder God's providence, it cannot prevent the fulfillment of a covenant that the unchanging God has established with an oath.

This rule does not merely apply only to the Israelites, but also to us today. In the plains of Moab just before the Israelites' entrance into Canaan, Moses gathered the people and spoke of God's covenant made through an oath with His people saying, "Now not with you alone am I making this covenant and this oath, but both with those who stand here with us today in the presence of the LORD our God and with those who are not with us here today" (Deut 29:14–15). Here, the phrase, "those who are not with us here today," refer to the future descendants of Israel and ultimately, to all the believers in Jesus Christ who are the spiritual descendants of Abraham (Rom 4:11, 16; Gal 3:7, 29). Thus, this covenant will be eternally in effect until the kingdom of God is completely established.

The Israelites committed a countless number of sins from the time of Abraham until the time of David. They broke God's heart during the 430 years of slavery and the 40 years of the wilderness journey with unbelief and grumblings of every kind. In addition, during the spiritually dark times of the judges, they pounded nails into the heart of God by worshipping idols of all sorts. Even through this time of sin by His chosen people, God did not forsake His providence for salvation. He punished His people, made them repent and turn back, and forgave them and bestowed mercy upon them. From Abraham until David, the violent attacks of Satan and ferocious winds of darkness could not quench the lamp of the covenant. Rather, it burned endlessly toward Jesus Christ, who is at the apex of the redemptive history. This is based on the oath of the God who does not extinguish even a dimly burning wick (Isa 42:3). The covenant that God establishes with an oath will surely be unchanged and be fulfilled.

God's oath, which appears in His covenants, is the driving force behind the work of salvation. Furthermore, this oath is revealed through the zeal of God who fulfills the covenants. God with His fervent zeal advances the work of salvation in order to fulfill His covenant.

3. God's Zeal to Fulfill the Work of Salvation

It is the zeal of God, which keeps working without rest, that does not allow the lamp of the covenant to dim and burn out but fulfills His providence in order to save fallen mankind.

> Isaiah 9:6–7 states, "For a child will be born to us, a son will be given to us; and the government will rest on His shoulders; and His name will be called Wonderful, Counselor, Mighty God, Eternal Father, Prince of Peace. There will be no end to the increase of His government or of peace, on the throne of David and over his kingdom, to establish it and to uphold it with justice and righteousness from then on and forevermore. The zeal of the LORD of hosts will accomplish this."

These verses are primarily prophecies regarding the first coming of Jesus Christ. Jesus Christ is the Word made flesh; He was conceived by the Holy Spirit and came as a child, as a Son (John 1:14; Matt 1:18), but He is the Almighty God, the Eternal Father and the Prince of Peace. However, these verses are also prophecies regarding the second coming of Christ. When Jesus comes again, there will be no end to the increase of His government or of peace. As the Prince of Peace, He will firmly establish God's kingdom and will uphold it with justice and righteousness forevermore. Thus, Isaiah 9:6–7 sums up the essence of God's administration in the history of redemption, which includes both the first and the second coming of the Lord.

The amazing truth is that it is God's zeal that fulfills all this. The word *zeal* is קִנְאָה (*kin'â*) in Hebrew and means "ardor" and "jealousy" (Num 25:11). This is not the jealousy that slays the simple (Job 5:2), but God's authoritative and exclusive love that saves His people and makes them to love only Him. It refers to a love on the universal scale that restores all of His creation that is out of order (2 Cor 5:14), and a love so great that compels God our Father who is greater than all, to come in the flesh (John 3:16).

Isaiah 59:17 describes God who is full of this love as having "wrapped Himself with zeal as a mantle." This zeal is the lamp, fiery and tall, burning brightly inside God's heart for the salvation of fallen mankind.

This lamp of zeal was brightly illuminated through the covenants of the Old and New Testaments until it finally reached its summit with the cross of Jesus Christ. God demonstrates His own love toward us, in that while we were yet sinners, Christ died for us (Rom 5:8).

Even at this moment, God's lamp of salvation burns vigorously for all eternity from the cross of Jesus Christ. In every place that these flames reach, the winds of repentance rise up. People will pound their hearts in repentance and a countless number of His holy people will freely come before God (Ps 110:3).

There is no force on this earth that can stand in the way of the unquenchable zeal of God's love. No force or enemy in heaven or earth can separate us from the burning love of Jesus Christ, no matter how strong it may be (Rom 8:35, 38–39).

Psalm 68:16 states, "Why do you look with envy, O mountains with many peaks, at the mountain which God has desired for His abode? Surely, the LORD will dwell there forever." Here, the "mountains with many peaks" refer to the mountains that make up the mountains of Bashan (Ps 68:15), but symbolically they refer to all the forces of Satan that oppose God's covenant and act as a hindrance to its fulfillment. On the other hand, "the mountain which God has desired for His abode" is Mount Zion and refers to the Church and God's people with whom He resides (Ps 2:6; 9:11; 74:2; 87:1–2; 132:13–14; Isa 4:5; 31:4; 60:14; Joel 3:17, 21; Zech 8:3).

The "many peaks" were also originally God's mountains (Ps 68:15), because God created the high mountains and their majestic grandeur comes from God. However, they exalted themselves from the beginning thinking they were high (Dan 8:11; 11:36), and became proud in their disbelief and challenged God. This is a description of the hostile attitude and desire of the forces of Satan that seek to destroy God's covenant and tear down the Church and His people. These forces became jealous of God's people and the Church. The word *envy* in "Why do you look with envy" in Psalm 68:16 is רָצַד (*rāṣad*) in Hebrew and means "to be jealous," "to look with envious hostility" (to look with eyes filled with evil intentions to fight) and "to watch stealthily." At first glance, it may appear that the mountains of Bashan will overcome Mount Zion in battle.

However, Mount Zion will surely win this battle. This battle is not won by the number of soldiers or by their might (Ps 33:16; 1 Sam 14:6; 17:47). Mount Zion will triumph because it is the mountain in which God abides eternally and the mountain that the myriads of angels guard over (Ps 68:16–17; Gen 32:1–2; 2 Kgs 6:16–18; Ps 34:7; Dan 6:22; Zech 1:8, 11; 6:1–7; Heb 1:14; cf. Ps 5:12; 33:20).

Although all the forces of Satan, the "many peaks," gather in an attempt to quench the lamp of the covenant and oppose it, the Church and God's people will triumph because the God who works with burning zeal is with them.

God's fervent zeal will unquenchably burn as the lamp of the covenant will continue to burn until the day that God's administration in the history of redemption is completed, until all those who had become Satan's spiritual prisoners and captives of sin return to God (2 Kgs 19:30–31; Ezek 39:25), and until the people of God are resurrected and transfigured at the sound of the last trumpet when Jesus Christ returns (1 Cor 15:51–54).

O Lord our God, the Lord of hosts,
May the lamp of Your zeal and the lamp of the covenant
Burn brightly in the hearts of all Your people
Among all the nations of the world,
And throughout the entire universe
Until the day of Your redemptive administration
is completely fulfilled!

עמלק

מדבר צין הוא קדש

ים המלח

עתר
מקדה

עיר כרמל

מדבר סיני

שבט יה

מדבר פארן

מדבר שור

באר שבע
שבט שמעון

שבט

ארץ פלשתים

ארץ גשן
פתם
שרה
צען
רעמסס

אלכסנדרי

ים

לוח המסעות במדבר
אשר על פי׳ הסעו ועל פי׳ היחנו

כט׳ חרהגדגד	טו׳ רחמה	א׳ רעמסס
ל׳ ילבתה	טז׳ רמן פרץ	ב׳ סכת
לא׳ עברתה	יז׳ לבנה	ג׳ אתם
לב׳ עציונגבר	יח׳ רסה	ד׳ פיהחירת
לג׳ מדברצין	יט׳ קהלתה	ה׳ מרה
לד׳ ההרההר	כ׳ הרספר	ו׳ אילם
לה׳ צלמנה	כא׳ חרדה	ז׳ ים סוף
לו׳ פונן	כב׳ מקהלה	ח׳ מדברסין
לז׳ אבת	כג׳ תחת	ט׳ דפקה
לח׳ דיבןגד	כד׳ תרח	יו׳ אלוש
לט׳ עלמןדבלתי	כה׳ מתקה	יא׳ רפידם
מ׳ הרי עברים	כו׳ חשמנה	יב׳ מדברסיני
מא׳ ערבתמואב	כז׳ מסרות	יג׳ קברתהתאוה
	כח׳ בני יעקן	יד׳ חצרת

Commentaries and References

Dr. Yeong-Su Ye

President of the International Christian Academy
President of the International Council of Churches and Ministries
Former President of Hanshin University Graduate School

As a scholar, coming across a good book brings me great happiness. Not only does a good book display the author's background and culture, it is a representation of his life. Every time I open the pages of *The Unquenchable Lamp of the Covenant*, I am pleased to note that the author is as sharp as ever even now that he has become a mature and seasoned man of God. The author's untiring effort to research the material is clearly evident in this great book.

When we open this book, we see the heading "God Who Is Greater Than All," and the following text describes the vast panorama of the universe. Author Rev. Abraham Park explains that God's *agape* love is incomparably greater than the vast and perfectly conducted planetary movements of the universe. This everlasting love exists solely in the hope that it will save even one solitary soul; therefore, this saving grace is too precious to be put into words.

The author proclaims that the genealogy of Jesus Christ is part of God's work of Salvation in which God, the creator "who so loved the world" sent His only son, Jesus Christ, so that the people of the world may "believe in him and they will gain everlasting life." Not only does the author clearly reveal the lives of Joseph's 41 ancestors shown in Matthew 1, and Mary's 77 ancestors in Luke 3, but he also compares their ancestries to prove God's perfectly calculated redemptive administration. The author also explains the historical, economic, political, and even religious settings of each important individual's time period in God's redemptive plan. The interesting definitions of the characters' names illuminate how the names affected their personalities, and even influenced their actions.

This book also illustrates how God's redemptive administration is linked to our own lives and salvation. It is awe-inspiring to see God's plan unfold through this progression of characters that led to the coming of our savior, Jesus Christ. Each individual carries a role that is perfectly synchronized with God's puzzling, yet perfect plan for a redemptive salvation.

Rev. Abraham Park made a hit in the Christian community when he released *The Genesis Genealogies* in 2007 and *The Covenant of the Torch* in 2008. He surprised the community once again with this third book, which follows the theme of Jesus' genealogy seen through the lens of God's redemptive plan. We cannot help but be in awe of the author's passion for reviving the gospel and striving to find God's life-giving plan. In this succinctly written book, there is a truthful dedication in each and every word that is unique to the author. Like a final confession, his writing is full of earnest sincerity.

The author also shares his individuality by explaining his victories against many trials and tribulations that he encountered during his long life of 80 years with the great love of Jesus Christ. This book burns with a passionate faith for Jesus Christ from beginning to end. Dear readers, this book plainly exposes the abstract substance of faith through God's redemption.

Simply put, this book is the nexus of theology and ministry, logic and evidence, and sermons and scientific theories. The unfortunate truth is that many preachers deliver a sermon without any theological elements. A message that is focused on practicality may move the hearts of the congregation at times, but can also stray from the background of theology and cause an injurious effect. On the other hand, many theologians fail to affect their audiences due to their heavy reliance on theories and research. Pastor Abraham Park's superb book deftly sidesteps these potential flaws, combining ministerial and theological elements. I am deeply confident that this book will aid individual researchers of the Bible and further assist congregational studies performed in churches.

Above all, this book's strength lies in its faithful exposition of God's redemptive administration. The large cast of biblical characters is presented in order to teach, remind, and correct. Although many biblical figures boasted great achievements, their greatness should be strictly reflected towards the Glory of God. Be it a story of a character's good faith, or even the decline of the unfaithful, both narratives point towards God's ultimate plan. Despite Satan's evil doings and numerous sinful deviations, wicked characters, and human failings, God's plan has never stopped or faltered. The excitement only continues to grow as we await the triumphant and majestic return of Jesus Christ, which will be the final step to completing God's redemptive plan. These historic proceedings have been brilliantly examined in the author's groundbreaking study of Jesus Christ's genealogy.

The author has given us the names of all the biblical figures in Jesus Christ's genealogy, supporting bible verses, brief explanations, an outline of genealogical characters, a list of generations, details of the flight of David, David's lineage, and so on, allowing readers to thoroughly understand the genealogy. No other theologian or preacher has ever attempted to trace Jesus' lineage in such detail. The author's decision to delve into the Bible shows that he's been blessed with rare and remarkable spiritual insight—evidence of a lifetime spent in prayer and the study of God's word. The author's theology is based upon redemption and the covenant. This work claims that the entire history of the Old Testament was purposefully written for Jesus Christ's redemptive plan, and furthermore examines the various covenants that God made after the fall of man.

Ultimately, this book's finest conclusion is that once God has made a covenant, no amount of sinful intrusion should weaken our faith that God will fulfill His promise. Although we strive to live with faith, often times we fall and surrender to our human frailty. I can think of countless instances of failure in my own life, but the proclamation that God uses both victory *and* failure in order to complete His redemptive plan should give us all a new hope and strength. This book's conclusion is is reflected by its title. It's a declaration that we can continue to hope upon the unquenchable lamp of the covenant. Jesus spoke to His frightened disciples in Matthew 10:26, "So have no fear of them, for nothing is covered that will not be revealed, or hidden that will not be known." This was a proclamation made by the Lord that confidently assures us that the gospel is the true wisdom and there will come a day when it will be revealed to the entire world.

I sincerely hope that this precious book will open a path for the gospel, still stained with the blood of Jesus Christ, to spread throughout the entire world and be used as a tool in God's plan for salvation. As the author concluded, "God's fervent zeal will unquenchably burn along with the lamp of the covenant until the day that God's administration in the history of redemption is completed." I hope that readers will join the author in his unrelenting effort for sharing Jesus Christ's work of redemption.

Yeong-Su Ye

Bishop Kwang-Young Jang

First President of the Bishops Association of the Methodist Church

This is Rev. Abraham Park's third book in the History of Redemption series: *The Unquenchable Lamp of the Covenant*. Many Christian books have flooded the market but the unfortunate reality for readers is that there are not many books that inspire and move the hearts of their readers. When I first started to read this book I figured it would be just another one of those kinds of books, but I was surprised to feel my heart being touched as I found myself being totally immersed into the book.

Rev. Abraham Park makes it easy for the reader to understand theological themes or biblical contents as he explains them with simplicity in the view of the history of redemption. The fascinating thing is that as you read this book, you are able to experience all of the characters and events of the history of redemption as if you were seeing the magnificent panoply from one choice vantage point.

I believe that a book of this weight and depth must only be the result of Rev. Abraham Park's life-long spiritual experience of Bible study and prayer, coupled with his extensive research.

This great work explores the genealogy of Jesus Christ, which traces back to the Old Testament. I am certain that it is by God's grace that the author, through deep meditation and research into the original language, was able to explore the lives of even the most obscure biblical characters and deftly tie them into God's spiritual vein that runs throughout the Bible.

His theology, in simple terms, is covenantal and redemptive. The Bible is a book of covenants, starting with the promise of the woman's seed after the fall of Adam and Eve in Genesis 3:15 until the fulfillment of the new covenant of Jesus Christ. The author explains this clearly through the genealogy of Jesus Christ.

As he shows in the introduction, this book expresses the author's philosophy and theology. The History of Redemption series is like a well-ripened fruit of the author's faith because the books are written with truthful life of prayer and intimate fellowship with God. I believe this is a "must-read" book for all, and recommended for all pastors and laypeople.

Kwang-Young Jang

Dr. Ki-Ho Sung

Former President of Sungkyul University

During my years of studies, the most difficult time during history class was memorizing people's names and dates. It was particularly difficult to memorize foreign names and places. I feel it is the same now when I come across difficult biblical names and places.

One of the reasons that believers give up reading the Bible part way through is that the contents are often confusing, dry, and repetitive. In Genesis the expressions "It became evening and it became morning, it was so and so day," are hard to get past. In Matthew it repeats the expression, "someone bore somebody," throughout the genealogy. Therefore, some people recommend that first-time Bible readers should read Mark first because there is no genealogy in the Gospel of Mark.

However, Rev. Abraham Park has been continuously publishing books about those genealogies and their years, making it easier for ministers and even lay people to understand them. Having spent tens of his ministerial years in praying two hours and reading the Bible three hours daily, Rev. Park has published *The Genesis Genealogies, The Covenant of the Torch*, and now, *The Unquenchable Lamp of the Covenant*. They are truly the great fruit of the author's efforts, and I highly anticipate the remaining books of the series that have not yet been published.

Because the third book in the History of Redemption series, *The Unquenchable Lamp of the Covenant* covers the genealogy of Jesus Christ, its roots extend all the way up to the eternal God.

Almighty God's plan for the redemption of mankind is clearly revealed in the genealogy of Jesus Christ. *The Unquenchable Lamp of the Covenant* illustrates how God's covenants have been fulfilled throughout history, and continue to be upheld today.

The lives of the patriarchs who were put in the genealogy of Jesus were very complex and turbulent at times; however this precious book reveals how the plan of God's salvation continued its undaunted march toward fulfillment.

This book's well-organized genealogical summaries, be it the ascending genealogy in the Gospel of Matthew concerning Jesus' father Joseph or the descending genealogy concerning Mary's family that reaches all the way up to God, clearly show Jesus Christ as the descendent of Abraham and David.

The Unquenchable Lamp of the Covenant is the product of Rev. Abraham Park's extensive biblical knowledge and deep research, and is leading many believers on the path of righteousness. He clarifies various challenging topics through research on the original languages, commentaries of other biblical scholars, and other sources. The richness and significance of the subject matter causes the reader to take interest in the often overlooked and rarely understood subject of genealogies and chronologies. Readers are now able to examine God's profound administration, which has been hidden like a mystery. This fine book reveals Rev. Abraham Park's true merit, and I heartily recommend it.

成耆虎
Ki-Ho Sung

The 42 Generations in the Genealogy of Jesus Christ at a Glance

Matt 1:17 Therefore all the generations from Abraham to David are fourteen generations; and from David to the deportation to Babylon fourteen generations; and from the deportation to Babylon to the time of Christ fourteen generations.

Πᾶσαι οὖν αἱ γενεαὶ ἀπὸ Ἀβραὰμ ἕως Δαυὶδ γενεαὶ δεκατέσσαρες, καὶ ἀπὸ Δαυὶδ ἕως τῆς μετοικεσίας Βαβυλῶνος γενεαὶ δεκατέσσαρες, καὶ ἀπὸ τῆς μετοικεσίας Βαβ υλῶνος ἕως τοῦ Χριστοῦ γενεαὶ δεκατέσσαρες.

	The First Period (1,163 years)	
	THE GENEALOGY IN MATTHEW 1 (14 GENERATIONS FROM ABRAHAM TO DAVID)	THE GENEALOGY IN LUKE 3 (FROM THE SAME TIME PERIOD—14 GENERATIONS)
Time of the patriarchs	1 **Abraham /** אַבְרָהָם **/** Ἀβραάμ (Matt 1:2; 1 Chr 1:27, 34)	1 **Abraham /** Ἀβραάμ (Luke 3:34)
	2 **Isaac /** יִצְחָק **/** Ἰσαάκ (Matt 1:2; 1 Chr 1:28, 34)	2 **Isaac /** Ἰσαάκ (Luke 3:34)
	3 **Jacob /** יַעֲקֹב **/** Ἰακώβ (Matt 1:2; 1 Chr 1:34; 2:1)	3 **Jacob /** Ἰακώβ (Luke 3:34)
	4 **Judah /** יְהוּדָה **/** Ἰούδας (Matt 1:2-3; 1 Chr 2:1)	4 **Judah /** Ἰούδας (Luke 3:33)
Time in Egypt	By Tamar (Matt 1:3)	
	5 **Perez /** פֶּרֶץ **/** Φαρές (Matt 1:3; 1 Chr 2:4; Ruth 4:18)	5 **Perez /** Φαρές (Luke 3:33)
	6 **Hezron /** חֶצְרוֹן **/** Ἑσρώμ (Matt 1:3; 1 Chr 2:5; Ruth 4:18-19)	6 **Hezron /** Ἑσρώμ (Luke 3:33)
	7 **Ram /** רָם **/** Ἀράμ (Matt 1:3-4; 1 Chr 2:9-10; Ruth 4:19)	7 **Ram /** Ἀράμ (Luke 3:33)
	8 **Amminadab /** עַמִּינָדָב **/** Ἀμιναδάβ (Matt 1:4; 1 Chr 2:10; Ruth 4:19-20)	8 **Amminadab /** Ἀμιναδάβ (Luke 3:33)
Time during the wilderness journey and the conquest of Canaan	9 **Nahshon /** נַחְשׁוֹן **/** Ναασσών (Matt 1:4; 1 Chr 2:10-11; Ruth 4:20)	9 **Nahshon /** Ναασσών (Luke 3:32)
	10 **Salmon /** שַׂלְמוֹן **/** Σαλμών (Matt 1:4-5; 1 Chr 2:11; Ruth 4:20-21)	10 **Salmon /** Σαλμών (Luke 3:32)
Time of the judges	By Rahab (Matt 1:5)	
	11 **Boaz /** בֹּעַז **/** Βοός (Matt 1:5; 1 Chr 2:11-12; Ruth 4:21)	11 **Boaz /** Βοός (Luke 3:32)
	By Ruth (Matt 1:5)	
	12 **Obed /** עוֹבֵד **/** Ὠβήδ (Matt 1:5; 1 Chr 2:12; Ruth 4:21-22)	12 **Obed /** Ὠβήδ (Luke 3:32)
	13 **Jesse /** יִשַׁי **/** Ἰεσσαί (Matt 1:5-6; 1 Chr 2:12-13; Ruth 4:22)	13 **Jesse /** Ἰεσσαι (Luke 3:32)
Time of the unified kingdom	14 **David /** דָּוִד מֶלֶךְ **/** Δαβίδ Βασιλεύς (Matt 1:6; 1 Chr 2:15; Ruth 4:22)	14 **David /** Δαβίδ Βασιλεύς (Luke 3:31)

*The first and the second periods of the genealogy are distinguished by the two different periods of David's reign—7 years and 6 months in Hebron and 33 years in Jerusalem (2 Sam 5:4-5; 1 Chr 3:4; 29:27; 1 Kgs 2:11).

The Second Period (406 years)

Period	No.	The Genealogy in Matthew 1 (14 Generations of Kings from David to Babylonian captivity)	No.	The Genealogy in Luke 3 (from the same time period)
Time of the unified kingdom	1	**David** / דָּוִד / Δαβίδ (Matt 1:6; 1 Chr 2:15; Ruth 4:22)		
		By the wife of Uriah (Matt 1:6)		
	2	**Solomon** / שְׁלֹמֹה / Σολομών (Matt 1:6-7; 1 Chr 3:5)	15	**Nathan** / Ναθάν (Luke 3:31)
Time of the divided kingdom	3	**Rehoboam** / רְחַבְעָם / Ῥοβοάμ (Matt 1:7; 1 Chr 3:10)	16	**Mattatha** / Ματταθά (Luke 3:31)
	4	**Abijah** / אֲבִיָּה / Ἀβιά (Matt 1:7; 1 Chr 3:10)	17	**Menna** / Μεννά (Luke 3:31)
	5	**Asa** / אָסָא / Ἀσά (Matt 1:7-8; 1 Chr 3:10)	18	**Melea** / Μελεᾶ (Luke 3:31)
	6	**Jehoshaphat** / יְהוֹשָׁפָט / Ἰωσαφάτ (Matt 1:8; 1 Chr 3:10)	19	**Eliakim** / Ἐλιακείμ (Luke 3:30)
	7	**Joram** / יוֹרָם / Ἰωράμ (Matt 1:8; 1 Chr 3:11)	20	**Jonam** / Ἰωνάν (Luke 3:30)
		Kings omitted from the genealogy **Ahaziah** / אֲחַזְיָה (1 Chr 3:11) **Athaliah** / עֲתַלְיָה (2 Kgs 11:1-3; 2 Chr 22:12) **Joash** / יוֹאָשׁ (1 Chr 3:11) **Amaziah** / אֲמַצְיָה (1 Chr 3:12)	21	**Joseph** / Ἰωσήφ (Luke 3:30)
			22	**Judah** / Ἰούδας (Luke 3:30)
	8	**Uzziah** / עֻזִּיָּה / Ὀζίας (Matt 1:8-9; 1 Chr 3:12)	23	**Simeon** / Συμεών (Luke 3:30)
			24	**Levi** / Λευί (Luke 3:29)
	9	**Jotham** / יוֹתָם / Ἰωθάμ (Matt 1:9; 1 Chr 3:12)	25	**Matthat** / Ματθάτ (Luke 3:29)
	10	**Ahaz** / אָחָז / Ἀχάζ (Matt 1:9; 1 Chr 3:13)		
	11	**Hezekiah** / חִזְקִיָּה / Ἐζεκίας (Matt 1:9-10; 1 Chr 3:13)	26	**Jorim** / Ἰωρείμ (Luke 3:29)
	12	**Manasseh** / מְנַשֶּׁה / Μανασσῆς (Matt 1:10; 1 Chr 3:13)	27	**Eliezer** / Ἐλιέζερ (Luke 3:29)
	13	**Amon** / אָמוֹן / Ἀμώς (Matt 1:10; 1 Chr 3:14)	28	**Joshua** / Ἰησοῦς (Luke 3:29)
	14	**Josiah** / יֹאשִׁיָּה / Ἰωσίας (Matt 1:10-11; 1 Chr 3:14)	29	**Er** / Ἤρ (Luke 3:28)
		Kings omitted from the genealogy **Jehoahaz** / יְהוֹאָחָז (2 Kgs 23:31; 1 Chr 3:15; 2 Chr 36:1-2) **Jehoiakim** / יְהוֹיָקִים (2 Kgs 23:34, 36; 1 Chr 3:15; 2 Chr 36:4)	30	**Elmadam** / Ἐλμωδάμ (Luke 3:28)

*There may be some inevitable errors in the years of the 41 generations from Mattatha to Jesus in Luke's genealogy because the Bible does not expound on their lives.

The Third Period (593 years)	
THE GENEALOGY IN MATTHEW 1 (14 GENERATIONS FROM POST-BABYLONIAN CAPTIVITY TO JESUS CHRIST)	THE GENEALOGY IN LUKE 3 (FROM THE SAME TIME PERIOD)
1 Jeconiah / יְכָנְיָה / Ἰεχονίας (Matt 1:11-12; 1 Chr 3:16)	31 Cosam / Κωσάμ (Luke 3:28)
King omitted from the genealogy Zedekiah / צִדְקִיָּה (2 Kgs 24:18; 1 Chr 3:16)	
2 Shealtiel / שְׁאַלְתִּיאֵל / Σαλαθιὴλ (Matt 1:12; 1 Chr 3:17)	32 Addi / Ἀδδί (Luke 3:28)
3 Zerubbabel / זְרֻבָּבֶל / Ζοροβαβέλ (Matt 1:12-13; 1 Chr 3:19)	33 Melchi / Μελχί (Luke 3:28)
→ Hananiah (1 Chr 3:21)	34 Neri / Νηρί (Luke 3:27)
→ Shecaniah (1 Chr 3:22)	35 Shealtiel / Σαλαθιήλ (Luke 3:27)
→ Shemaiah (1 Chr 3:22)	36 Zerubbabel / Ζοροβάβελ (Luke 3:27)
→ Neariah (1 Chr 3:23)	37 Rhesa / Ῥησά (Luke 3:27)
→ Elioenai (1 Chr 3:24)	38 Joanan / Ἰωαννά (Luke 3:27)
4 Abihud / אֲבִיהוּד / Ἀβιούδ (Matt 1:13)	39 Joda / Ἰωδά (Luke 3:26)
	40 Josech / Ἰωσὴχ (Luke 3:26)
5 Eliakim / אֶלְיָקִים / Ἐλιακείμ (Matt 1:13)	41 Semein / Σεμεῒ (Luke 3:26)
	42 Mattathias / Ματταθίας (Luke 3:26)
6 Azor / עַזּוּר / Ἀζώρ (Matt 1:13-14)	43 Maath / Μάαθ (Luke 3:26)
	44 Naggai / Ναγγαί (Luke 3:25)
7 Zadok / צָדוֹק / Σαδώκ (Matt 1:14)	45 Hesli / Ἐσλί (Luke 3:25)
	46 Nahum / Ναούμ (Luke 3:25)
8 Achim / יוֹקִים / Ἀχείμ (Matt 1:14)	47 Amos / Ἀμώς (Luke 3:25)
9 Eliud / אֱלִיהוּד / Ἐλιούδ (Matt 1:14-15)	48 Mattathias / Ματταθίας (Luke 3:25)
	49 Joseph / Ἰωσήφ (Luke 3:24)
10 Eleazar / אֶלְעָזָר / Ἐλεάζαρ (Matt 1:15)	50 Jannai / Ἰαννά (Luke 3:24)
	51 Melchi / Μελχί (Luke 3:24)
11 Matthan / מַתָּן / Ματθάν (Matt 1:15)	52 Levi / Λευί (Luke 3:24)
	53 Matthat / Ματθάτ (Luke 3:24)
12 Jacob / יַעֲקֹב / Ἰακώβ (Matt 1:15-16)	54 Eli / Ἡλί (Luke 3:23)
Mary's husband 13 Joseph / יוֹסֵף / Ἰωσήφ (Matt 1:16)	55 Joseph / Ἰωσήφ (Luke 3:23)
By Mary 14 Jesus / יֵשׁוּעַ / Ἰησοῦς (Matt 1:16)	56 Jesus / Ἰησοῦς (Luke 3:23)

Side labels (left margin):
- Time of the Babylonian captivity
- Time of reconstructing the temple and the wall
- The inter-testamental times

*The estimated time span of the third period is from the time of the Babylonian captivity until the inter-testament period.

Outline of the 42 Generations in the Genealogy of Matthew—First Period

– 14 Generations from Abraham to David

People	History
1st Generation **Abraham** אַבְרָהָם 'Αβραάμ Father of a multitude, father of many nations	① Abraham is the first person to be listed in the genealogy of Jesus Christ. His father is Terah, and his heir who continues the lineage is Isaac (1 Chr 1:27, Matt 1:2, Luke 3:34). ② Abraham's original name was *Abram*, which means "exalted father," and he was renamed at the age of 99 as *Abraham*, meaning "father of a multitude" and "father of many nations" (Gen 17:5). As the name signifies, Abraham is not only the Jews' forefather; through Jesus Christ, he is the father of faith for all peoples of the earth (John 8:53; Rom 4:1, 16, 18; Gal 3:7, 29). ③ He first received God's calling in Ur of the Chaldeans (Acts 7:2–4). He received his second calling in Haran when he was 75 years old and finally arrived in Canaan (Gen 12:5). At the age of 84, he received confirmation about the land and his descendants through the covenant of the torch (Gen 15:1–21). At the age of 86, he became the father of Ishmael by Hagar (Gen 16:16). At the age of 100, he became the father of the promised son, Isaac, by Sarah (Gen 21:5). ④ The promise of a descendant that God spoke to Abraham (Gen 13:15–16) ultimately refers to the one seed, Jesus Christ, who would later come through his lineage (Gal 3:16).
2nd Generation **Isaac** יִצְחָק 'Ισαάκ To laugh	① Isaac is the second person in the genealogy of Jesus Christ. His father is Abraham, and his heir who continues the lineage is Jacob (1 Chr 1:28, 34; Matt 1:2; Luke 3:34). ② Isaac is the promised son, born through Sarah at the appointed time of which God had spoken, that is, when Abraham was 100 years old (Gen 17:18–21; 18:10; 14; 21:1–5; Rom 9:7–8). ③ At the age of 40, Isaac married Rebekah, the daughter of Bethuel (Gen 24; 25:20). At the age of 60, as the result of his prayer, he became the father of twins, Esau (the firstborn) and Jacob (the second born) (Gen 25:21–26). ④ After Isaac, the generation of faith continues down to Jacob. Outwardly, it seems as though Isaac was deceived by Jacob and unknowingly blessed him with the blessings of the firstborn, but in actuality it was by God's sovereign providence (Gen 25:23; 27:26–40; Rom 9:10–13; Heb 11:20).

People	History
3rd Generation **Jacob** יַעֲקֹב Ἰακώβ The one who takes by the heel, supplanter	① Jacob is the third person in the genealogy of Jesus Christ. His father is Isaac, and his heir who continues the lineage is Judah (1 Chr 1:34; Matt 1:2; 1 Chr 2:1; Luke 3:34). ② He dwelled in the same tents with his grandfather Abraham and his father Isaac for 15 years (Heb 11:9), where he inherited their covenantal faith. Although Esau was clearly the firstborn, he lost the blessing to his younger brother Jacob (Rom 9:10–13) because Esau despised the birthright (Gen 25:31–34). ③ Jacob was 76 years old when he left Canaan to flee from his older brother Esau (Gen 28:1–5). For 20 years, from 76 to 96 years of age, Jacob served in his uncle Laban's household. He got married when he was 83 years old (Gen 29:18–30), and at the age of 90, he had his 11th son, Joseph, through Rachel (Gen 30:22–24). ④ Jacob's godly act of drawing in his feet on his deathbed (Gen 49:33) speaks of his great unwavering faith in settling accounts before God from his walk of life right until his very last step.
4th Generation **Judah** יְהוּדָה Ἰούδας To praise	① Judah is the fourth person in the genealogy of Jesus Christ. His father is Jacob, and he had five sons. Among the five sons, Perez was listed in the genealogy of Jesus Christ (Matt 1:2–3; Luke 3:33; 1 Chr 2:1–4). ② From his father, he received the blessings of the "scepter," which symbolizes a king's sovereignty and power. It also represents the blessing of the coming of Messiah who is symbolized by "Shiloh" (the giver of peace and rest). Just as Jacob prophesied in this blessing, Jesus was born in the tribe of Judah (Matt 1:3; Heb 7:14; cf. Mic 5:2). ③ Judah had three sons, Er, Onan and Shelah, from his wife (the daughter of Shua; Gen 38:2–5). Later, he had Perez and Zerah by Tamar, his daughter-in-law (Gen 38:27–30). With divine zeal, Tamar risked her life to obtain a covenantal descendant to succeed Abraham, Isaac and Jacob, and hence erected Judah's failing family line. For this, the Bible acknowledged her as "righteous" (Gen 38:26; Ruth 4:12). ④ The name *Tamar* (תָּמָר) originated from the root "to be erect," and means "pillar, palm tree."
5th Generation **Perez** פֶּרֶץ Φαρές Breach, break through	① Perez is the fifth person in the genealogy of Jesus Christ. His father is Judah, and his heir who continues the lineage is Hezron (1 Chr 2:4; Matt 1:3; Luke 3:33; Ruth 4:18). ② Perez is one of Judah's twins by Tamar, his daughter-in-law. He became the firstborn by bursting out before Zerah, who had the scarlet thread on his hand (Gen 38:27–30). ③ After succeeding Judah in the genealogy of the Messianic lineage, Perez became the father of two sons, "Hezron and Hamul" (1 Chr 2:5).

People	History
6th Generation **Hezron** חֶצְרוֹן Ἐσρώμ Surrounded by a wall, fence	① Hezron is the sixth person in the genealogy of Jesus Christ. It is written that his father is Perez, and his son is Ram (1 Chr 2:5; Matt 1:3; Luke 3:33). ② Hezron had five sons; Jerahmeel his firstborn (1 Chr 2:9, 25), Ram the second (1 Chr 2:9), Chelubai the third (Caleb; 1 Chr 2:9, 18), Segub the fourth (1 Chr 2:21), and Ashhur the fifth (1 Chr 2:24). ③ Hezron's first wife bore him Jerahmeel, Ram, and Chelubai (1 Chr 2:9). His second wife, the daughter of Machir, whom he married when he was 60 years old (Abijah; 1 Chr 2:24), bore him Segub and Ashhur (1 Chr 2:21).
7th Generation **Ram or Aram (Arni)** רָם Ἀράμ Exalted, high	① Ram is the seventh person in the genealogy of Jesus Christ. It is written that his father is Hezron, and his son is Amminadab (1 Chr 2:9–10; Matt 1:4; Luke 3:33). ② Although he was the second son, he was listed as the direct descendant in the genealogy of Jesus Christ. Ram had four more brothers (Jerahmeel, Chelubai, Segub, Ashhur) (1 Chr 2:9, 21, 24). ③ In the genealogy of Luke, he is recorded as Ram (NASB, NIV, NKJV), Aram (KJV), and Arni (NLT, NRSV) (Luke 3:33). The name *Ram* is Ἀράμ (*Aram*) in Greek, meaning "high place."
8th Generation **Amminadab** עַמִּינָדָב Ἀμιναδάβ My noble kinsman	① Amminadab is the eighth person in the genealogy of Jesus Christ. It is written that his father is Ram, and his son is Nahshon (1 Chr 2:10; Matt 1:4; Luke 3:33). ② Amminadab's daughter Elisheba marries Aaron, and thus becomes related to the household of Aaron the high priest (Exod 6:23). Between Elisheba and Aaron, there were four sons, "Nadab, Abihu, Eleazar, and Ithamar" (Exod 6:23). ③ The genealogy of Matthew lists only the four generations of Hezron-Ram-Amminadab-Nahshon for the 430 years of slavery in Egypt. All other generations were not listed in the genealogy.
9th Generation **Nahshon** נַחְשׁוֹן Ναασσών Know from experience, diligently observe, that foretells	① Nahshon is the ninth person in the genealogy of Jesus Christ. It is written that his father is Amminadab, and his son is Salmon (1 Chr 2:10; Matt 1:4; Luke 3:32). ② He was the leader of the tribe of Judah during the wilderness years (Num 1:7; 2:3; 10:14). The men over the age of 20 who were numbered in the census totaled 74,600 for the tribe of Judah (Num 1:27). Moses and Aaron designated Nahshon by name and appointed him as leader among them (Num 1:17). ③ As the leader of the tribe of Judah, Nahshon always took the lead when presenting offerings (Num 7:12), or marching in the wilderness (Num 10:14).

People	History
10th Generation **Salmon** שַׂלְמוֹן Σαλμών Garment, coat, cloak	① Salmon is the tenth person in the genealogy of Jesus Christ. It lists his father as Nahshon, and his son as Boaz (1 Chr 2:11; Matt 1:4–5; Luke 3:32). ② He was one of the two spies that Joshua had sent to spy on the city of Jericho at the beginning of the conquest of Canaan (Josh 2:1). ③ Salmon married Rahab, the harlot who hid the two spies safely, placing him in the genealogy of the Messiah (Ruth 4:20–21; Matt 1:5; Luke 3:32). ④ Rahab (רָחָב) originated from its root רָחַב (rāḥab), which means "to grow large," "to widen," and "to enlarge." Hence it has the meaning of "wide," "large," and "roomy." Rahab risked her own life to meet the spies in peace and hide them. Knowing that Jericho, her homeland, would soon face its judgment, she confessed in conviction, "I know that the LORD has given you the land" (Josh 2:9). Even though she was a Gentile, she had a great enough faith to confess that "the LORD your God is God in heaven above and on earth beneath" (Josh 2:11).
11th Generation **Boaz** בֹּעַז Βοός Excellence/ keenness, a mighty man of wealth	① Boaz is the eleventh person in the genealogy of Jesus Christ. It is written that his father is Salmon, and his son is Obed by Ruth (1 Chr 2:11–12; Matt 1:5; Luke 3:32). ② Historically, Boaz's time was part of the dark age of the judges, which was characterized by idolatry and sinfulness. ③ Ruth was a widow who had lost everything, and she was a Gentile, a Moabite woman forbidden to enter the assembly of the Lord (Deut 23:3). However, she met Boaz, the influential kin who could redeem the inheritance.
12th Generation **Obed** עוֹבֵד Ὠβήδ To serve, servant	① Obed is the twelfth in the genealogy of Jesus Christ. It is written that his father is Boaz, and his son is Jesse, the father of David (1 Chr 2:12; Matt 1:5; Luke 3:32). ② He was born to Ruth the Moabite woman and Boaz, who married Ruth to fulfill his obligation as a kinsman redeemer. Obed was named by the neighbor women (Ruth 4:17), and Naomi, his grandmother, became his nurse (Ruth 4:16). ③ The neighbor women said to Naomi that Obed will be "a restorer of life and a sustainer of your old age" (Ruth 4:15). ④ Just as the neighbor women had said "may his name be famous in Israel" (Ruth 4:14), Obed was called "the father of Jesse, the father of David" (Ruth 4:17) and his name indeed became famous.

People	History
13th Generation **Jesse** יִשַׁי Ἰεσσαί God exists, God lives	① Jesse is the thirteenth in the genealogy of Jesus Christ. It is written that his father is Obed, and his son is David (1 Chr 2:12; Matt 1:5; Luke 3:32). ② Jesse had eight sons and two daughters. Among them, the youngest son, David, became the king of Israel (1 Sam 16:10–12; 17:12; 1 Chr 2:13–16). ③ Jesse was the closest one to witness God's providence in the process of establishing his own son, David, as the king of Israel (1 Sam 16:3–13, 17–23; 17:17–58; 22:1). By witnessing God's Word coming to fulfillment exactly according to His words, he probably experienced that God truly lives. ④ The prophecy that the Messiah would come from the nameless "stem of Jesse" (Isa 11:1) foreshadowed how the Messiah would come in a lowly and poor state, under physical conditions that are not very attractive to people's eyes (Isa 53:1-3). It also foreshadowed the hopelessness of the times at His coming.
14th Generation **David the King** מֶלֶךְ דָּוִד Δαυὶδ τὸν βασιλέα Beloved, friend	① David is the fourteenth in the genealogy of Jesus Christ. It is written that his father is Jesse, and his son is Solomon (1 Chr 2:13–15; Matt 1:5–6; Luke 3:32). ② Before he was enthroned, he fled from King Saul and lived as a fugitive for about 10 years. David's humiliation and suffering during the years of refuge remind us of the severe suffering and mockery Jesus Christ endured for our sins. ③ Throughout his 40-year reign (1010–970 BC), David had 6 sons during the 7 years and 6 months of reign in Hebron (2 Sam 3:2–5; 1 Chr 3:1–9) and 13 sons during the 33 years of reign in Jerusalem (2 Sam 5:13–16; 1 Chr 14:3–7). He also had a son named Jerimoth (2 Chr 11:18) and other sons from his concubines (1 Chr 3:9). ④ The title "king" is given only to David in the genealogy of Jesus Christ (Matt 1:6) in order to signify that only Jesus Christ is the King of all kings. Also, David was counted twice—once at the end of the first period and second time at the beginning of the second period—foreshadowing that Jesus Christ would come and fulfill the Old Testament law and begin the new works of the New Testament.

The Chronology of the Period of the Judges

As we have previously observed, if all the years of the reigns of the judges are added to-gether without taking into account the years that overlap, then the period of the judges spans 410 years. This exceeds the time given for the period of the judges (1390–1050 BC) by 70 years, so there must be an overlap in the reigns of the judges.[68]

We have already observed that the reigns of Ehud and Shamgar overlap as do the reigns of Tola and Jair. Also, the periods of affliction by the Ammonites and the op-pression by the Philistines coincide in parts. Besides, there are other issues related to the period of the judges that need to be examined.

1. The Problem of the "300 years" Mentioned by Jephthah

Judges 11:26 While Israel lived in Heshbon and its villages, and in Aroer and its villages, and in all the cities that are on the banks of the Arnon, three hundred years, why did you not recover them within that time?

Jephthah refutes the king of Ammon when Israel was attacked after 18 years of affliction at the hands of the Ammonites (Judg 10:8). Here, Jephthah confronts Ammon with the injustice of his claim over the land that the Israelites had ruled for 300 years.

Just before entering Canaan, the Israelites conquered Heshbon, Aroer, and all the land east of the Jordan River. Then, they crossed and arrived in Gilgal on the tenth day of the first month in 1406 BC (Josh 4:19). Thus, 1406 BC has to be the beginning of the 300-year period of which Jephthah spoke and the year that the Israelites entered Canaan. Consequently, the end of the 300-year period is 1106 BC, or even 1105 BC to 1104 BC if the years are counted according to calendar years. If the end of the 300 years is extended to 1104 BC, the 300 years mentioned by Jephthah perfectly coincide with the regnal years of the judges.[69]

2. Problems of Oppression by the Philistines and the Reign of the Judges

As we have previously observed, the 18-year affliction by the Ammonites (Judg 10:8, 1121–1104 BC) and the 40-year oppression by the Philistines (Judg 13:1, 1121–1082 BC) began at the same time (Judg 10:7–8).

At this time, Samson, who was from Zorah near Philistia, had been serving as a judge for 20 years in the regions around Philistia (Judg 15:20) while other regions to the north had been under affliction by the Ammonites. Samson continued to work in the northern regions of Israel through the 18 years of the Ammonite affliction and two more years near Philistia.

(1) The judges after the 18 years of the Ammonite affliction

The judges of Israel who ruled after the 18 years of affliction by the Ammonites, in the order of their rule, were as follows: Jephthah (6 years; Judg 12:7), Ibzan (7 years; Judg 12:8–9), Elon (10 years; Judg 12:11), and Abdon (8 years; Judg 12:13–14). Thus, it can be inferred that the reign of the last judge, Abdon, ended in 1077 BC.[70]

(2) History after Samson's 20-year rule

① Death of Eli the priest

It appears that Samson ruled during the first 20 years of the 40-year oppression of the Philistines. It can be inferred that the battle at Aphek (1102 BC) in which the Philistines captured the Ark of the Covenant was in retaliation to Samson's destruction of the temple of Dagon (Judg 16:30; 1 Sam 4:1–11).[71] At the battle of Aphek, Eli's two sons, Hophni and Phinehas, died (1 Sam 4:11, 17). Upon hearing the news about his sons' deaths, Eli, who had judged Israel for 40 years, fell backward off his chair and died at the age of 98 (1 Sam 4:15, 18).

② The emergence of the prophet Samuel

It was 1102 BC when Samuel's presumed age was 12 years. 1 Samuel 3:1 states, "Now the boy Samuel was ministering to the LORD before Eli. And word from the LORD was rare in those days, visions were infrequent." Josephus, a Jewish historian, uses the phrase, "was ministering to the LORD" to deduce that Samuel must have been 12 years old at the time.[72] This is because the Israelite society regarded a person to be an adult from the age of 12. Thus, Samuel must have begun his duties in the house of the Lord at the age of 12.

③ The 20 years and 7 months without the Ark of the Covenant

The Ark of the Covenant, which was captured by the Philistines at the battle of Aphek, was in the country of the Philistines for seven months (1 Sam 6:1) before it was moved to the house of Abinadab in Kiriath-jearim where it remained for 20 years (1 Sam 7:2).

④ Battle of Mizpah

Samuel was 12 years old when the Ark of the Covenant was captured in the battle of Aphek, and the battle of Mizpah occurred about 20 years later when Samuel was 32 years old (1082 BC).

Before the battle of Mizpah occurred, Samuel had urged the Israelites to repent (1 Sam 7:3). When the people listened to Samuel's urging and removed the Baals and the Ashtaroth and served the Lord alone, Samuel directed them to gather at Mizpah (1 Sam 7:4–5). At Mizpah, the Israelites drew water and poured it out before the Lord, fasted and prayed in repentance (1 Sam 7:6).

When the Philistine army heard that the Israelites had gathered at Mizpah, they came up to attack them. Samuel took a suckling lamb and offered it as a whole burnt offering to the Lord and cried out to the Lord on Israel's behalf (1 Sam 7:9). The word *cried* is זָעַק (zāʿaq) in Hebrew and means "to shout" or "to cry out for help." The Lord heard Samuel's earnest prayer for help, and He thundered with a great thunder which confused the Philistines, so that the Israelites were victorious (1 Sam 7:10).

Then Samuel took a stone and set it between Mizpah and Shen saying, "Thus far the LORD has helped us" and named it Ebenezer. Ebenezer is אֶבֶן הָעֵזֶר ('eben hā'ēzer) in Hebrew, meaning "the rock of help" and is thus the confession that Israel's victory was totally the result of God's help. Afterwards, all the land that the Philistines had taken, from Ekron to Gath, was restored. God protected Israel and prevented the invasions of the Philistines during all the remaining days of Samuel's life (1 Sam 7:12–14).

⑤ **Saul's accession to the throne**
After this, Samuel continued to judge Israel (1 Sam 7:15). He went on annual circuits to Bethel, Gilgal and Mizpah and judged Israel in all these places (1 Sam 7:16). In 1050 BC, the prophet Samuel poured oil upon Saul and anointed him king (1 Sam 10:1).

The following chart is a summary of the period of the judges, starting from the entry into Canaan (1406 BC) until the appointment of King Saul (1050 BC).

Chart: The Chronology of the Period of the Judges

✳ Organized and presented for the first time in history

Oppressors or Judge	Years of Duration	Bible Reference	Time of Reign or Oppression	
Canaan conquest & distribution of inheritance	16 years	Josh 24:29 Judg 2:8	1406–1390 BC	
Oppression by Cushan-rishathaim, king of Mesopotamia	8 years	Judg 3:8	1390–1383 BC	
The Beginning of the Period of the Judges				
Judge Othniel	40 years	Judg 3:11	1383–1344 BC	300 years
Oppression by Eglon, king of Moab	18 years	Judg 3:14	1344–1327 BC	
Judge Ehud	80 years	Judg 3:30	1327–1248 BC	of which
Judge Shamgar	?	Judg 3:31	(included in the time of Ehud)	
Oppression by Jabin, king of Canaan	20 years	Judg 4:3	1248–1229 BC	Jephthah
Judge Deborah	40 years	Judg 5:31	1229–1190 BC	spoke
Oppression by Midian	7 years	Judg 6:1	1190–1184 BC	(Judg 11:26)
Judge Gideon	40 years	Judg 8:28	1184–1145 BC	
Oppression by Abimelech	3 years	Judg 9:22	1145–1143 BC	
Judge Tola	23 years	Judg 10:2	1143–1121 BC	
Judge Jair	22 years	Judg 10:3	(included in the time of Tola)	

40 years of oppression by the Philistines (1121–1082 BC)	Oppression by Ammon, 18 years	1121–1104 BC	Judge Samson (1121–1102 BC)
	Judge Jephthah, 6 years	1104–1099 BC	
	Judge Ibzan, 7 years	1099–1093 BC	Prophet Samuel (1102–1050 BC)
	Judge Elon, 10 years	1093–1084 BC	
1082 BC	Judge Abdon, 8 years	1084–1077 BC	

King Saul enthroned	1050 BC
Approx. 340 years in the period of the Judges	1390–1050 BC

- The overlapping years of the judges are unclear, and the calculation for this chronology is an estimation based on probability.
- The beginning year of the new period and the ending year of the old period are rendered as years that overlap.

This is the first study that has ever attempted a comprehensive comparison between the 300 years of which Jephthah spoke (Judg 11:26) and the time period of every judge.

Notes

1. In some translations, such as NRSV, this passage is in verse 13. It is also indicated as verse 13 in the Greek text (Novum Testamentum Graece, Nestle-Aland 27h Edition. Copyright © 1993 Deutsch Bibelgesellschaft, Stuttgart.)

2. οὕτως or οὕτω (a rarely occurring variant): a relatively high degree, presumably in keeping with the context—"so, so much."

3. Youngyup Cho, *Doctrine of God, Man and Sin* (Seoul: Lifebook, 2007), 99-102.

4. O. Palmer Robertson, *The Christ of the Covenants* (Grand Rapids: Presbyterian & Reformed Publishing, 1980), 27-30.

5. The teaching that the father is the one who represents his family, his descendants.

6. Abraham Park, *The Covenant of the Torch: A Forgotten Encounter in the History of the Exodus and Wilderness Journey* (Singapore: Periplus, 2010), 27.

7. The most widely accepted designation for a diverse collection of Greek literature encompassing: (1) translations of the contents of the Hebrew Bible; (2) additions to some of its books; and (3) works written originally in Greek (or in some instances in Hebrew) but not included in the Hebrew canon. The word "Septuagint" (from Latin, septuaginta = 70; hence the abbreviation LXX) derives from a story that 72 (other ancient sources mention 70 or 5) elders translated the Pentateuch into Greek; the term therefore applied originally only to those five books.

8. Youngyup Cho, *Christology*, (Seoul: Lifebook, 2007), 92.

9. Textus Receptus (Latin: "received text") is the name subsequently given to the succession of printed Greek texts of the New Testament which constituted the translation base for the original German Luther Bible, for the translation of the New Testament into English by William Tyndale, the King James Version, and for most other Reformation-era New Testament translations throughout Western and Central Europe. The series originated with the first printed Greek New Testament to be published; a work undertaken in Basel by the Dutch Catholic scholar and humanist Desiderius Erasmus in 1516, on the basis of some six manuscripts, containing between them not quite the whole of the New Testament. Although based mainly on late manuscripts of the Byzantine text-type, Erasmus's edition differed markedly from the classic form of that text.

10. John Albert Bengel, *Bengel's New Testament Commentary*, vol. 1, *Matthew – Acts* (Grand Rapids: Kregel, 1981), 54-56.

Norval Geldenhuys, *Commentary on the Gospel of Luke: The English Text with Introduction Exposition and Notes* (Grand Rapids: Eerdmans, 1951), 151-152.

11. There are people who explain this with the lunar calendar, in which a month is 28 days. They explain the three parts of the 42 generations as the 14 days when the moon increases (the period of Israel's growth), then the 14 days when the moon diminishes (the period of Israel's decadence), and the 14 days when the moon recovers (the period of Israel's recovery). (Disciples Publishing House, ed. *The Oxford Bible Interpreter [Seoul: Disciples Publishing House, 2006], 64.*)

12. The number 7 is used in the Bible with a special meaning. However, more than the number itself, we need to think about its meaning viewed through the history of redemption. For example, God had rested on the 7th day after creating the heavens and the earth

(Gen 2:1-2). In order to commemorate this day, He set it as a day of rest and had consecrated and set it apart. Also, as a period of consecration, the feast of unleavened bread was kept for seven days (Lev 26:6-8). Abraham set seven ewe lambs of the flock in order that it may be a witness of digging a well between Abimelech and himself and made a vow. When Joseph had interpreted Pharaoh's dream we come across seven cows, seven stalks of wheat, seven years of abundance and seven years of famine (Exod 25:37; 37:23; Num 8:2). The year of Jubilee is the 7th year, the Sabbath year (Lev 25:8). Elijah told his servant to "go and look towards the sea" seven times. When Elisha raised the son of a woman's boy from Shunem from the dead, he sneezed seven times before he opened his eyes. As a symbol of complete atonement, blood was sprinkled seven times (Lev 4:6, 17; 8:11; 14:7, 16, 27, 51; 16:14, 19; Num 19:4). When they marched around the city of Jericho on the 7th day they marched around seven times (Josh 6:4). When Naaman the leper dipped himself in the Jordan River seven times according to the command of Elisha the prophet, his flesh was restored like the flesh of a child (2 Kgs 5:14, 18). David praised seven times in a day (Ps 119:94). The Word of God is pure like silver refined in the furnace that is refined seven times (Ps 12:6). Jesus taught that they should forgive not seven times but rather seven times 70 times (Matt 18:21-22; cf. Luke 17:4). The seven eyes of the Lord range to and fro throughout the entire earth (Zech 4:10; Rev 4:5; 5:6) Aside from that, the number seven is used to symbolize God's salvation and judgment (Rev 1:4, 16; 2:1; 5:1, 6; 6; 8-11; 15:1).

13.   The name Semite was suggested by the fact that most of the nations listed in the Table of Nations (Gen 10:21 ff.) were descendants of Shem. The origin of the term has been credited to A. L. Schlozer (1781).

14.   Kyeong-Yeon Jun, *Matthew's Theology* (Seoul: Lifebook, 2007), 99-102.

15.   John Nolland, *Word Biblical Commentary*, vol. 35A, *Luke,* (Dallas: Word Books, 1989), 174.

16.   Deuck Joong Kim, *A Commentary on the Gospel of Luke* (Seoul: The Christian Literature Society of Korea, 1993), 235-236.

17.   Abraham Park, *The Genesis Genealogies: God's Administration in the History of Redemption* (Singapore: Periplus Editions, 2009), 136-138.

18.   More than anything, it is trying to understand Jesus as the second Adam by putting a relationship between the time of Adam and Jesus through typology. (Byung-Soo Cho, 107.)

19.   Marshall D. Johnson, *The Purpose of the Biblical Genealogies* (New York: Cambridge University Press, 1969), 236.

20.   The beginning of Jesus is God. The genealogy of Jesus has its roots in God. In other words, Jesus is the result of God's roots growing and bearing fruit. This is in an important theme in the genealogy of Jesus. (Byung-Soo Cho, 106.)

21.   *Dālet* (ד) is the fourth letter and *wāw* (ו) is the sixth letter in the Hebrew alphabet. Thus, the sum of the numerical values represented by the letters in David's Hebrew name דָּוִד (4 + 6 + 4) is 14.

22.   Donald Guthrie, *New Testament Theology* (Leicester: Inter-Varsity Press, 1981), 253.

23.   The history of a linguistic form (as a word) shown by tracing its development since its earliest recorded occurrence in the language where it is found, by tracing its transmission from one language to another, by analyzing it into its component parts, by identifying its cognates in other languages, or by tracing it and its cognates to a common ancestral form in an ancestral language.

24.   Deuk-Joong Kim, *The Gospel Theology* (Seoul: Concordia, 1995), 56-57. Deuk-Joong Kim, *The Theology of the Gospels Seen Through Main Topics,* (Han-Deul Publisher, 25-26).

25. Deuk-Joong Kim, *The Gospel Theology*, 56.
Deuk-Joong Kim, *The Theology of the Gospels Seen Through Main Topics*, 25-26.

26. The word *bosom* is κόλπος (*kolpos*) in Greek, meaning "the front of the body between the arms." This word has a connotation of warmth or special grace and love. It is used four times in the New Testament (Luke 6:38, John 1:18, 13:23, Act 27:39). In particular, "the only begotten Son, which is in the bosom of the Father" (John 1:18) expresses Jesus' oneness with God , which is His divinity. Also, "leaning on Jesus' bosom, one of His disciples, whom Jesus loved" (John 13:23) indicates that this disciple, whom Jesus loved, was so close to Jesus that he received special grace and love.

27. Abraham Park, *The Covenant of the Torch*, 316-317.

28. Abraham Park, *The Covenant of the Torch*, 89.

29. The expressions may vary in different translations, but there is consistency in each version.

30. Abraham Park, *The Covenant of the Torch*, 256-261.

31. The word enaim means "two springs."

32. Sprios Eodhiates, *The Complete Word Study Dictionary New Testament* (AMG Publishers, 1994), 248.

33. HALOT, 1980.

34. BDB 770.

35. Also spelled *Aminadab* in the Bible

36. ISBE, 2:519, 4:61.

37. See p. 321, Reference 4: "The Genealogical Chart of King David."

38. In 1 Chr 2:13-15 it is recorded that Jesse had seven sons. It is probably because one son died young without a child. (C. F. Keil and F. Delitzsch, *Commentary on the Old Testament* [Peabody: Hendrickson, 2002], 3:410)

39. See p. 321, Reference 4: "The Genealogical Chart of King David"

40. Abraham Park, *The Covenant of the Torch*, 48-49.

41. Eui-Won Kim, Young-Jin Min, *A Commentary on Ruth and Judges* (Seoul: The Christian Literature Society of Korea, 2007), 42.

42. Leon J. Wood, *A Survey of Israel's History* (Grand Rapids: Academie Books, 1986), 171, 178-179.

43. J. D. Douglas, ed., *New Bible Dictionary* (Wheaton: Tyndale House, 1982), 641.
Leon Wood, 171, 184.

44. Abraham Malamat, "The Period of the Judges," *World History of the Jewish People*, ed. Benjamin Mazar (Tel Aviv: Massada, 1971), 157.
Walter Kaiser, *A History of Israel: from the Bronze Age Through the Jewish Wars* (United States: Broadman & Holman, 1998), 178-179.

45. See p. 310, Reference 3—Chart: "The Chronology of the Period of the Judges"

46. James Strong, *The Exhaustive Concordance of the Bible: Showing Every Word of the Text of the Common English Verion of the Canonical Books, and Every Occurrence of Each Word in Regular Order* (Ontario: Woodside Bible Fellowship, 1996), H8044.

47. Matthew Henry, *Matthew Henry's Commentary*, vol. 2, *Joshua to Esther* (Hendrickson Publisher, 2006), 117.

48. In the NASB, Judges 5:15 reads, "…Among the divisions of Reuben There were great resolves of heart"; whereas in the NLT, it reads, "…But in the tribe of Reuben there was great indecision."

49. Eui-Won Kim, Young-Jin Min, 485.

50. "Judges 10:7 implies that Jephthah, occupied with the Ammonites east of the Jordan, and Samson, concerned with the Philistines on the west, were contemporary in activity." (Leon Wood, 171.)

"Of particular significance is the fact that the 40-year Philistine oppression (13:1) in W. Palestine continued uninterruptedly from the deaths of Tola and Jair (10:7), through the judgeships of Jephthah, the three minor judges, Eli and Samson, down to the victorious advent of Samuel." (Douglas, 640.)

See p. 310, Reference 3—Chart: "The Chronology of the Period of the Judges"

51. See p. 310, Reference 3—Chart: "The Chronology of the Period of the Judges"

52. The MT reads "seventh." In Hebrew there is a difference of only one letter between the words רְבִיעִי (rĕbîʿî, "fourth") and שְׁבִיעִי (šĕbîʿî, "seventh"). Some ancient textual witnesses (e.g., LXX and the Syriac Peshitta) read "fourth" here.

53. The Hebrew word for "press…hard" is צוּק (sûq), meaning "to constrain," "to press upon," and "to bring into straits." According to *The New Oxford American Dictionary*, the word press has the meaning "to make strong efforts to persuade or force (someone) to do or provide something" [*The New Oxford American Dictionary*, 2nd ed., ed. Erin McKean (New York: Oxford University Press, 2005), 1341s.]

54. David purchased the threshing floor of Araunah and oxen for 50 shekels of silver (2 Sam 24:24), and Solomon imported a chariot for 600 shekels of silver and a horse for 150 (1 Kgs 10:29; 2 Chr 1:17). Comparatively, 5,500 shekels is a great amount.

55. Because kings, prophets, and priests were appointed with sacred oil poured on their heads (anointing) in the Old Testament times, they were called "the anointed."

56. *The New Oxford American Dictionary*, 2nd ed., ed. Erin McKean (New York: Oxford University Press, 2005), 875.

57. Leon Wood, 205

58. *The New Oxford American Dictionary*, 1406.

59. Disciples Publishing House, ed. *The Grand Bible Commentary: With Comprehensive and Synthetic Exegetical Study Methods* (Seoul: Bible Study Material Publisher, 2000), 5:331.

60. In 1 Samuel 21:12-13, it is recorded that David pretended to be insane not in front of Abimelech but in front of Achish king of Gath. The Hebrew word for Abimelech is אֲבִימֶלֶךְ (ʾăbîmelek), which is a compound word of two nouns: אָב (ʾāb), meaning "father," and מֶלֶךְ (melek), meaning "king." Thus, the name *Abimelech* means "father of the king," and it is understood that this was a common noun used to refer to Philistine kings, not a proper name for a specific person (Gen 20:2; 21:22; 26:1). On the other hand, *Achish* was a proper name of a Philistine king and *Gath* was a name of a city in Philistia. Therefore, the two seemingly different names in 1 Samuel and Psalms are simply different titles of the same person.

61. According to the King James Version, Saul went into the cave "to cover his feet."

62. Disciples Publishing House, *The Grand Bible Commentary*, 5:250.

David was anointed king in approximately 1025 BC, but he actually became a king in approximately 1010 BC.

63. The Ark of the Covenant was taken away from the Israelites in the war of Aphek in 1102 BC. Afterwards, it was in the country of the Philistines for seven months (1 Sam 6:1) and then moved to the house of Abimelech (1 Sam 7:1-2). After that, David became a king in Hebron in 1010 BC and reigned there for seven years and six months. Then, he began his reign in Jerusalem in 1003 BC. It was after David had begun his reign in Jerusalem in 1003

BC, that the Ark of the Covenant was moved. Thus, the ark was in the house of Abinadab at least 99 years. It is more logical to say that Uzzah and Ahio were Abinadab's grandsons rather than sons. The Hebrew word for son, בֵּן (*bēn*), also used to mean "grandson."

64. The New Jerusalem Bible (NJB) translates, "The entire population was weeping aloud…" (2 Sam 15:23).

65. Disciples Publishing House, *The Grand Bible Commentary*, 9:53.

66. One million talents of silver are equivalent to 34,000 tons, and 100,000 talents of gold are equivalent to 3,400 tons.

67. 5,000 talents of gold weighs 170 tons; 10,000 darics of gold weighs 84 kg.; 10,000 talents of silver weighs 340 tons; 18,000 talents of brass weighs 612 tons; and 100,000 talents of iron weighs 3,400 tons. There were different kinds of precious stones that were brought as well.

68. Disciples Publishing House, ed. *The Oxford Bible Interpreter* (Seoul: Bible Study Material Publisher, 1989), 20:29.

69. See p. 310, Chart: "The Chronology of the Period of the Judges."

70. See p. 310, Chart: "The Chronology of the Period of the Judges."

71. Eui-Won Kim, Young-Jin Min, 42.

72. Flavius Joseph, *Josephus: With an English Translation by H. St. J. Thackeray, M.A. and Ralph marcus, Ph.D.*, vol. v, *Jewish Antiquities, Books V-VIII* (Cambridge: Harvard University Press, 1988), 157.

Index

Jehoshaphat, 74, 192
Jephthah, 154, 185–89, 307
Jephthah's daughter, 187–88
Jeremiah, covenant, 41–42,
47–49
Jerusalem, 250–52
Jesse, 70, 71, 79, 134–39,
146, 215–16, 306
Jesus Christ, baptism, 69;
birth, 57; blood, 15–17,
32, 42, 46–47, 123–24;
conception, 57; covenant
with Abraham, 44–45,
284; with David, 46–47,
254, 284; with Jeremiah,
47–49; with Noah, 43–
44; divine origin, 68–69;
entry into Jerusalem, 120;
foreshadowed by David,
141–42; fulfiller of cov-
enant, 43–49; genealogy,
53, 59–62, 70–77, 78–81,
84–85; see also specific
names; genealogy Luke 3,
59–60, 63–69, 113–14,
299–301; genealogy
Matthew 1, 54–56, 59–
62, 113–14, 299–306;
history of redemption, 55,
62, 73, 77, 127, 281–84;
Messiah, 53, 56, 78, 84;
new covenant, 42, 43–49;
obedience, 94, 96, 114;
only begotten Son, 30–
31; Savior of the world,
44, 85, 89, 129; second
coming, 287; self-hum-
bling, 72–73, 114, 193;
self-sacrifice, 94–95;
Sinaitic covenant, 45–46;
son of Abraham, 56–57,
78, 84; son of David,
56–57, 78, 84
Jews, Abraham as father, 88;
importance of genealogy,
52–53
Jezebel, 80
Joab, 249, 257, 260, 264,
270–71
Job, on works of God, 25
Joel, 210
Jonathan, 213, 224–26,
234–35
Joram, 74
Joseph (Jacob's son), 98–102
Joseph (Mary's husband), 76

Joshua, 39, 79, 121, 123,
146, 157, 199, 219, 274,
283
Josiah, 74, 300
Jotham, 74, 300
Judah, 66, 70, 71, 99, 101–
4, 281–282, 283, 303
Judah (tribe), 118–20,
201–02; David made king,
247–48
judges, 79, 146–47, 148–
52; chronology, 153–55,
307–11; see also Ref. 3

Keilah, 233–34
king, requested by Israelites,
210–11
Korea, importance of genealogy, 52

Laban, 98
lamp of the covenant, 14,
259, 284–86
law, human hearts, 41–42;
Sinaitic covenant, 39–40
Lazarus, 89
Leah, 98
life eternal, in John's gospel,
31–32
love, in John's gospel, 29
love of God, 13, 29, 72–73,
247, 288
Luke 3, genealogy of Jesus,
59–60, 63–69, 113–14,
299–301. See also Ref. 1;
Ref. 2

Machir, 263–64
Manasseh, 74
Manasseh (tribe), 119, 169
Maon Wilderness, 235–36
Mary, 60–61
Matthan, 76, 301
Matthew 1, genealogy of
Jesus, 54–56, 59–62,
113–14, 299–306. See also
Ref. 1; Ref. 2
Matthew's gospel, link with
Genesis, 52
Mephibosheth, 265–66
Messiah, Jesus Christ, 53,
56, 78, 84; prophecies,
137–39
Messianic covenant, 142–43,
284
Michal, 218, 219, 252

Midianites, 171–73, 175–79
Mizpah, 186–87, 212,
230–31, 308–09
Moabites, 125–27, 129–30,
161–62, 230, 283
moon, 23
Moses, covenant, 39, 45,
286; tabernacle, 119
Most High Ruler, 22

Nabal, 239–41
Nahshon, 70, 71, 78–79,
118–20, 299–304
Naioth, 223–24
names, genealogy of Jesus,
63–67, 80–81; meanings,
64–67, 80–81. See also
specific names
Naomi, 125–26, 131–33,
283
Naphtali (tribe), 119,
168–69
Nathan, rebukes David,
257–58; secures throne for
Solomon, 269–70
Negev, 157
neighbors, serving, 132–33
Noah, covenant, 37–38,
43–44
Nob, 226–27

oath, in covenant, 40,
285–86
Obed, 70, 71, 79, 128–29,
131–33, 305
Obed-Edom, 252
obedience, 214. See also
disobedience, Abraham, 90–92,
94; Isaac, 94–95; Jesus
Christ, 96
Onan, 102–3, 116, 303
Othniel, 148, 154, 156–59,
310

Paradise, 89–90
Paran Wilderness, 238
parents, honoring, 132–33
Perez, 103–4, 105–7, 282,
303
persistence, 178–79, 163–
68. See also generations
Philistines, 136, 155,
163–64, 198–205, 307–9;
battled by Saul, 212–13,
216–18, 236; David's